Choreophobia

Bibliotheca Iranica
Performing Arts Series No. 5

No. 1
Parviz Sayyad
Theater of Diaspora
Two Plays: *The Ass* and *The Rex Cinema Trial*
Edited by Hamid Dabashi

No. 2
Othello in Wonderland
and
The Mirror-Polishing Storytellers
Two Plays by
Gholamhoseyn Sa'edi
Edited with an Introduction by
M.R. Ghanoonparvar

No. 3
Traditional Persian Art Music
The *Radif* of Mirza Abdollah
Musical Notation, Commentary, and Performance by
Dariush Tala'i
(Includes 5 compact discs)

No. 4
Sadeq Hedayat
The Myth of Creation
A Puppet Show in Three Acts
Translated by M.R. Ghanoonparvar
Illustrated by Kaya Behkalam

Choreophobia

Solo Improvised Dance
in the Iranian World

೦೩⃝ಟಿಐ

Anthony Shay

MAZDA PUBLISHERS
1999

Mazda Publishers
Academic Publishers
P.O. Box 2603
Costa Mesa, California 92626 U.S.A.
www.mazdapub.com

Library of Congress Cataloging-in-Publication Data
Shay, Anthony, 1936-
Choreophobia: Solo Improvised Dance in the Iranian World / Anthony Shay.
p. cm—(Bibliotheca Iranica, Performing Arts Series; No. 5)
Includes bibliographical references (p.) and index.

ISBN:1-56859-083-0
(cloth: alk. paper)

1. Dance—anthropological aspects—Iran. 2. Improvisation in dance—Iran. 3.
Folk dancing—Iran. I. Title. II. Series.
GV1588.6.S53 1999
792.8—dc21
99-28112
CIP

This book is for Jamal

Contents

Acknowledgements

First, I wish to thank Sally Ann Ness, who gave countless hours of her precious time, and who in many ways, helped to shape the final form of this study. Her encouragement and patience during my graduate years have been invaluable. I also wish to thank those who served on my examination and dissertation committees: Paul Gelles, Heidi Gilpin, Dariush Haghighat, Ethan Nasreddin-Longo, Nancy Lee Ruyter, and Marta Savigliano. I also thank those colleagues, Jennifer Fisher, Daniel Bradburd, Garay Minicucci, and Audrey Shalinsky, who listened to my wilder ideas and suggested ways to articulate them into coherent thought. Thanks go as well to Professor Dale Eickelman, Dartmouth College, and Professor Gilbert Behague, University of Texas, Austin, who believed in my academic work enough to accept me into their respective National Endowment for the Humanities Summer Seminars for Scholars where I had the opportunity to test out some of my theoretical ideas and have access to valuable library collections. I also thank Dr. Robert Georges, Professor Emeritus, UCLA for his many years of encouragement.

Thanks also go to the many students who participated in my classes in Iranian dance at the University of California, Riverside and Pomona College, Claremont, especially Marjan Haghnia. The members of the AVAZ International Dance Theatre, Brandy Maya Healy, Cay Lundy, Mary Esther Espinoza, Lori Parker, and Karen Ochoa, to name a few, provided constant inspiration in my search for new ways to move. AVAZ board members Parvaneh and Ahmad Azad so believed in this study that they spent countless hours in Iran searching and finding difficult-to-obtain, out-of-print materials. Pary Azad, in particular, encouraged me to undertake this study because of her deep love for Iranian dance and her fight against choreophobia. I hope that this study fulfills her hopes.

I have been greatly honored by my colleagues in the dance world who awarded me a James Irvine Dance Fellowship for 1998. I am grateful to the Graduate Students Association at the University of California for three mini-grants as well as a social sciences research grant from the University of California, Riverside.

My deepest gratitude must go to the many individuals in the Iranian-American community who took the time to talk to me and who provided me with valuable insights. I must especially mention Ardavan Mofid who shared his profound knowledge of traditional theatre and photographs, master calligrapher, Masoud Valipour, who listened to me for many hours, gave me the precious gift of books, and also created many of the visual examples for this study, Rezvaneh and Abbas Chamanara, who gave the gift of music, and the families of Afsar and Mansour Moghaddam and Mojgan and Farzin Rahbar for information and photographs.

My heartfelt thanks go to my family. My mother, Margaret M. Shay, and my sisters, Kitty Walters and Penny Shay, have given unstintingly of their love.

Above all, my particular gratitude goes to Jamal who selflessly gave everything possible to make certain that I returned to school, listened to my ideas for endless hours, and contributed the kinds of rich insights every researcher longs to hear.

Introduction

*"When you see a nation
dance, you know the character
of the people."*
Confucius

*I*n the Iranian culture sphere, including the Iranian diaspora community, the performance of the solo improvised dance form (sometimes referred to as *majlesi* (social or party) often evokes powerful negative reactions.[1] This is reflected both currently and historically in attempts to ban its public performances and marginalize its professional performers. For this reason I feel that this area of the world sometimes exhibits what I call a "choreophobic mentality." However, the very people who might condemn a particular performance by a particular individual in certain contexts will themselves perform this dance. In spite of the political ban in both Iran and Afghanistan and the possibility of severe punishment, people will put themselves at risk by dancing.[2] A photograph taken by one of my informants shows people riding in a bus in rural Iran and dancing in the aisles to a contraband music tape. The curtains are pulled down and one of the passengers is on the look-out for the highway patrol.[3] Another image is one that was smuggled out of Iran and seen on Iranian television (*Sima-ye Ashena* program at New Year, March 20, 1994), showing a small group of men clandestinely dancing this solo dance form and playing music in the countryside away from the watchful eyes of authorities—a breath of illusory freedom. (A second, similar performance was shown in the same program for the *No-ruz* broadcast of 1996.) In this respect this dance form appears to constitute an ambiguous, powerful, and highly negative symbol in Iranian society, but nonetheless it is also loved and performed both in the United States, and throughout the Iranian culture sphere before it was banned in Iran and Afghanistan.

The central project of the study is to identify and analyze what factors currently contribute and have historically contributed to the ambiguous position this dance form occupies in an Iranian context. Many of my examples and observations come from personal experiences in

1

Iran, Afghanistan, Tajikistan, Uzbekistan, and Azerbaijan, as well as the
Iranian diaspora in California, where my most recent research has been
focused. For purposes of this study I have coined the term "choreophobia," which I utilize to describe the negative and ambiguous reactions of
Iranians to certain performances and performers of solo improvised
dancing in both public performance and social contexts.

*But, in many ways this is my story, too, for I have lived through and
with this dance tradition for over forty years: I have danced it and created it, defended it and inscribed it. One of my qualifying examination
committee members, an Iranian, shared a story of "choreophobia" in
his own personal experience, of which we were both aware, with other
committee members. He described me as an "agent of change" within
the Iranian community, for I have shaped both the dance itself, as well
as the Iranian community's perception of it. Therefore, I will choreo-
graph and weave personal experiences and stories that people have
shared with me into the pattern and design of the study.*

This study approaches the reactions and responses of a population
which largely perceives dance, particularly the solo improvised form, in
what I term "choreophobic" terms. Only Karin Van Nieuwkerk's recent
study (1995) deals with the topic of similar negative reactions in her
study of professional Egyptian dancers. Van Nieuwkerk, however, focuses specifically on attitudes of Egyptians toward professional belly
dancers rather than the dance form itself, which like that of the Iranian
culture sphere, is performed privately and domestically as well as publicly and professionally. This study is concerned with the dance and its
performers, both as a social activity and as a performance phenomenon,
as well as its perception by a variety of Iranians living in the United
States. Until this time, virtually all of the major ethnographic studies on
traditional or folk dance have been concerned with dance where it is
considered as a positive and legitimate activity, and in some cases, an
indispensable expression of ethnicity or ritual. This study is a major
departure from those past studies. I assert that this study of ambiguous
attitudes toward dance will yield different and valuable viewpoints of
Iranian society, and by extension, other Middle Eastern, Central Asian
and North African societies, or those societies in which dance is not regarded as a positive or important activity. This will, in turn, provide
new ways in which researchers may look at dance in a manner not addressed in the past. I suggest that dance receives a variety of responses
in different societies and students of dance have much to learn about
societies which are indifferent to or feel negatively toward this form of
human expression, one that has long been represented as positive, aesthetic, and valuable in Western studies.

I also look at the role of Islam in the context of how Moslems, and
other Iranian minorities such as Jews, Baha'is, Christians, and Zoroas-
trians, regard dance.[4] Surprisingly in this era of increased consciousness

about Islam, there are still students of dance who ignore this important topic. For example, Melissa Cefkin's (1995) recent dissertation on Turkish dance groups almost totally avoids discussion of the crucial issue of Islam. She claims that in Turkey "dance is poised specifically to stand for Turkish culture" (1995: 30). Turkey, a neighboring country of Iran, has long cultural and historical connections with the Iranian culture sphere, and currently manifests an important Islamicist revival that is creating political news. Cefkin portrays dance performance in Turkey in a highly positive way, a very different attitude from that which I am theorizing for the Iranian culture sphere. Cefkin's study contrasts with long-time Turkish dance scholar Metin And's numerous studies of Turkish dance (1959; 1976), and Van Nieuwkerk's study of Egyptian belly dancers, which like mine, address the crucial issues of Islam and Moslem attitudes. Metin And, for example, credits Islam as an unquestioned blanket reason for negative reactions of Turks toward dance (1959:13). In Chapter Three I address the issue of Islam in some detail.

An important aspect of this study is to establish the intellectual construct of the Iranian culture sphere. Cowan, Van Nieuwkerk, and Cefkin all view dance through established, internationally recognized, national and local political units. I am suggesting that this narrow view, in a subtle manner, creates the notion that these dance forms are in some way unique to these specific areas, and additionally reifies these entities as eternal historical verities. I am suggesting the opposite: that to view this dance form only in terms of the current Iranian state borders would be as restrictive as studying Iranian literature within that same context— a context that would give a false sense of the extent of its practice and would be similar to omitting Rudaki or Jalal-al-din Rumi from a study of Iranian literature because they never dwelled in the current territory of the nation-state of Iran. Such an omission would clearly be unacceptable to students of Iranian literature.

Throughout the process of elaborating and analyzing the data I present in this study, I will turn to certain aspects of the theories, concepts, and findings of scholars from a variety of disciplines in order to better illuminate and clarify these ideas and data, as well as demonstrate their limitations for the theories and models that I am developing. The choice of theoretical concepts with which to illuminate the data has been carefully considered, for as literary theorist Terry Eagleton sagely observed: "any set of data can be explained by more theories than one" (1983:86). Certain theories, such as the theory of "art as a cultural system," in which Geertz cogently demonstrates the cultural and historical specificity, as well as the ethnographic linkages that exist between art and its specific environment, will serve as the overarching conceptual framework within which I present my data. Particularly useful for the examination of the sparse historical evidence that exists is his notion of the "period eye." Edward Said's concept of Orientalism must be addressed on a number of levels in order to more fully understand certain writings about and public performances of this dance form. Issues such as representation through dance, sources of auto-exoticism, and auto-orientalism will be addressed in detail in Chapter Six to assess how orientalism and auto-orientalism affect the presentation of solo improvised dance in the Iranian diaspora.

"Art as a Cultural System:"
Cultural Specificity of Iranian Solo Improvised Dance
In his essay, "Art as a Cultural System" (1983), Clifford Geertz points out that art, like many other aspects of life in other times and places, is "local knowledge," and forms an aesthetic system which is specific to a particular time and place.

> The chief problem presented by the sheer phenomenon of aesthetic force, in whatever form and in result of whatever skill it may come, is how to place it within the other modes of social activity, how to incorporate it into the texture of a particular pattern of life. And such placing, the giving to art objects a cultural significance, is always a local matter; what art is in classical China or classical Islam, what it is in the Pueblo southwest or highland New Guinea, is just not the same thing, no matter how universal intrinsic qualities that actualize its emotional power (and I have no desire to deny them) may be. The variety that anthropologists have come to expect in the spirit beliefs classification systems, or the kinship structures of different peoples, and not just in their immediate shapes but in the way of being-in-the-world they both promote and exemplify, extends as well to their drummings, carvings, chants, and dances. (1983:97)

Geertz' statement strongly suggests that in order to understand the dance tradition I am investigating, a necessary step is to analyze how Iranians express themselves about it, through words, reactions, painting, and poetry. This search for the meaning that dance constitutes for Iranians forms the central focus of my investigation because, as Geertz suggests concerning local arts: "...what enables us to talk about them usefully [is that] together they all inscribe a communal sensibility, present locally to locals a local turn of mind" (1983: 12).

Geertz's essay provides insights I will utilize in order to establish linkages between the various Iranian art forms and their local environments. He states that: "The question is not whether art (or anything else) is universal; it is whether one can talk about West African carving, New Guinea palm-leaf painting, quattrocento picture making, and Moroccan versifying in such a way as to cause them to shed some sort of light on one another" (1983: 11).

While Geertz argues the possibility that diverse cultural expressions using diverse media might illuminate important aspects of culture, my project is similar but more modest in scope. In Chapter One I discuss several forms of Iranian aesthetic expression to illuminate and establish what I argue are cross-genre expressive and performative impulses, such as practices of improvisation which characterize Iranian theatre, story-telling, and music, as well as dance, and the way in which geometry informs a wide variety of aesthetic expressions such as dance, calligraphy, and architecture.

Further, Geertz's notion of the "period eye" (after Baxandall 1983:103-109) suggests an important insight in analyzing the materials and data which I am presenting, particularly the use of art such as the Persian miniature, as proof of specific movement practices. This consideration extends both to the results of interviews and participant observation as well as to the analysis of Iranian iconographic sources—the chief native historical "voice" which depicts dancing. Geertz observes that "all sorts of cultural institutions were active in forming the sensibility of quattrocento Italy which converged with painting to produce the 'period eye'" (1983:104). At the core of this observation is that the artist worked not only with his or her own skills and materials, but above all "the painter's true medium: the capacity of his audience to see meanings in pictures" (1983:104). I address this issue both in dance and in the examination of iconographic sources in the Iranian culture sphere because some observers have turned to these pictorial sources and have treated them as a reflection of some kind of historical "reality" or "truth." Roland Barthes suggests that such a "truth" is suspect:

> The starting point of these reflections was usually a feel-
> ing of impatience at the sight of the "naturalness" with
> which newspapers, art and common sense constantly
> dress up a reality which, even though it is the one we live
> in, is undoubtedly determined by history—I wanted to
> track down, in the decorative display of *what-goes-
> without-saying*, the ideological abuse which, in my view,
> is hidden there. (1972: 11) (emphasis in the original)

Thus the reading and analysis of current aesthetic practices, as well as the quest for the Iranian "period eye," becomes crucial in analyzing the often conflicting and ambiguous meanings that dancing represents for contemporary Iranians as well as the way it has been portrayed in historical renderings such as miniatures. For example, the Timurids and the artists who served them in the fourteenth and fifteenth centuries, as Lentz (1989) amply demonstrates, were masters of portraying their dynasty in highly artful and idealized representations, a reminder that

Madison Avenue and "spin doctors" are only the latest in a historical series of attempts to depict a "special kind of reality." Reality is thus layered and must be unpeeled to demonstrate a range of "truths" and "realities." Barthes' and Geertz's studies suggest important ways for eliciting local truths, those that are not "natural" but "cultural."

Islamic art scholar Gulru Necipoglu underscores Barthes' notion by pointing out that scholars of Islamic art who essentialize this form attempt to portray the "natural" bent for geometric design that characterizes Islamic society:

> Rather than a single doctrine and cosmology that gave rise to uniformity in artistic expression throughout the Islamic world, there was a multiplicity of competing doctrines and cosmologies that informed the formulation of diverse visual idioms in different court milieus. (1995: 108)

Geertz explains how the art of the Renaissance, in both a Western time and place, as well as art in other societies, requires an ethnographic or "period" eye for its comprehension. He evaluates different forms of aesthetic expression in a variety of cultures, both large- and small-scale, using the same criteria. Thus, Geertz states that from this point of view, Western art is no different from aesthetic expression in other societies:

> Anthropologists... say... Primitives confuse the realms of their experience into one large, unreflective whole, but it does not apply to more developed cultures where art emerges as a differentiated activity responsive mainly to its own necessities. And like most such easy contrasts between peoples on different sides of the literacy revolution, it is false, and in both directions: as much in underestimating the internal dynamic of art in—What shall I call them? Unlettered societies?—as in overestimating its autonomy in lettered ones. (1983: 102)

This point is crucial because most Iranian societies have never been "closed" or "isolated" and each Iranian historical period requires inquiry into its specific and unique "eye." The Iranian culture sphere is not a "small-scale" society but one that is, and has always been, open to multiple cultural influences across the millennia—from Mesopotamia, Greece, China, India, and Europe, among other sources. Geertz addresses this issue, rather than limiting his theory to isolated small-scale societies.

Choreophobia

When I first contemplated the topic of my dissertation in 1992, I was interested in the historical aspects of solo improvised dance. I was especially fascinated by the prospect of seeking inspiration and evidence for this dance tradition in art forms, particularly the Persian miniature. I telephoned a professor of Islamic Art at UCLA who informed me that she knew of an Iranian doctoral student who had received a highly-prized grant to investigate a similar issue in music: to look at the Persian miniature for evidence of the existence of particular musical instruments in particular historical periods. I contacted this student, who, upon discovering that I was looking into dance, contemptuously declared, "raqs! (dance!) hamash faheshegi-ye! (it's all prostitution)."

A major theme of this study is the exploration of Iranian attitudes towards dance. Any individual conducting research on dance in the Middle East is soon confronted with widespread negative and ambiguous attitudes and reactions toward the subject. *In my case this was evident in the difficulty I had finding an Iranianist for my dissertation project. Several academics of Iranian background simply did not return telephone calls, respond to draft proposals of my project that they had specifically requested, or show up for agreed-upon appointments. They were not ready to state overtly that dance as a topic was beneath their dignity, distasteful, or even dangerous because it is currently banned by Iran's Islamic regime, but their reactions made that clear.* I coined the term "choreophobia" to describe the negative and ambiguous reactions and feelings toward solo improvised dancing expressed by Iranians and other individuals and groups from the Middle East. I have certainly been aware of and have attempted to analyze such attitudes ever since I began learning this dance tradition over forty years ago. Instances of such reactions, some of which I have personally witnessed and others that have been related to me by many generous informants, will serve as illustrations throughout the study.[5] I cannot sufficiently stress the fact that in the case of the Iranian culture sphere, including the Californian Iranian and Iranian-American population, what I call choreophobic attitudes are complex. Individual and societal attitudes vary greatly regarding which individuals may or may not dance without censure, and in which social and psychological contexts this may occur. Individual attitudes may vary towards different dance styles and traditions as well.

"Mr. Shay," a polite and apologetic-looking man addressed me before one of my classes in Iranian dance. He was accompanied by one of my young, female students, who was looking very embarrassed in front of her friends and classmates who had encouraged her to enroll. "I have seen you on television and I appreciate all that you are doing for Iran and my culture, but, you understand, I cannot let my daughter dance" (April 12, 1994).

Classical European ballet, and having one's daughters (but not one's sons) learn it, holds a considerable cachet for some Iranians. Others smile indulgently upon the Rousseauian innocence of "simple" tribal people performing regional dances, while decrying the loose behavior of professional dancers at a wedding party. Others frown upon all forms of dance. Children are frequently encouraged to dance in public contexts such as large parties. "But when I reached the age of twelve I was sat down by my mother and told that 'Ladies do not dance in public'" (Farzaneh [pseudonym]: personal interview Feb. 2, 1996). A half dozen women narrated variations of this incident to me.

These attitudes stem in part from the historical and current reactions toward professional dancers and their actual or perceived associations with commercial sex. Taj Al-Saltana, a Qajar princess (1884-1936) at the turn of the century, wryly noted in her memoirs:

> That night 'Abdi Jan's troupe had been called so that the harem occupants could watch the show. Of course, you remember 'Abdi well. Let me, nonetheless, give you a description of his looks. He was a lad of about twelve or thirteen, with large, black eyes, languid and incredibly beautiful and attractive. His face was tanned and good-looking, his lips crimson, and his hair black and thick. Renowned throughout the town, the boy had a thousand adoring lovers. Being a dancer, however, he was unworthy of being anyone's beloved. (1993:163)

In his notes to Taj Al-Saltana's memoirs, historian Abbas Amanat observes that Taj's husband "pawned off pieces of their fortune perhaps to spend lavishly on his new lover, a male dancer called Tayhu" (1993: 54).

Thus, it is perhaps not surprising that a complex and confusing message is sent: dance is encouraged for an individual at specific times, but denied to the same individual at other times. Like learning ta'arof, the unwritten, complex system of politesse, Iranians must internalize ways in which choreophobia is articulated and learn how to negotiate the shoals of its ambiguous boundaries. Unlike ta'arof, however, there is no encompassing term to describe the elements that comprise these complex ambiguous and negative attitudes and reactions, which is why I coined the term "choreophobia." In Chapter Five I argue that choreophobia is a system like language or ta'arof and its "structure, be it language or another sign system like culture, is not given empirically but has to be discovered and defined in relational terms" (Strinati 1995:92).

I posit that because dance in Iranian and Iranian-American society is not a basic, but a marginal activity, the unspoken "rules" of choreophobia are less familiar, and more amorphous than the unstated rules of ta'arof, for example, creating potential problems for the unwary. Zari, an Iranian student in her twenties, joined my company, AVAZ, as a dancer in the 1995-1996 season. Prior to a major concert, for which she had been practicing assiduously, Zari enthusiastically asked for fifty tickets which she would "easily be able to sell" to friends and family members. Two days later she sheepishly returned all of the tickets, greatly surprised by her mother's powerful negative reaction. Her mother had told her, "I don't care that you make a spectacle of yourself in public, but you will not let the people that we know find out that you are dancing on the stage." She ended up performing, but she was deeply hurt because no one special to her was there to watch her. After the performance she said that she could not continue to dance "because of her studies."

Another dancer, Pari, also underestimated the negative power of choreophobia. According to Negin, another girl in the company, Pari's father spoke frequently on the telephone with the parents of Negin, expressing his concern that his daughter, Pari, might not find a proper husband because of her dancing in public. It was not that he was personally against the activity, but he worried about what others would think. Thus, Pari, too, felt the familial and social pressure to give up an activity she very much enjoyed. Unfamiliarity with, underestimating, or ignoring the "rules" of choreophobia brought upon these two young women, and others, unpleasant reactions. The discovery, description, and analysis of choreophobia form a major element of this study.

Other studies have sought single explanations to account for these widely recognized negative attitudes. Some studies (Hamada 1978, for example) have explored the attitude of Islam toward dance, while others seek an answer in prevailing social attitudes (Friend and Segal 1986), but the search for *the* reason for these attitudes will elude the student of dance because it obscures the complexity of this phenomenon, and tends to neglect the wide range of individual attitudes that exist. Moreover, single individuals express different attitudes and display different reactions toward this dance form in varying contexts. Attitudes toward dance are thus dynamic, and when considering the influence of a new environment for the Iranians of Southern California, the careful scholar will note that changes in behavior and reactions can often be anticipated.

"When I first saw your dance company, almost twenty years ago now, I saw that you were performing a special service for both Iranian dance and the Iranian community. I decided then to do whatever I could for you and the company. When I told the president of the Iranian B'nai Brith Organization, a highly-placed and cultured woman, that I was encouraging my daughter to dance with AVAZ and suggested that she do the same, I saw by her reaction that she was shocked. If I had less confidence in myself, at that point I would have forced Mastaneh to leave. But, I believe in my convictions, and so I encourage her to participate" (Afsar Moghaddam: personal interview July 16, 1996).

One thing is certain. However they may feel towards this dance tra-

dition, all Iranians who are "culturally competent," to paraphrase Stanley Fish's concept of literary competence (1980:4-5; 13-16), are aware
that such ambiguous and negative feelings are a cultural generality in
the Iranian culture sphere, including the diaspora. Most individuals are
able to express their particular attitude along the continuum that we may
call the "horizon of expectations," a useful concept introduced by Hans
Jauss (Holub 1984:58-63). These concepts of "cultural competency,"
which parallels Geertz's notion of the "period eye," and the "horizon of
expectations" allow us, to some degree, to account for both the generality of attitudes and reactions, as well as those of specific individuals
within the Iranian community of Southern California. I have borrowed
these concepts from scholars of reader response and reception theory
who have struggled to resolve individual responses within the generality
in the field of literary criticism. In analyzing attitudes toward the solo,
improvised dance tradition within the Iranian culture sphere, it is important to account for both without totalizing the attitudes of a large and
diverse group of people. And yet, we must be able to account for
clearly widespread attitudes and reactions as well as individual responses and variations. For this purpose it is crucial to establish what
Fish (1980) terms an "interpretive community," a concept I address in
Chapter Four by profiling the Iranian community of Southern California, the largest outside of Iran.

I do not attempt to find the origins of negative and ambiguous reactions toward this dance tradition, a project doomed by the paucity of
historical evidence. Many writers, as I show in Chapter Three, assert
that Islam is responsible for these negative feelings and that dancers
were honored artists in pre-Islamic times. Were they? I am not so certain that no negative feelings existed toward dancers in pre-Islamic
times as well, and like many attitudes and elements of aesthetic expression in Islamic contexts, their roots may be found in Sasanian and Byzantine sources.[6] There exists some degree of proof that attitudes toward
dance and dancers were no different before Islam than after. A tendency
to idealize pre-Islamic Iran, encouraged throughout the Pahlavi period,
has a strong hold on many Iranians, including not a few scholars, producing the widespread notion that somehow, everything was different
(and better) before the Islamic period. As Hamid Naficy observes,
many aspects of television images in exilic programming "highlight the
link to the secular, fetishized past by borrowing from ancient pre-
Islamic Persian motifs..." (1993:135). One hears many callers on radio
talk shows valorizing pre-Islamic Iran, "when the arts were venerated."

Although it has often been noted that a connection exists between
prostitution and this dance tradition, not only in the Iranian culture
sphere, but also throughout the Middle East, this study is not concerned
with accounting for a specific historical reason, or reasons, for why this
attitude exists. Such searches must remain speculative and unverifiable.

Rather, I am interested in documenting what these complex, sometimes contradictory attitudes can tell us about contemporary Iranian society. It is also important to note that these attitudes are dynamic and subject to change as the performance of this dance engenders new meanings for the Iranians living in a new environment, as well as for those in the Iranian culture sphere. Students in my Iranian dance class, who state that their reason for enrolling is to express their Iranian heritage, exemplify this new meaning. In Iran, venues for performing in secret, or even publicly, in defiance of the Islamic Republic's ban, supply ample evidence that the performance of this dance creates a space for resistance to the regime. It is significant that Iranian women from throughout the diaspora chose to taunt the Islamic regime through the vehicle of dance at the International Women's Conference in Beijing in September, 1995. Thus, we are looking at a dynamic and complex phenomenon whose interpretation does not permit easy answers, but rather demands a careful investigation with sometimes multiple, layered analyses.

The History of this Study
The period of research for this study has been a long one with several phases in which I developed an increasingly specific focus on the research topic. Earlier, through a few self-reflective passages, I indicated a long association with the Iranian-American community. In late 1954, I began to learn Iranian solo improvised dance, as well as regional dances, a process that continues over forty years later.

The first Iranian party I attended, in late 1954, was really a rehearsal that became a party. It was held at the home of Maryam (pseudonym), my first teacher, and attended by a dozen homesick young Iranian students who came to watch the dancing, eat some home-cooked Iranian food, and reenter, if just for a few hours, an Iranian environment. To this day, the pungent smell of spices filling the air, the haunting beauty of the violin music of Saba, and Mobasheri's orchestra— played on already old 78 records—and the rich sounds of the Persian language, whose mysteries I was just beginning to penetrate, come back in a nostalgic rush—especially when I attend contemporary parties where, as often as not, keyboards and synthesizers and modern Persian pop music provide a brassy, more Westernized accompaniment. With a sense of surprise, and perhaps a hint of betrayal, all those young men, who for weeks had said they did not know how to dance, got up and danced. Some of them were highly proficient dancers. And so their denials of knowing how to dance, and the subsequent display of proficiency in a semi-private, "safe" environment, provided the first inkling of the ambiguity surrounding the propriety of dancing in my mind.

Over the next four years there were many parties, rehearsals, and appearances, culminating in a multi-city tour of the United States in the spring of 1958, sponsored by the Iranian Students' Association, in which Maryam and I were the chief performers, and later that year, a command performance for the late shah and Iranian diplomatic corps at the University of Minnesota. It was arranged between the shah and Dr. Ali Amini, then Iranian ambassador to the United States, that because of my fluency in Persian and intense interest in Iranian culture, I would go to Iran to study on an Iranian government stipend. I left for Iran in the summer of 1958. Many of those I interviewed for this study and with whom I have maintained friendships date back to that period.

While in Iran, among my many artistic and academic activities, I was able to travel to many areas where I saw a great deal of regional folk dancing, because I was engaged as an interpreter for a pair of American filmmakers preparing a travelogue of Iran. It was my understanding that this project had Iranian government support, and so I entered tribal and village areas to which I might otherwise never have had access. Much dancing was filmed because it provided the filmmakers an opportunity to record colorful natives, costumes and social events to enliven their filmed document. Not incidentally, it also provided me with golden opportunities to see, learn, and experience these dances in the field. *I vividly remember entering the village of Ghassemabad in the Caspian Sea province of Gilan, much to the surprise of the inhabitants, who were engaged in their daily tasks. They refused to dance without the permission of their landowner, who lived in Rasht. I took the local bus many miles back to Rasht to obtain his permission before the dancers would unfurl their skirts, made with yards of material and trimmed in ribbons, and dance against the dramatic backdrop of the Caspian sea and its emerald forests, creating a memorable choreographic image. Even more colorful were a group of Turkmen near Gorgan in northeastern Iran, dancing in front of their black tents, known as yurts, accompanied only by their own stamping and guttural explosions of breath.* In addition to this sojourn of several weeks, I attended many gatherings, large and small, in Tehran and other cities, in which I saw and participated in a wide variety of dance experiences.

When I returned to the United States in 1960, I entered a new phase of documentation and research, focused on recording the movements of all the dancing I could encounter—a project that continues. The aim of this earlier project was the creation of choreography for the companies that I directed and the one I currently direct, the AVAZ International Dance Theatre.[7] I currently conduct a large part of my life in an Iranian-American environment.

In 1993, when I entered the newly-created Dance History & Theory doctoral program at the University of California, Riverside, I planned to write a history of Iranian dance, but I soon realized that the research questions that I would pose would involve the deeper social and cultural meanings of Iranian solo improvised dance rather than a chronological history. As I sharpened the focal and theoretical aspects of this study, the phrases, observations, and experiences covering a forty-year period began to create a holistic meaning of how, and in which contexts, solo improvised dance creates a negative and ambiguous symbol among Iranians and Iranian-Americans. For example, some weeks ago, a woman caller to *Radio Seda-ye Iran* (Voice of Iran) characterized the behavior of the Iranian-Americans of Southern California as *raqas-bazi* (acting like dancers). This is a phrase indicating irresponsibility, a lack of ethics and morals, and out-of-control behavior, which I have heard for years, but since the inception of this research, and in light of my theory of choreophobia, it and other phrases like it have taken on added meaning.[8] However, dancing does not always constitute a negative symbol. Some Iranians, at great personal risk, perform solo improvised dance in Iran, where it is now banned. The meaning of this dance—joyful or shameful, entertaining or aesthetic, normative or transgressive, or even, occasionally, rebellious and out-of-control, flows from the specific context and the individuals involved. Thus, the meaning and how the particular behavior involved is judged becomes a highly involved and complex phenomenon requiring hours of observation and analysis. Such determinants as gender, age, social class and position, context, and the variable of individual character must be weighed and sifted.

Dance Events
"Dance events" form useful framing units for the analysis of various contexts for dancing, and as such they have constituted the primary unit of analysis for virtually all major ethnographically-oriented dance studies over the past twenty-five years. Anya Peterson Royce states that we can resolve the difficulties of defining what "dance" is "by thinking in terms of *dance events* (her emphasis) rather than of dances and dancing," that is, "taking whole events as the unit of analysis rather than individual dances" (1977:10). She points out that "the analyst's divisions may be arbitrary and so once again we must discover the boundaries that are culturally meaningful" (1977: 12).

Royce warns, "a culture may not have a major category that corresponds to 'dance event'" (1977:13). This is certainly true for Iran. Royce also points out that in addition to determining what kind of social or aesthetic gathering might comprise a "dance event" in a given culture is "the problem of determining the significance of dance in any particular society or culture. It is obvious that not all aspects of culture are given equal weight" (1977:13). In the Iranian culture sphere, including the diaspora, one informant cogently stated that "dance is the least of the arts, if an art form at all" (Khosrow Jamali: personal interview, April 4, 1994). Therefore, it is perhaps better to state that within this sphere there are events in which one may encounter dancing, rather than argue for the existence of dance events.

Dancing does not occur as an integral part of any specific occasion.

For example, one would not expect dancing to take place at the weddings of those who are religiously or socially conservative, but even here one is never certain. Such individuals often find dancing offensive, but not always. *A young woman in* hejab, *a form of dress identified as modest Islamic covering, approached me after a concert* (November 18, 1995). *I had helped her via fax and telephone in a class project concerning Iranian traditional clothing, but we had not met in person. I automatically held out my hand to greet her as I do with other Iranian women of my acquaintance, but she refused to take the hand of a strange man, for which she apologized. She said how much she had enjoyed the performance, because it was her first experience of dance where the dance and the dancers were appropriately and modestly portrayed in a public space, but that she was made uncomfortable by what she perceived as hostile stares and comments of other Iranian audience members, particularly women, who inquired, "what was a 'hejabi' doing attending a dance concert?" And did I share their views? She left after stating that she was returning to Iran for a short visit, kindly inquiring if she could bring back costume pieces to help us.*

Among other groups, such as families, groups of friends, social meetings of professional societies of attorneys and physicians in the Iranian diaspora in Southern California, dance is an expected activity at most weddings and parties, and musicians are hired to play for this activity. Certain singers and their orchestras are known for encouraging audiences to come to the dance floor and dance. Historian Gene Garthwaite stated that in Iran, even under a strict interdiction, dance is very important to wedding celebrations for many individuals, in order to express appropriate happiness. In the city of Shiraz, which he visits regularly, people bribe the local authorities and pay guards at considerable cost and risk to look out for anyone who might expose their illicit dance activities (personal interview: July 7, 1995). Several informants who have recently visited Iran stated that dancing in private, within safely secure sites, is commonplace in Tehran and other cities (Parvaneh Azad [March 30, 1996], Loghman and Jani Adhami [April 21, 1996], Houshang Chehabi [Nov. 15, 1995], Cynthia Word [Nov. 5, 1995], among others: personal communication). I argue that this is one way in which dance has begun to assume for some individuals the status of a symbol of resistance to the Islamic regime.

For many individuals, especially in cities in the Iranian culture sphere, solo improvised dance constitutes at once the folk dance, the art dance, the social dance, and the entertainment dance, and this dance tradition thus forms a blurred genre: to the trained eye, the dance performed at a party by a highly talented dancer may appear the same as that performed by a professional stage dancer. Indeed, the two *are* the same, except in context. In contrast, in the United States or Western Europe, these genres usually form discrete categories. Few people would feel it appropriate to suddenly encounter a *pas-de-deux* at a wedding reception or disco dancing at the Music Center (although this is theoretically possible).

Thus, although I will use "dance event" for the sake of brevity, what I mean by that term is an event in which dance occurs, for example, at a wedding party, and I will analyze the varying events in which dance occurs in the Iranian diaspora in the same way. In Chapter Five I look at participatory events, while in Chapter Six I present data on performance events for the sake of contrast and to discuss the issue of orientalism. It is not uncommon to find events in which both participatory and performance elements are present. Thus the division of Chapters Five and Six are, to some degree, as Nahachewsky suggests (1995), arbitrary and artificial, although most participants can make the distinction between dancing prepared for public performance and dancing found in social events. In fact, for many individuals it forms a dividing line between acceptable and unacceptable contexts.

In contrast to practices in Iran, dance and other activities, such as the wearing of Iranian folk and traditional clothing, increasingly serves in the diaspora as a method of representing one's "Iranian-ness." In addition to attending family events, young Iranian-Americans, some of whom can no longer speak Persian, flock to discotheques and concerts of popular singers to perform a modern version of this dance. A musical industry thrives in Los Angeles by primarily producing music to which this dance can be performed. Tapes of this music circulate in a huge black market in Iran and the Persian Gulf area, where contraband audio and video tapes are prized items. Solo improvised dancing serves as a major form of cultural expression for this young group; however, the stigma of the professional dancer still obtains, even among the young. For example, most of the backup dancers in Iranian videos are non-Iranians.

This study of solo improvised dance constitutes a portrait of this dance genre and serves as a lens for viewing the wider Iranian world, including the diaspora, in both social and aesthetic contexts, by scrutinizing critical aspects of gender, ethnicity, religion, and social class in the research process. The concept of choreophobia will be suggestive of future studies, both in Middle Eastern contexts and in general social science issues, such as the negative reactions of fathers toward sons who wish to take dance classes, historic reactions of Americans and Western Europeans toward women who dance in public, or studies of performers in various classical dance traditions such as Kabuki, Kathak, and classical Western ballet.

Chapter 1

Solo Improvised Dance: Its Movement, Practices and Aesthetics

Introduction

> One Western resident here (Tehran), a woman,
> would tell me: "You must watch a Persian woman
> dance in her home·before her guests, displaying her
> gold and jewels to show that her husband is doing
> well and that he loves her enough to buy such things.
> You can see traces of this behavior in five-year old girls -
> how these girls move with their bodies!
> It is implanted in their genes.
> Politics has no effect over these things."
> (Kaplan 1995 :184)

*I*n 1954, I first encountered Iranian classmates, and a new dance
form—different from anything I had ever seen or imagined.
Over the next few years as I learned this dance, I entered a sur-
real world of geometry and movement, design and pattern: a world of
lines and curves, webs and intersecting points, jeweled and brilliant,
beckoning the dancer to stretch, reach, and touch the sources of jeweled
light at their points of intersection. Ushered into this new sphere by the
plangent tones of Saba's violin playing on a lovingly protected old 78
record by my teacher, Maryam, I followed her in a series of filigreed
gestures of the hands and fingers, geometrically informed movements
that follow the curves of the intricate Persian calligraphy and the arabesques contained within its sphere. I sought the answer to the web and
its infinite structure, but always elusive, it continued, and still continues,
to throw out lures beckoning me to resolve the problem of its creation,
at whose possible solution it enticingly hints and beckons. I began by
following my instructors, Maryam and Asad,[1] and I continue through my
own dancing, and through that of those who learn with and from me, to
try to solve the enigma of this world, hauntingly reflected in the intricate

16

mirrored walls, naves, and ceilings of the shrine of Imam Reza in Mash-
had, the intricate masonry of the dome of the Lotfallah mosque in Isfa-
han, or the turquoise minarets of Khiva and Samarqand. I now search
through these writings to seek an understanding of the aesthetic spell
this dance tradition has cast over me for more than forty years.

The freedom was intoxicating for one whose dance experiences were
those of the folk dances of the West, where each movement of the feet
and hands is dictated and somehow bound. In this new world I could
reach and stretch when and where I wanted; I was able to create new
patterns in a never-ending quest for creating new designs. Each minute
movement of the eyebrow or lip forms a pattern and meaning as signifi-
cant as a ballet leap or modern dance contraction. The freedom of ex-
pression seems endless, at first frightening, and finally liberating in the
vast possibilities the dance offers.

Not all who see and experience this dance enter this world I have
found. I was surprised that my new Iranian friends at Los Angeles City
College were uncomfortable that this was an aspect of Iranian culture
that enticed me—for them it had other, less aesthetic, meanings. They
were pleased when I learned to speak Persian and sing classical songs,
which, after all, are related to poetry, the supreme Persian art, but they
could not enthusiastically enter into the enchantment that I felt with this
new world of movement.

A study of dance should properly begin with its source: the dancing
body. In this section I wish to examine the movement tradition and
certain choreographic aspects of the solo improvised dance form, to
draw its portrait. In order for the reader to better understand this tradition I wish to present certain aesthetic and movement characteristics of
this dance form, for an understanding of the movement aspects of this
tradition is crucial in determining how much they contribute to the ambiguity with which this dance is often perceived, in contrast to how
much contextual and societal elements play a role in this perception. As
I stated in the introduction, this ambiguity consists of the love of performing solo improvised dance, which many Iranian individuals avidly
feel, while at the same time accounting for the negative attitudes held by
those same individuals toward professional dancers or even individuals
who are perceived as dancing in a transgressive or out-of-control fashion in a social context. In either case, the dancing body becomes an
active constructor and conductor of meaning.

Although I will discuss the process of improvisation in detail in the
next subsection, it is important to draw attention to its role, which is of
paramount importance because it is in the performance of the improvisational movements of highly proficient dancers that both the aesthetic
and potentially transgressive aspects of this dance form are visually
most clearly manifested. I argue that the improvisational character of
the dance contributes to the sense of ambiguity, because one never

knows what is coming next. (A similar observation has been made about the parallel performative elements in the traditional improvised comic theatre by the actor, Ardavan Mofid, personal interview, April 4, 1994).

In the following subsections I begin with observations to establish this dance form, in contrast to other patterned movement practices in the Iranian culture sphere, and then proceed to a discussion of: 1) the movements that are characteristic of the solo improvised dance tradition 2) the process of improvisation and 3) the relationship between this dance tradition and other performative forms of expression, such as theatre, storytelling and music, and visual expressions, such as calligraphy and the decorative arts.

Iranian Dance Types, Regional Folk Dances

I want to briefly recapitulate what I described in the introduction: that there are two basic types of dance performed throughout the Iranian culture sphere, and indeed, throughout the Middle East generally. The first type is regional folk dancing, which is most often performed, but not exclusively so, in groups. In the folk dances of the northern and western regions of this vast cultural region, which includes Georgia, Armenia, Daghestan, Azerbaijan, Kurdistan, and Luristan, the dancers are often linked by hand and arm holds of various sorts. The performance of these dances in line, semi-circular and/or circle formations thus forms the eastern terminus of a "belt" which begins in Europe and ends in this northwestern region of the Iranian culture sphere, in which such patterned line and circle dances constitute the most common form of choreographic expression. (See Hasanov 1988 and Lisitsian 1956, 1972 for descriptions of dances of the northwestern districts of the Iranian culture sphere.) By contrast, in the eastern and southern districts of this area, such as Khorasan, Fars, the Persian Gulf region, Baluchistan, Afghanistan, Turkmenia, Uzbekistan and Tajikistan, the regional dances are performed in groups, but the dancers do not touch one another, and often carry scarves, sticks, or other objects with which to embellish their movements. In the latter area, some scope for improvisation is possible because of the relative freedom of the body; however, the dancers conceive of themselves as part of a group that moves together. (See Hamada 1978 and St. John 1993 for descriptions of typical regional dances from the eastern regions of the Iranian culture sphere.) All of these dances are most often associated with the countryside, even though they may sometimes be seen in urban areas, particularly the line and circle dances. Because of the many participants associated with these dances, they are more commonly associated with outdoor performances. Briefly, these dances are characterized by regional specificity of style and short, patterned choreographic phrases that are repeated and embellished with variations, in contrast to the solo improvised dance, which is based totally on improvisation and solo performance.

Regional dances, particularly those of the first type, which are performed in lines and circles, may be seen at various events in Southern California where large communities of Azerbaijanis, Kurds, Assyrians, and Armenians live and gather for communal celebrations. Peoples from the eastern and southern regions of the Iranian culture sphere are not as numerous or as tightly organized on community lines in Southern California as the above mentioned groups; nevertheless, one can readily find individuals from these areas who can demonstrate regional dances.

Solo Improvised Dance

The second type of dance is solo improvised dancing, which is associated more often with urban life than the specifically regional forms that are more commonly performed in village and tribal areas. In contrast to the regional dances, this dance form is performed in a strikingly uniform manner, within the wide scope of its potential movement practices, both in its performance and in the aesthetic and creative impulses that form its basis throughout this vast region. Such dancing can be seen from Tiflis in Georgia to Western China, from Khiva in Uzbekistan to Shiraz in southwestern Iran, as well as the diaspora. This dance form is potentially limitless in its improvisational creativity within its specific stylistic framework, and as I have previously stated, it serves, in all of its ambiguous manifestations, as the topic of this investigation.

A tour group I led to the former Soviet Union in 1986, and again in 1989, which contained several Iranian friends, was thrilled by the amount of dance events we attended. In Bukhara, after a concert of highly choreographed dance selections, and in Baku, the capital of Azerbaijan, where we were the guests of the koreografskii *institut (a version of the high school for the performing arts), after a recital, we were invited to join in a dance. That dance, was, of course, the solo improvised dance. Iranians and non-Iranians alike were startled that the dance appeared the same in two locales thousands of miles apart. We saw the same dance at two weddings in Tajikistan on a bus ride through that republic. The Uzbeks and Azerbaijanis with whom we danced were also surprised to see how well we executed the movements of their dance. After all of the choreography they learn, professional dancers, like all others, turn to the solo improvised dance when an event takes on a social aspect.*

The Movements

> *An Iranian woman dancer in AVAZ*
> *demanded more solos. When told*
> *that her years of training in jazz*
> *dancing were preventing her from*
> *dancing Persian dance with precision,*
> *she replied, "I dance Persian dance*
> *perfectly, because it's in my blood."*

Let me state at the outset that I am extracting for analytical purposes what I have identified as basic movement elements from this dance tradition. In the actual performance, the performer is rarely self-consciously considering his or her next movement, for dancing is as "natural" to the dancer as his or her native language—in other words, it is another form of culturally learned behavior. The person who is dancing rarely sustains the same movement for a prolonged period; rather, the movements flow from one to another with no perceptible boundary except, perhaps, for a brief and artful pose. (Occasionally, one encounters an individual who dances so poorly that he or she can only sketch one or two basic movements, which are then sustained for long periods.)[2]

The constant flow of movement in all of the arts is of paramount aesthetic value, in both the performative expressions of dance and music and in the visual arts such as calligraphy, rug-making, and ceramics. In a preliminary Laban Movement Analysis report, I found that this dance form, like many of the visual and aural forms of expression, is marked by Effort that alternates between "bound" and "free," indicating a sense of "movement" and flow marked by tension and release. This intrinsic feature of "movement" is one that is almost universally observed and remarked upon by scholars in such fields as music and art history. (See especially Pope 1964, Farhat 1965, Hill and Grabar 1964, and Yusofi 1994.)

It is extremely difficult to extract meaningful movement elements as separate analytical units to use in the classes in which I teach Iranian dance, because they are generally very individual and idiosyncratic to specific dancers.[3] Nevertheless, certain movements are common to most dancers. Whereas non-Iranian students can more readily learn and "read" such artificially isolated movements, Iranian students are hard-pressed to articulate and isolate from the flow of movement these actions, which they instinctively know and have learned from childhood. This is analogous to the manner in which many native speakers of a language cannot always articulate its grammar, because its linguistic organization and rules are embedded in their mental structure. Just as a child learns a language which is culturally specific and, although it seems "natural" because it is a deeply ingrained learned experience, it is not "natural," as Barthes (1972) suggests, but "cultural," in this same way a child learns movement, including dance. During this process, a child also learns which words and phrases he or she may, or may not, politely say in given circumstances and contexts. The child also learns that certain kinds of movements acquire a cultural value of good and bad, appropriate and inappropriate to one's gender and social standing. This is important to grasp in dealing with a society in which dance can often, but not always, carry negative connotations, because this will frequently determine not only the movement characteristics of how an individual dances, but which contexts are appropriate for performance. When they dance, the Iranians just allow the movements to flow in the same way their words do as they speak. Many state that they cannot dance without "appropriate" music.

What I present in the following descriptions are *generic* movements that are common in the tradition, but that no two dancers perform alike, with the possible exception of theatrical performances. Even in such performances, achieving uniformity is difficult due to the nuances that characterize Iranian movements. Like the classical music tradition in which elements from regional folk music and popular urban music may be woven into a musical composition, individual dancers may utilize movements from a variety of sources, including regional dances.

Feet. In this dance tradition, the footwork is not as important as the carriage and movements of arms, especially the hands and fingers. The foot movements that I describe are basically a repeated step pattern of right-left-right, then left-right-left (or the opposite) in no set direction, i.e. three steps in a single 6/8 musical phrase. It is the most basic step employed in the domestic dance form *(majlesi)*. In performance, the vast majority of dancers, or those who watch them, pay little attention to their footwork, unless it is intrusively awkward. Most dancers perform with the feet maintained in a parallel rather than turned-out position. Men sometimes step on one foot, placing their full weight on it, while bending the knee of the other leg and lifting that foot onto the toe with no weight, and alternating feet in a stationary position or moving slowly in a forward direction. This step can be exaggerated or made transgressive by the performance of deep knee bends. For most dancers, the primary weight is mostly on the ball of the foot, but they can also employ the full foot. In the Caucasian variant of this style, the most elaborate in the region, the male dancer may dance on his toes, bent back and encased in specially constructed boots for support.

Individual dancers display a wide variety of choice in how far they lift the heel from the floor; some female dancers, especially, rise high on the toes, while many male performers touch the heel to the floor. The surface on which the dance is performed also plays a part. Rugs, an almost invariable feature in an Iranian living room, present a different challenge from grass, cement, wood, or other flooring. Another factor is whether or not the dancer wears shoes; very often in an indoor setting, the dancer is barefoot or wearing stockings. In the next section, improvisation, I will describe how a dancer might change and alter the footwork during a performance.

An additional element which determines the size of the step and whether a dancer will perhaps mark time with the feet, or even remain stationary, is the size of the space in which the dancers perform and how many other performers are occupying it. For example, in a crowded wedding party, with limited space for dancing and many dancers moving in an uncoordinated fashion, little footwork is employed except to move in a small space, in which the foot pattern might constitute a simple weight shift from the left foot to the right foot in time to the music or performing the step I described above in one place. An individual performing a solo with adequate space may take alternatively large and small steps, remain stationary to perform a backbend or kneel to execute some intricate gesture with his or her upper limbs and bring the focus of the viewer to his or her arm or facial movements. He or she might move about the space and acknowledge the onlookers.

In the domestic form of the dance, the feet rarely leave the dancing surface, but professional dancers will lift their legs, perhaps lifting the knee forward as they execute a backbend, or extending the leg behind in order to create a long linear figure in conjunction with an extended opposite arm. Male dancers, in the style familiar from the Caucasian tradition, may perform squats and kicks, an element of many regional dance styles (i.e., Khorasan, Baluchistan, Gilan, Azerbaijan, Georgia, and Armenia).

Most dance music, often called *reng*, is conceived of and executed in 6/8 rhythm, called in Persian *shish-hashtom*. (In point of fact, the rhythm often "drifts" between 6/8 and 7/8, the latter being especially common to Eastern Iran and Afghanistan.) The dancer moves to and maintains this rhythmic pattern.

Arms, hands, and fingers. In this choreographic form, the hands and fingers form the primary center of interest in the performance and the movements of the arms and hands can range from motionless, especially by males, to very articulated rotations of the wrists and hands and intricate gestures of the fingers, culminating in a position, held momentarily, in which the thumb and middle finger create a "c" shape. This intricate movement is more common in the female style, but there is no set rule, and some men employ intricate hand movements, though rarely with the very ornate finger gestures that characterize highly proficient female dancing. Males tend to extend both of their arms to the side, rotating the wrists and hands on the first beat of the music for emphasis. Females more commonly extend one arm while keeping the other near the head or face. Alternating hands and arms, she will often move gently from side to side to accommodate this movement.

A typical movement performed by most dancers in this tradition: both arms sweep gently to the right during one pas-de-basque, i.e., one full musical measure of 6/8, (right foot, left foot, right foot). In this movement, the arms move sagitally across the front of the torso, finally extending with slightly bent elbow of the right arm and strongly bent elbow of the left arm. On the second measure, starting on the left foot, both arms sweep gently to the left. In other words, the movement to the right is repeated to the left.

The arms and hands may also be used to frame the face and head and call attention to movements of the head, face, or torso. In accomplished dancing, the arms and hands generally create geometrically balanced forms that can bear a marked similarity to calligraphic forms and strokes of such Persian letters as *sin, lam, be,* and *he (jimi).* These movements are likened to the calligrapher's movements in forming these letters (for which I observed master calligrapher, Masoud Valipour, Sept. 13 and Dec. 6, 1995); in the performance of an experienced dancer in this tradition, the arms and hands may be held or moved either in opposition to one another or in parallel positions. For example, one arm may extend diagonally right, forward, and high, the other diagonally backward and low, in the opposite direction. As the arms flow from position to position, for example, from diagonally, forward, right high, to low, left, back, they create arcs, the trace forms of which may resemble the letters I mention above, as well as other letters or geometric forms such as arabesques. They may move within a wide range of space surrounding the body, the kinesphere, and the dancer may reach, extend or hyper-extend above the head and body, or reach and extend forward, backward, or to the side. These limbs may be held close to the body or they may stretch and extend to the maximum possible physical range. The most accomplished dancers use the entire range of possible directions and elevations. This, like the foot movements, is largely determined by spatial constraints, and the ability of the dancer. More than any other part of the body, the hands, arms, and fingers are in almost constant and harmonious movement, with the elements moving together, for example, the dancer may rotate the wrists and hands toward one another or away from each other. These movements are largely created by deep rotations of the hands and wrists, and articulation of the wrist and elbow joints, which require considerable muscular effort and control.

The geometric elements of the dance become most apparent in an accomplished performance when the dancer's movements may be punctuated by effective pauses, which create momentary poses, generally in some interesting geometric form, such as turning to the side and curving both arms in an arc, with the hands placed near the head, or alternatively extending the arms and hands away from the body in a linear figure extending from the shoulders, the torso and head leaning away from the extended arms, creating a long diagonal figure. One of my

outstanding students, Marjan Haghnia, who is a highly proficient performer of the domestic style of this dance, states that she is aware of this
geometric symmetry in her dancing and that of other outstanding performers, but does not think in geometric, or any other terms, during a
performance. Rather, she "just lets the movements flow" (personal interview: November 4, 1995). These brief pauses and poses may seem to
the observer like a momentary breath in the playing of a woodwind
player, and then the performer continues, creating ever-new figures.
Perhaps this time, the dancer creates undulating, sinuous, or wave-like
movements by rotating the wrist or articulating the elbow and wrist
joints.

The more experienced dancers, particularly female performers, articulate their fingers, ultimately completing the poses with intricate and
elegant gestures of the fingers. The most popular figure is a "c" created
by closing the thumb and middle finger. However, this gesture may be
extremely rounded or executed with the fingers extended in a flattened
"c." In addition, the most accomplished dancers carry their arms farther
away from the body and demonstrate great flexibility in the manner in
which they extend their limbs, rotate the wrists, and articulate the joints,
creating arcs and spirals of the arms and hands, whereas many of those
who dance only occasionally tend to maintain their arms close to the
body and perform fewer movements. This is especially manifest in the
inability of dancers with little experience to perform full rotations of the
wrist or create elegant finger positions.

Torso and head. For purposes of both movement analysis and aesthetic conceptualization, the body may divided into two halves at the
mid-line. In preliminary Laban movement analysis examinations of this
dance genre, it became clear that this mid-line forms a useful center
point around which the "rules" of logic of choice, which I describe below, unfold. Thus, the torso becomes a focal point for the analysis of
movement practices in this dance tradition.

During the course of the dance, highly experienced dancers employ
shoulders, hips, torso, head and even nuanced movements of lips and
eyebrows. Some highly proficient and accomplished dancers are aware
of the positioning of the spine in order to create a bearing that is highly
aesthetic, reflected also in the way in which the arms are carried and the
distance at which these limbs are maintained from the body. However,
unlike many Western dance practices, the shoulders are maintained in a
highly relaxed position so that they can be employed in the movement
sequences. Such awareness is more common among those who have
experience in Western dance forms such as ballet, or those who have
had professional experience in a performing company. Older traditional
dancers also demonstrate this awareness in the uncompromising up-
rightness of the upper body with which they dance. They are very conscious that a firm control of the spine allows them a more graceful and

commanding carriage of the arms and the ability to perform extensions of the torso and arms. *I especially remember Nino Ramishvili, who served as the director of the Georgian State Ensemble for many decades. She performed a solo with eight men who were performing enormously difficult acrobatics, but with minimal movements of the hands, arms, and fingers, she managed to command the stage, drawing my eyes to her and all but obliterating the male octet with whom she shared the stage. Her majestic carriage and bearing, which she created through her posture and strength and which was most clearly manifest in her almost rigid spinal position, coupled with her artistic authority, turned the general order of these performances upside down: the woman was in charge. I do not know if any other person in the audience was as forcibly struck by the sheer force of Ramishvili's presence on the stage as I was. Generally, it is my experience as a choreographer and audience member that if a male or group of males performs highly athletic, acrobatic and gymnastic movements, female dancers often disappear from the observer's attention. That is why I was particularly struck by Ramishvili's performance: she was middle-aged, with a highly prominent nose, she was striking, and she was performing minimal versions of several of the movements I described above, and yet, in this performance, I could not take my eyes from her, in spite of the best efforts of the highly athletic male dancers who flanked her.*

During the course of a performance a dancer might move the torso in a number of ways. One example is the dancer who moves the torso from the front-center to an alternating side-to-side pattern, so that the dancer creates a 45-90 degree angle turning right and then left (or the opposite). Dancers often use a combination of bending the knee and gently extending the pelvis diagonally forward, alternating sides. In the execution of this movement, the weight is carried on one foot, the other extended forward, with no weight, resting on the toe. The torso movements found in a domestic performance are supple and undulating, but generally do not approach the open sexuality seen in Egyptian belly dancing, except in a cabaret dancer who is recognized as performing foreign movements in a transgressive manner. When the dancer does employ such a movement, known in Persian as *gheir*, which in English can be rendered colorfully and colloquially as "bump and grind," or indeed, any coquettish, sensual, or sexy gesture, especially of the torso, the movement can lead to transgressive and out-of-control behavior. Such movements are evoked in several traditional, popular *tasnif* (rhythmic songs) which celebrate worldly parties with wine and professional entertainers (*motreb*). A typical refrain is:

ela saqia, mey biar	(to the wine-bearer, bring wine)
ela motreba, ney bezan	(to the *motreb*, strike up the flute)
pas boro, pish bia	(go this way, come that)
naz nakon, gheir biar	(don't act coy, perform a *gheir*)

A typical male movement of the pelvis occurs in traditional comic theatre or in the dance called *shateri*, a dance associated with the male urban
underclass. In this figure the dancer extends his arms to the sides at
shoulder level, places his weight on one foot and slowly rotates the pelvis in a half circle, starting the rotation by moving back, which he extends as far as the body permits without moving his feet from their stationary position.

Another common movement is the raising and lowering, or moving
forward and backward, of one or both shoulders—each type of such
movement creates a different impression, depending on the relative size
of the gesture, sometimes very subtle and elegant if minute movements
are made, sometimes vulgar or comic if large, gross gestures are employed. In the Persian Gulf region, intense shimmying movements of
the shoulders and torso and/or hip movements, sometimes associated
with Egyptian belly dancing, are performed. In the 1970s these movements became popular in Tehran and other large cities, in much the
same manner that Latin American dances became popular in Anglo
contexts in the United States from 1920, beginning with the tango, up to
the present with salsa. In addition, Egyptian and Indian musical films
with elaborate dance scenes were popular in Iran until the fall of the
Pahlavis in 1979. In these films, particularly those of India, large casts
of dancers, numbering in the dozens, performed highly polished dance
routines employing movements that appealed to many Iranians. Such
movements as swiveling the head from side to side, intricate turning
figures, elaborate arm and hand gestures, and sensual torso movements,
such as articulating the pelvis in the manner of Egyptian belly dancers,
increased the movement vocabulary of some dancers in both the Iranian
culture sphere and in the California diaspora. For example, one of the
young Iranian women in my class uses these movements far more than
any of the other Iranian students because of her "interest in belly dance."

The range of torso movements, especially regarding how often the
torso is employed, varies perhaps more than any other type of movement among dancers. Mernissi (1975) argues that Islam, unlike Christianity, acknowledges sexual urges, and through this recognition, its
authorities are highly concerned with maintaining sexuality within
proper spaces and contexts. Women and men may perform transgressively in sexually segregated spaces, but not in mixed spaces, or run the
risk of being considered out-of-control. Pelvic movements are recognized as sexual, the torso and pelvis form a site of sexuality in Iranian
society, and prudent women and men in mixed situations are careful of

the way in which they use articulated movements of the pelvic area. Many dancers feel uncomfortable performing torso movements that approach those seen in belly dancing, preferring instead to concentrate on the graceful movements of the hands and arms, while others, particularly younger dancers, unhesitatingly perform torso movements with great gusto.

The head may be moved from side to side, swiveling on the neck, by both men and women, and men especially will sometimes jut their heads forward and back. Such movements often produce highly comic effects. The most proficient dancers can make their eyebrows "dance," moving them alternately up and down, or seemingly creating a sinuous effect of the eyebrow moving along the brow. The lips can be used to great effect by some dancers who create sensuous or comic effects by pursing or twitching movements or sinuously rolling them sideways.

It is in the category of movements of torso, head, and facial features that the greatest potential for transgression lies. If the performer is highly skilled, he or she can imbue these movements with either comedy and wit, or a sensuality that can be condemned by those who are not amused. For example, in the comic theatre, *ru-howzi*, the black-face clown and other male characters jut their buttocks or pelvis in a variety of transgressive gestures. It is rare that movements of the hands, arms or feet carry such transgressive meaning.[4]

Turns and spins. During the course of a performance, a dancer might execute a single or double turn, generally slowly, but occasionally rapidly. A turn provides spice to a performance, giving another dimension of movement, a type of flavoring. It permits the dancer to suddenly alter direction, face another group of onlookers, and change the mood from serious to comic. If the turn is slow, he or she may demonstrate new ranges of movement for the all-important hands, arms, and fingers. A highly proficient dancer, particularly in a stage performance, might execute a series of rapid spins. In a performance captured on film by the American University Field Services, a professional Afghan male dancer executes many rapid turns. Rapid spinning is a basic element of the choreographies of the Uzbek professional dance companies, based on the domestic practice of former professional entertainers. In domestic settings the possibilities for turning are always limited by spatial considerations and the skill of the individual dancer.

The movement vocabulary, as I will try to demonstrate, is potentially enormous and capable of accommodating the individual movement styles of a wide variety of performers and performance contexts. As Farhat, an ethnomusicologist (1965), remarked about Persian classical music, Iranian solo improvised dance is a subtle and detailed form of expression, and to the untutored eye it may appear repetitive. I argue that the same aesthetic creative impulses and improvisational format are universal throughout the urban areas of this region, creating the exis-

tence of a single dance tradition. As ethnomusicologist Joanna Spector
pointed out earlier in a parallel fashion for music, I assert that dance is
also performed in a myriad of individual styles that nevertheless display
a remarkable uniformity.

In sum, solo improvised dance consists of a large and rich reservoir
of movement practices, and during the course of the dance, highly experienced dancers, both professional and amateur, employ shoulders, hips,
torso, head and even nuanced movements of lips and eyebrows. Due to
the length and objectives of this study I was able to describe a few of the
most generic types of movement found in many Iranian social and public gatherings. This array of movement practice may be seen in often
prolonged performances showcasing an enormous variety of movement
combinations and moods—serious, playful, sensual, joyful, graceful,
ethereal. In such performances, the individual, skilled dancer has at his
or her disposal a reservoir of movements and movement formulae which
can be composed and recombined in a dizzying and almost limitless
variety, presenting the truly creative individual with the possibility of
endless performances of exciting creativity, freshness, and uniqueness.
It is in the use of the movements of torso and facial features such as the
eyebrows and lips that both the most transgressive and aesthetic potential exists. For purposes of this study the most important characteristics
of this dance tradition are its linkages with other performative practices
through the use of improvisation and with other visual forms through its
use of geometric elements, which inform many genres of Iranian art.

Improvisation
The process of improvisation (*fel-bedaheh or bedaheh*) is the core of all
of the traditional performing arts and performative creative expression
in the Iranian culture sphere, which includes the Iranian diaspora. (See
Farhat 1965 for music, Page 1976 for storytelling, and Beiza'i 1965 for
theatre.) To my knowledge, no one has investigated this feature of
dance in detail, much less distinguished between those dance forms that
are patterned and those that are improvised. It is the manner of improvisation which is key to the performance of this dance tradition. In this
discussion I wish to address two theoretical constructs of improvisation
which best conceptualize this process as it is manifested in solo improvised dance. Levi-Strauss' discussion of *bricolage* (1966) shows how
known units are recombined in new ways, and the Lord-Parry theory of
story telling and oral composition in the former Yugoslavia (Lord 1970)
suggests a model of the types of elements that are employed by storytellers, which I utilize to show how parallel strategies of composition of
movement phrases and formulae are elaborated, developed and embellished by performers of dance.[5]

As a simple illustration of an improvisational process, I will follow a
dancer through a movement action as the dancer improvises his or her

movements. Utilizing one of the basic step patterns, the performer may then pause to perform a backbend, the arms and hands may be carried across the body at chest level, then the dancer may raise them, and as the dancer performs a backbend, the hands will create intricate movements utilizing rotations of the wrists and hands, ending in the fingers creating a "c" figure. As he, or more generally she in this figure (men rarely perform backbends), rises, the dancer may execute a movement in which the head swivels from side to side, and, placing the right (or left) hand above the eyebrows, and the opposite hand below the chin, the dancer might execute minute twitching movements with the lips, or cause her eyebrows to rise and fall in opposition. Or, conversely, the performer might choose a whole different set of movements, either from among those I have described, or from an array of other actions and gestures. For example, the dancer might face the palms of her two hands outward, and maintain the wrists close together, at a 90 degree angle to the elbow, while the hands and fingers are moved side to side as they are articulated to the greatest possible mobility within that position. As the dancer creates that movement she may raise her hands upward. Alternatively, the dancer might place one hand at waist level, with a rounded arm, the other placed in opposition behind. If the right hand is in front, or the center of the body, the dancer flicks the fingers away from the body as she turns to the right. Instead of flicking the left hand, she may elect to place it on her waist, or behind her head. Or, she may create the flicking movement from low front, center and move to high front center, perhaps turning only a quarter of a turn as she executes the figure. The dancers select movements and figures depending largely on the audience, the music, the venue, the space, and the context.

In the above example, the pattern of the feet (right-left-right then left-right-left [or the opposite]) is a "set" (i.e., non-improvisational) figure, seen sometime during the course of the performance of most dancers. The rotation of the wrists to perform graceful hand and finger gestures, and the formation of a "c" with the middle finger and thumb, are also "set" figures, although the method and style usually change frequently during the performance, depending on factors such as musical tempo and context. The improvisational element in this example consists, partly, in how many times a figure, such as the rotating wrists or a backbend, is repeated; whether the dancer rotates the wrists and hands inward or outward; whether the arms move at high, middle, or low levels, forward, sideways, or back in direction; or the size of the movements (a proficient dancer often varies this element for contrast). I stress that each dancer has his or her own "set" figures and methods of improvising and recombining them.

Untangling the skein of what constitutes "set" movements from those that are improvised is a daunting and time-consuming task. Each individual has developed his or her own "set" phrases, and the observer,

after considerable time, can begin to discern individual styles and identify which of the gestures, figures, movements, and actions constitute
the "set" figures for a specific dancer and how that dancer typically improvises upon them.

One of the major objectives of this study is to ascertain when a specific dancer is performing in a transgressive, or even out-of-control
manner. Since, as I make specific throughout Chapter Five, this judgment is contingent on context and the performance of movements that
onlookers judge to be transgressive, it follows that a close familiarity
with the specific movement patterns of an individual dancer become
crucial in making such a determination. For instance, in Chapter Five, I
describe several instances where, during the course of dancing, certain
individuals were considered to be performing in a transgressive fashion,
and in some more extreme cases, out-of-control. In the case of "Nazi,"
this determination was made possible both through my familiarity with
her dancing style over several years, as well as the reactions of other
members of the event, many of whom were also familiar with her style.
In the case of "Jaleh," the dancer who was considered out-of-control,
such a determination was aided by the fact that she rarely danced in
public, and then performed movements, particularly of the pelvis, that
even a non-Iranian might have considered shocking. (Indeed, this was
true, since I spoke with several such individuals who had been considerably startled by Jaleh's performance.) Hence, familiarity with a specific dancer's usual movement style and practice enables an investigator
to analyze, through both movement analysis as well as social context,
when an individual can be deemed to be performing in a transgressive or
out-of-control manner.

Improvisation, as I mentioned, may consist of patterns (or a lack
thereof) of repetition, varying directions of movement and different elevations of arms or feet, intricacy or simplicity of hand or finger gestures,
or size of steps and figures. The generic figures I described above belong to the movement vocabularies of the majority of Iranian dancers.
By contrast, one young woman in my class typically places one hand
lightly on her forehead, looks down, and begins to turn, extending the
other hand in front. While this movement is by no means unique to her,
it is also not common. The "set" element in this performance is the
placing of the hand on the forehead.

The improvisational elements are: the turn may be rapid or very
slow; instead of turning, she might choose to move forward, or move a
few steps first to one side and alternate to the other side; she may move
the extended hand high or low, forward or sideways; she may rotate the
wrist of the extended hand inward or outward; she might elect to repeat
all or parts of this sequence on the other side, beginning the sequence by
placing her other hand on her forehead.

As a third example, a dancer might place his or, more typically her in this movement, right hand and arm, bent at the elbow at a ninety degree angle, diagonally to the right and extend the left arm, also bent at the elbow, across the body at chest level, the fingers of the left hand lightly touching the right elbow. The "set" portion of the figure is the position of the arms. The dancer, while moving from one side to the other, may choose to execute a different position of the hands and fingers with each movement, for example, altering the direction of the palms in or out. She may hold the position for several measures as she turns in place toward the vertically held arm. She may choose to move her head, or emphasize the movement of her alternating arms by extending her hips and pelvis from side to side as she moves. The performer may select a moving foot pattern or one that is stationary.

Improvisation informs the total range of movement practice in the Iranian solo improvised dance from demure and domestic to transgressive and professional. It is not knowing what comes next that provides the chief opportunity for transgressive and potentially "out-of-control" behavior. An understanding of the process of improvisation will aid the observer in analyzing and determining such behavior. In the next section I will discuss the process by which a dancer selects the choreographic elements he or she employs.

Logic of Choice "Principles"

Within the improvisational process, the discerning eye of the careful observer may begin to analyze and establish certain patterns and movement "strategies" that a large number of individuals utilize during the improvisational performance. I will loosely call these "principles" of the logic of choice, by which I mean that certain aesthetic elements within the dance tradition are translated into movement by a performer. I will describe three "principles" or "rules" that I believe illustrate this point: 1) alternation, 2) opposition, and 3) simultaneity. I wish to stress that in no way do these "rules" or "principles" constitute any kind of articulated practice: the majority of men and women who dance do so in an unconscious fashion. By unconscious, I mean that the process of performing is so rapid that the dancer does not plan his or her movements. Nevertheless, these "principles" form common elements that constitute some of the "aesthetic building blocks" of this tradition that the careful student may observe in countless performances of many dancers. I must also stress that all three "principles," or any combination of them, may be employed at the same time, which I attempt to make clear in the following descriptions. In this way the use of these elements is highly fluid. Although I use specific movement examples to illustrate the logic of choice, the "principles" that I describe, in my opinion, underlie the entire movement edifice of this dance tradition and are not attached specifically to any particular set of movements, figures, or positions. Although I have identified three "principles" for the purpose of this study,

further analysis and observation might uncover and articulate the presence of many more, and so those that I present below are intended to be
suggestive of the possibility of other such examples within a larger
framework, and as such may form the subject of a future study.

   Alternation. This principle manifests itself in a large variety of
ways, some of which I described above. For example, a man may rise to
dance. He extends both arms and hands to the side (opposition) and he
slowly rotates his hands around, first his right hand, and then his left, or
vice versa. He may embellish this movement by raising his right shoulder forward and up, and then alternate this movement with his left
shoulder. He may push the alternation principle by alternating the
shoulder movement with that of the hands and wrists, or simultaneously
perform both. He may further demonstrate alternation by swiveling his
head first right then left. In a moment of high humor he may throw
imaginary breasts into the air, alternating his right hand with his left. *A
young Iranian woman from my group, saw Jamal execute this movement
in a performance where he was enacting the role of a* jahel [tough guy],
*to whom this movement figure is common, and, without realizing its
meaning or impact, she later performed this highly transgressive figure,
considerably startling the guests at a party she attended. She said later
"they were most forgiving and amused" when they realized that she did
not understand the meaning of this highly transgressive movement (interview: June 17, 1996).* The dancer may perform these movements in a
stationary position or move about the dance space alternating the foot
pattern I described above, right-left-right and then left-right-left. During
this performance, he may alternate the use of the movements of the
head, shoulders, arms, and hands in a variety of combinations.

   As a general observation, male dancers tend to move from position
to position more slowly than females. The males also tend to employ
fewer varieties of movement than female performers, thus alternation
occurs more frequently, and visually in a clearer manner, than is the
case of a skilled female performer. This is, however, a very general
observation, and throughout this study I wish to make clear that there
are many skilled male dancers who exhibit great inventiveness, while
there exist unskilled females who demonstrate limited movements during the course of a performance. All of this is tempered by the social
aspects of the particular gathering and the social status of an individual.
An individual dancer may exhibit great inventiveness and uniqueness
among a group of intimates, but appear limited or even awkward among
strangers with whom the individual is not comfortable.

   As another example of alternation, a dancer of either sex may rise
and, as he or she moves about the space where the dance is occurring,
use the foot pattern of right-left-right, left-right-left (or the opposite).
He or she may extend the right arm fully to the side at shoulder level
and at the same time move the left arm across the chest, bent at the el-

bow. The performer then alternates the position of the arms by next moving with the left arm extended and the right arm bent. As the dancer moves, the arms alternately move across the body, and commonly, he or she may rotate both hands around the wrists (simultaneity).

A highly skilled dancer may manipulate the eyebrows by alternating the lifting of the right eyebrow and then the left eyebrow.

Opposition. Opposition generally refers to the positioning of the arms in relation to one another; that is, while the right arm is raised, the left is lowered or vice versa. Opposition therefore stands in contrast to alternation, by which I refer to the sequence of movements. By opposition I mean, for example, the occasion when a performer extends the right (or left) hand up and the opposite hand down or one hand and arm forward and the other behind. This movement is very basic, and even considered by some to be old-fashioned, and is frequently used in historical miniatures as a symbol that dance is occurring. (See illustrations.) Thus, the limbs are in opposition to one another. Alternation also occurs, because it is usual to alternate the movement of the arms during the course of a performance. Simultaneity may also occur as the dancer rotates the hands around the wrists of both arms at the same time. All of this may take place during a single movement or figure.

Simultaneity. As I have shown above, when an individual performs with both hands moving at the same time, he or she exhibits my "principle" or "rule" of simultaneity. A dancer may choose to place both hands together at wrist level and move them together, perhaps rotating them around the wrist, or creating a wave-like motion by pushing the heel of the hand forward as far as possible, and then releasing it, and alternating the hands from one side of the body to the other.

It is hoped that these few examples will serve to demonstrate a larger phenomenon of patterning, and how this patterning model may be extended in a unique manner by each performer. I again reiterate that within specific stylistic parameters, which are always being pushed by some individuals, this is a highly idiosyncratic style of dance.

Having described some of the basic movements and aesthetic "principles" of this tradition as experienced in domestic settings, it remains to state that this dance tradition can also be performed in a carnivalesque and even grotesque fashion. This style of improvisation is very important since it contributes to the negative and ambiguous attitudes which many Iranian-Americans exhibit toward dance. This style of improvisation can occur either in a professional performance by professional actors in the traditional improvised comic theatre; or, in contrast, such informally, transgressive improvisation may occur when a group of male friends in a night club or a dancer at an intimate party might toss imaginary breasts in the air in the manner of a juggler, or dance with the comic movements of an infirm old man. It may also be seen when a woman participating in women's domestic theatre in the intimacy of the women's quarters, and among close female friends and family, might don her husband's hat and coat, puff out her chest and strut about the dance space in a hyper-masculine style, twirling a nonexistent moustache, thus using improvisation for fun and transgressive wit (Shay 1995b).

> With Batul-Khanom there was someone with whom to sew, visit the baths, and enjoy the jokes, games, and clowning with which women entertained themselves in a bit, fancy andarun [harem] like Ezzatdoleh's. My mother was too strict a Moslem to clown, but she enjoyed watching the others' horseplay, especially one of Ezzatdoleh's maids, who could paint her naked buttocks to look like two eyes and, dancing with them to the onlookers, would roll them so that the two eyes crossed. This made my mother, her little sisters, Batul and her daughters, and all the other women laugh until their sides ached. (Farman Farmaian 1992:37)

As we see in the example of Ezzatdoleh's maid, this dance tradition contains highly transgressive possibilities of expression.

The rules or principles of logic of choice may be associated with several modes of dance styles. These principles of logic of choice may be used in a number of interpretive modes: they may be employed in a transgressive performance, as I described with the dancer "juggling" imaginary breasts, or conversely, these "principles" can be also discerned in a serious performance of highly aesthetic expression. The dancer might attempt, through idiosyncratic mimetic movements, but more generally abstract movements, to express the lyrics of a song or poem. The range of transgression can include a harmless performance by an elderly woman who has, on the spur of the moment, decided to "kick over the traces," and move in a manner considerably outside of her normal dance performance, and yet be so minimal on a movement level that they might not draw the attention of an untrained observer who is unfamiliar with her specific, idiosyncratic style. Such a performance might, however, invoke a family member's rebuke or wrath after the event, or form the topic of gossip in the days following the event. By contrast, at the other end of the "transgressive scale," a nightclub performer of low social status, whose erotic or grotesque movements would never be tolerated in a domestic environment, might draw applause from the same outraged family member attending a cabaret performance where transgression is expected and encouraged. In this manner, transgression operates on a continuum contingent on context.

These same principles of logic of choice can be seen in a concert performance where a dancer who possesses a technical capacity of great skill performs a beautiful solo, or perhaps in a domestic setting, where a dancer might be inspired by the company and music to perform in an unusually moving manner.

Levi-Strauss and the Lord-Parry Theory
As I have attempted to demonstrate in the preceding section, improvisation forms a key element in the process of creating and performing solo improvised dance in the Iranian culture sphere. To best describe and analyze the manner of improvisation of Iranian solo improvised dance, I consider aspects of Levi-Strauss' notion of *bricolage* as he presents it in the *Savage Mind,* as well as the Lord-Parry theory of improvisation of the storytelling of bards in the former Yugoslavia within traditional frameworks (1970). I want to stress that the methods that Iranian storytellers use to formulate their tales, at least as far back as Ferdowsi, the national poet of the *shah-nameh,* the epic history of Iran (1010 AD), directly parallel the manner of improvisation in Yugoslavia (based on personal observations of both as well as detailed descriptions by Page and Lord and Parry), and that a similar formulaic base is utilized in dance, music, and theatre. (See Page, 1975 for an example of how Iranian storytellers improvise from formulaic motifs.)

Solo Improvised Dance as Bricolage
Bricoleur and Engineer/ Iranian Dancer and Modern Dancer
To paraphrase the aspects that I would like to abstract from Levi-Strauss' presentation, he likened the thought processes of people in "primitive" and, I would add, in "traditional," by which I mean much of the population of preindustrial societies such as Iran, to the *bricoleur,* a kind of tinker who plied his trade in the French countryside.[6] I wish to make clear that I make no value judgments, and indeed neither did Levi-Strauss, in characterizing types of performance or problem-solving mechanisms utilized by performers of Iranian solo improvised dance. For the purpose of this study, the distinctions I am attempting to create when I discuss the differences between academic modern dance and Iranian solo improvised dance, address issues such as the relative value of novelty for its own sake and what I call the conceptual "mind set" of an individual who creates within a dance tradition such as that of the Iranian-American community, and a modern dance performer or choreographer who is often trained to constantly look outside of tradition for "new" solutions. As we will see, Levi-Strauss makes clear that in spite of the difference in conceptions of problem-solving, the bricoleur, with whom I compare a dancer in the Iranian tradition, and the engineer, to whom I compare the practitioner of academic modern dance, both work within their own cultural and conceptual restraints.

The *bricoleur,* a type of tinker who roamed the French countryside, carried a large box filled with items such as nails, hammers, and other tools and materials with which to repair various household items. To

effect his repairs he had recourse only to those items in his box. His
genius lay in his ability to combine and recombine these elements from
his box in innumerable and creative ways. Levi-Strauss contrasts the
process of bricolage with the thinking process of an engineer, in which
solutions to problems are conceptually sought in new sources (although,
in fact, the engineer may solve a problem in the same manner as a bricoleur, by recombining known elements). It seems significant that the
vast majority of modern dancers, like Levi-Strauss' engineer, take formal training, either in classes in a university or college setting, in which,
as with the engineer, one may receive a degree, or within a dance company or in a studio. Iranian dancers, like the bricoleur, overwhelmingly
learn their skills in informal settings, like those I describe in the following section.

As Levi-Strauss astutely observes, whatever the engineer, or the
modern dancer may think, her or "his means, power, and knowledge are
never unlimited," thus squarely positioning the engineer and the bricoleur closer together in their search for solutions and problem solving
(1971:236).

> The engineer no doubt also cross-examines his re-
> sources...his means, power and knowledge are never un-
> limited...1) It might be said that the engineer questions
> the universe, while the 'bricoleur' addresses himself to a
> collection of oddments left over from human endeavours,
> that is, only a sub-set of the culture...2) The engineer is
> always trying to make his way out of and go beyond the
> constraints imposed by a particular state of civilization
> while the 'bricoleur' by inclination of necessity always
> remains within them. [The engineer] is no more able than
> the 'bricoleur' to do whatever he wishes when he is pre-
> sented with a given task. He too has to begin by making a
> catalogue of a previously determined set consisting of
> theoretical and practical knowledge, of technical means,
> which restrict the possible solutions. (1966:19)

I would like to address two issues in Levi Strauss' theory. The first is
how the Iranian dancers assemble, or learn, the elements which comprise their collection of choreographic bricolage; in other words, where
they learn the movements and figures which constitute their repertoire.
The second concerns how an Iranian dancer typically approaches the
learning and acquiring of their repertoire of movements, which I compare to the bricoleur, and contrast that manner of acquisition of movement elements with a modern dance choreographer in the United States
or Europe.[7] As I demonstrated in the previous section, there exists a
logic of choice in the Iranian tradition which pervades its performances.
I argue that one also exists within modern dance, which is equally a tra-

dition of movement and aesthetic practices, and the culturally competent individual in the United States or Europe, upon viewing a modern dance concert, can identify this tradition by the movement practices, costumes, and music found in many of its performances. If its practices were as original and diffuse as some of its adherents claim, there would be no category for "modern dance," because it would be unidentifiable as a specific form. That such a concept of uniqueness exists is clearly expressed by dance scholar Susan Leigh Foster, in describing the styles of such modern dance creators as Martha Graham and Merce Cunningham, for whom "Not only did each mark the body so deeply that a dancer could not adequately perform another technique, but each aesthetic project was conceived as mutually exclusive of, if not hostile to, the others" (1992:493).

Among many dance scholars in the United States and Europe, who have often received training in some form of classical ballet, or more often in modern dance, certain notions prevail that privilege modern dance as some form of superior, natural, and more highly-evolved choreographic form of aesthetic expression than classical ballet or traditional/ethnic/folk dance. Unlike Levi-Strauss, those involved in modern dance sometimes dismiss traditional dance forms as constituting an unthinking process in which the dancers in non-Western contexts move in a preprogrammed fashion, shaped by history—timeless and unchanging, like automatons. As anthropologist Raymond Firth remarked, "Exotic art has often been regarded as fixed by convention, unalterable in style" (1992: 34). Among such dance scholars there exists the notion that there is something more "authentic" about modern dance. They heed Martha Graham's dictum that "dances should express 'deep matters of the heart'" (Foster 1986:27). In contrast, George Balanchine, in describing his work in classical ballet, which amazingly parallels my own experience working with Iranian dancers and choreographing Iranian and Persian dances, and provides a perfect illustration of bricolage, stated, "I do not create. Only God creates. I only put the pieces together" (1986: 17), a disingenuous simplification of his genius, surely, but also a recognition that he views himself as a link in a historic chain of aesthetic movement practices. Because of Balanchine's aesthetic approach, Graham "remained dubious about the authenticity of his creative impulse" (1986:42). Thus, dance historian Selma Jeanne Cohen was able to state that "Unlike ballet. . .the modern dance was geared to stimulate creativity" (1993: 193). However, Firth has pointed out that "Anthropological studies, too, have demonstrated that considerable initiative has been shown by individual artists, initiative which, fed into the stream of local art production, has given significant potentiality for change" (1992:193). Thus, I suggest that the possibility exists that, due to a lack of familiarity with Iranian, Indian, or Japanese dance, some observers seem unable to identify the diversity of styles, subtlety, creativity, and potential for change and development that exists in these forms.

Susan Leigh Foster, for example, observes that "The ballet and many types of folk dance, including square dancing each have a lexicon of moves from which the vocabulary of a given dance is drawn" (1986:90). She contrasts this with "the major modern dance traditions" which "have developed certain principles for generating the steps of their dances" (1986:90). The implication is that the former traditions exhibit fossilized, unchanging vocabularies. In fact, change occurs and the parameters of the possible, within stylistic constraints, in Iranian dance, as with Persian classical music, are always being pushed by talented and creative performers of this choreographic tradition, as represented by Marjan Haghnia. Certainly, Iranian dancers do not approach each performance with, in Levi-Strauss' terms, "raw materials and tools conceived and procured for the purpose of the [specific] project" (1971:254), as Foster described above for the creators of modern dance. The dancer in the Iranian or Iranian-American context, as we saw with Marjan Haghnia, uses "whatever is at hand." Nevertheless, like the Iranian dancer's movements, they are the "result of all the occasions there have been to renew or enrich the stock or to maintain it with the remains of previous constructions" (1971:254). In an Iranian context this "stock" does not remain static. What is clear is that modern dance forms the hegemony of dance discourse in academia, and therefore is theorized, and modern dancers are trained to think about what they are doing aesthetically, philosophically, and creatively. For the most part, dancers in the Iranian tradition have not been given to aesthetic introspection. This study aims to theorize aspects of its aesthetic and creative practices and potential, and to demonstrate how Iranian dance, while less theorized and cerebral, is no less dynamic, innovative and complex in its aesthetic and movement practices than modern dance.

Dance scholar Randy Martin, like Foster, observes that "Classical ballet, hip hop, Balinese or Ghanaian dance certainly have a vocabulary established prior to a given work" (1993: 109). He cautions that "Especially for the latter three forms the question of how to situate the choreographic function is particularly complex in terms of the way it is instantiated in other cultural processes" (1993:109). I would add that this function differs in each of these societies and constitutes a culturally specific phenomenon. This is parallel to anthropologist Anthony Shelton's similar finding, a recognition regarding Huichol art that "Aesthetic judgments are predicated on a system of values, fixed, situated, and manipulated by rules which are, for the most part, culturally specific and historically determined" (1992: 209). Anthropologist Alfred Gell adds the important rider, "I consider the various arts—painting, sculpture, music, poetry, fiction, and so on—as components of a vast and often unrecognized technical system" (1992: 43), thus supporting my notion of Iranian dance as a component of the larger Iranian aesthetic, one that is dynamic with a rich potential for change and development—on its own terms.

Nevertheless, Martin privileges modern dance over traditional dance by continuing, "In contrast, the lexicon for modern and experimental dance is more diffuse" (1993:109), a statement that I would contest, since, like classical ballet, Balinese, and Iranian dance, modern dance is equally identifiable by the culturally competent as a body of stylistic movement practices, in spite of the claims of its creators and critics that each is unique. In a similar sense, each Iranian dancer is also unique. Dance historian Katy Matheson says of modern dance that: "The dance world has encouraged all kinds of experimentation, individual voices, new discoveries" (Cohen 1992:222). In my opinion, the major difference is the persistent conceptual search for novelty for its own sake by the modern dancer, while the Iranian dancer utilizes "what is at hand" to create a freshness in each performance through the use of his or her choreographic bricolage. For the outstanding Iranian dancer, like the Iranian musician, is also encouraged in Iranian and Iranian-American society to present fresh and unique performances and creatively improvise within shifting stylistic parameters. (As I point out in Chapter Two, Beiza'i, the theatre historian, indicated that when itinerant dancers settled in cities in the Safavid [1501-1725] period, they had to search for ways to keep their patrons entertained, which required new "choreographies" and dances.) Iranian dancers look within the tradition, one which is rich in movement possibilities and their combinations, which each talented individual helps to develop, for their creativity.

Like the engineer, the modern dancer often looks for "new" sources. Thus, "Laura Dean derived her inspiration for minimal structures from the repetitions and *simplified patterns* of folk dance (emphasis mine, Matheson in Cohen 1992: 218), while the Judson Dance Theatre "resorted to non-dancers in experiments that used ordinary movement" (1992: 195). Just how "new" such sources of inspiration are is open to interpretation. Such possibilities would not occur to individuals such as Marjan Haghnia. She would not, for example, borrow a movement or stylistic element from a Balinese dance she encounters at an international student performance or a classical ballet concert on television. An even less likely possibility would be for an Iranian dancer to turn to the pedestrian movements of the people around her as a source of inspiration. The stylistic parameters of this tradition beckon the dancer to elaborate on and alter familiar dance movements in a fresh and innovative manner.

Alongside the idea of a "frozen" and "set" tradition of movement, there exists a concomitant notion that there is something artificial about both classical ballet and classical forms in non-Western contexts, whereas one of the oft-repeated goals of modern dance choreographers is to create "natural" movement. "The early proponents of modern dance believed that they had discovered (or more correctly, rediscovered) the natural way of dancing" (Copeland and Cohen 1983:227). Certainly, as Barthes pointed out, "natural" is, in fact, cultural. Throughout the twentieth century, modern dancers, beginning with Isadora Duncan, invoked "naturalness" and "getting in touch with the earth" as "reacting in part against the artificial and hierarchical organization of ballet" (Foster 1992: 487). For example, Susan Leigh Foster describes Isadora Duncan's philosophy:

> For Duncan and those following in her tradition, the dancing body manifests an original naturalness. Unadorned by the contrived distortions of movement that modern society incurs. . . to cultivate the natural body and to allow it to relinquish affected habits, Duncan's approach advocates the study of "basic" human movements such as walking, running, skipping, lying down, standing, turning and jumping—all performed with a graceful, relaxed fullness, initiated by patterns of breath. (1992:487)

Later, Martha Graham "was looking for a movement style at once basic to man's nature and attuned to the rhythms of contemporary life" (Cohen 1992: 120). In a recent event held on the campus of the University of California, Riverside (1992), well-known avant-garde modern dance choreographer Anna Halprin "appeared and informed the gathering that in contemporary society, we have lost our ritual connections to the earth. There, she explained, she was going to direct us in a 'spontaneous ritual' to help reestablish those connections" (Novack 1995: 177). If this could be accomplished then it would "bring us greater harmony with the natural world" (1995:177). In order to accomplish this, she advised the participants, "Don't think about what you should do. Let the earth speak to you through your body. The earth will tell you what to do" (1995:178). Novack made an astute summary:

> Halprin's implicit assumption of bodily knowledge as essential, mindless truth, and of dancing as spontaneous expression, devoid of choreographic intent or inspiration, exemplifies a particular construction of the body and self popularized in countercultural events in the United States beginning in the fifties and sixties. (1995:178)

Such concepts clearly still exist, according to the program notes of several modern dance choreographers of today. I agree with Novack that "What has continued to disturb me about this event are the discrepancies between what was claimed and what occurred" (1995:178).

It would be difficult, if not impossible, to encounter a dancer in an

Iranian context who, like Martha Graham:

> In her struggle to intuit the appropriate development of
> her ideas, Graham becomes secretive, temperamental, and
> filled with doubt. During rehearsals she rages at the
> dancers and at herself. While making a dance, she claims
> to be possessed: seized by the idea inside her, victim to
> cycles of destruction and creation entailed by her creative
> act, she suffers through the birth of her dance. (Foster
> 1986:28)

Such notions and approaches seem alien to the type of creativity one
encounters with the dancer in an Iranian or Iranian-American context.
In fact, I suggest, following Joann Kealiinohomku's insightful article on
classical ballet as an ethnic dance form (1970), that modern dance, like
Iranian dance, is a form of ethnic dance for its practitioners—the major
difference between the two seems to lie in the manner in which its practice, as Levi-Strauss indicates, is culturally conceptualized by its creators and performers.

Stylistic Parameters
In order to deepen the discussion of the concept of bricolage, I would
like to use a parallel notion of the musicologist Leonard B. Meyer, who
describes style as a certain cultural "series of choices made within some
set of constraints" (1989:3), a concept which also supports Geertz's theory of the "period eye." In this way, one understands both the limitations and the logic of choices made by a dancer in an Iranian-American
context. Meyer demonstrates that the choices that form the constraints
of style are learned: "The constraints of a style are *learned* by compos-
ers and performers, critics and listeners" (author's emphasis, 1989: 10).
In his discussion of how items (movement elements for purposes of this
study) from among the range of choices are selected (1989: Chapter
Five), Meyer makes clear that most of the choices, as we have seen in
Marjan's dancing, are automatic, rather than consciously made. This is
in part due to the rapidity with which the dancer makes these choices.
"To take an example from music: Mozart evidently composed with such
astonishing facility that only a small portion of his choices could have
involved a deliberate decision among possible alternatives" (1989: 5).
Thus, in this manner we can find a connection between the *way* in which
both Mozart and Marjan Haghnia approach composition. While the rapidity of the choices in a particular composition occurs through context,
the other important contributing factor to this apparently automatic response results from the high level of technical control and competency
within their forms of expression that our two examples bring to their
experience of creating.
    The way in which an Iranian dancer performs is very much like the

concept of bricolage as set forth by Levi-Strauss, in which a well-known set of elements is combined and recombined in potentially unlimited combinations, but always from the wellspring of movements that have been learned by rote, a form of mimesis, although commonly less formally than the similar way in which musicians learn their art, namely the learning of short, formulaic musical phrases which are then elaborated through improvisation. (See Farhat 1965 for a discussion of how the process of improvisation occurs in Persian music.) Typically, a dancer creates and assembles his or her "box" of bricolage materials by learning short choreographic phrases, most often culled from copying adults within his or her immediate or extended family environment. Jamal recalls his sister-in-law "formally" schooling her daughters in how to move so that they would shine in social occasions, and she would sometimes lose patience when they failed to learn her movements and figures properly and with style (personal interview: Sept. 13, 1995).[8]

Islamic art historian Gulru Necipoglu, in analyzing the learning of architectural design techniques in a parallel manner with my discussion of learning and improvising dance movement, states that:

> ...originality is measured with respect to previously codi-
> fied models renewed in an ever-widening canon of inter-
> locked forms. Once internalized through an initial period
> of workshop training, the geometric repertory dissemi-
> nated in *girih* scrolls allowed designers to demonstrate
> their skill within preestablished structural molds that pro-
> vided a wide margin for improvisation. (1995:206)

While medieval and contemporary designers and architects learned in more formal workshop or guild contexts, dance is generally learned in an informal manner. Nevertheless, the way in which dancers acquire the movement vocabularies, or bricolage, with which they express themselves parallels that of the other expressive forms.

Elements for choreographic bricolage to add to the "box" may also be acquired from auxiliary sources such as films, as I indicated above, or performances of popular entertainers. When a famous performer performs in a unique style, some fans will pick up his or her characteristic gestures and movements and incorporate them, bricolage fashion, into their own dance performances.

Friends and classmates form another source for new movement elements. For example, Jamal stated that in the army barracks, dancing was one of the chief forms of entertainment. When confined to the barracks at night, the soldiers learned movements from one another, as well as arranging small performances with which to entertain one another, and occasionally, the officers (September 13, 1996). While living in Tehran, I often witnessed schoolgirls in my neighborhood dancing with friends, trying out new movements and figures. Performances of this dance tradition sometimes took place at the end of the school year in many of the girls' elementary and high schools, encouraging the girls to vary their repertoire of movement elements. The engineer, or modern dancer, learns his or her profession through formal schooling, and although classes in this tradition were available in Tehran, few persons attended; rather, the overwhelming majority of individuals learned through informal networks, especially through the extended family.

As a concrete example of learning movement practices, I use some of the movements of Marjan Haghnia. One of her most characteristic movements is one in which she holds her hands in the center of the body and in a strongly bounded movement, she alternately moves her hands from neck level to waist level as if pulling or drawing a string between the two hands. Her "set" figure, which I have observed often, is the "drawing" figure, so called because she appears to be drawing or pulling an imaginary string and stretching it with her hands. During the execution of this figure she improvises on this basic movement: she may move forward, or backward, or remain stationary, thus varying its overall look. At the end of each movement phrase she forms her hands in a graceful "c," relaxing momentarily the bounded effort. She has taken my class twice, and has appeared in three other classes to demonstrate how she moves. All of the students love this movement, which is now known as "Marjan's step," and they all attempt to perform some variation of it. (Marjan kindly consented to appear in each of my classes as a source of inspiration, and thus, several classes benefited from her expertise.)

Marjan, like the bricoleur, does not consciously look outside of her tradition or stylistic constraints for inspiration to "solve" choreographic problems. When she dances, her choreographic strategies and "solutions" consist almost entirely of movements that "she knows," in other words, movements and figures that she has acquired throughout her life both in Iran and in Southern California and which "feel right and natural" to her (personal interview: October 28, 1995).

In contrast, as we have seen, modern dancers, like engineers, actively seek choreographic inspiration from a variety of sources: everyday movement, folk traditions, and social dance forms, among others. The modern dancer typically learns through formal classes and training, like the engineer who studies at an institution of higher education where he or she learns "new" methods for approaching the field. Many colleges and universities throughout the United States offer not only classes in modern dance, but degrees as well.

Just as among bricoleurs there is probably considerable variation in the numbers and types of items in each box of bricolage, and individual skill in their use, so, too, those Iranian and Iranian-American individuals who love to dance, and there are many, according to my informants as well as personal observation, acquire many movements, gestures, and figures they use to assemble and furnish their choreographic box of bricolage from which they draw the inspiration with which to enhance their performances.

Lord-Parry's Theory of Song Composition
While for purposes of this study Levi-Strauss' theory shows how the mechanism of improvisation proceeds from the performer's ability to combine known elements to create something fresh, the Lord-Parry theory demonstrates which elements are incorporated into the process. The theory is named for Albert Lord and his mentor, Millman Parry, who were interested in the problem of the authorship of Homer's works. In order to show the process by which they theorized how epics were created in Homer's time, they turned to the contemporary storytelling practices of Yugoslav bards, whose practices they considered to be the modern-day counterpart of the process by which Homerian epics were composed. This theory stresses the process of the improvisational performance, as well as the kind of content in the form of "motifs." Dance movements, like literary images and melodic fragments, may be likened to:

> formulas [which] are not ossified cliches which they have the reputation of being, but that they are capable of change and are indeed frequently highly productive of other and new formulas...(Lord 1970:4)

I showed some typical formulaic developments in the movement section of my discussion of some of the typical types of movements that one might encounter in a performance of this dance tradition. As another example, a dancer might utilize the basic foot pattern outlined earlier and stop, perhaps abruptly, to turn in place, weight on the right foot and turning with the aid of the left (or opposite) similar to a "buzz" turn. During this turn, he or she may raise the arms from a low elevation, alongside the body, to touch the hands above the head. Using a series of undulating wrist movements, ending with the arms fully extended above the head, she creates an arc that frames the torso. When the dancer completes this movement, while retaining the hands momentarily in a fixed position above the head, he or she may lean sideways, extending the torso, first to one side and then the other. Using this formula, the dancer may further develop this theme by returning the arms and hands downward, using the same or different hand movements, and returning to the original position. From this position the dancer may resume the basic step, stepping first right and extending the right arm and hand forward in an arc-like gesture, first toward the center of the body and then away, the left hand and arm moving in opposition backward, and then the dancer changes arms, alternating left and right. This figure may continue for a few executions, until the dancer begins a new one. As one dances, each performed movement suggests a new one.

This final product, a dance performance or a song, is unique because "in a very real sense every performance is a separate song; for every performance is unique" (1970:4). I quote extensively from Lord because it bears directly on the performance and creativity found in dance and other performative expression in the Iranian culture sphere. Thus, Marjan Haghnia resembles the "singer of tales," who:

> ...is at once the tradition and an individual creator. His manner of composition differs from that used by a writer in that the oral poet makes no conscious effort to break the traditional phrases and incidents; he is forced by the rapidity of composition in performance to use these traditional elements. To him they are not merely necessary, however; they are also right. He seeks no others, and yet he practices great freedom in his use of them because they are themselves flexible. His art consists not so much in learning through repetition the time-worn formulas as in the ability to compose and recompose the phrases for the idea of the moment on the pattern established by the basic formula...What is important is not the oral performance but rather the composition during oral performance. (Lord 1970:4-5)

I would like to address several of the points that Lord made in the paragraph above with regard to solo improvised dance. As the singer of tales makes no effort to break with tradition, the dancer in this form, as I demonstrated in the example provided by Marjan Haghnia, does not consciously seek "new" solutions in the way that a performer of modern dance, like the engineer, searches for new concepts. And, as Necipoglu observed above in her discussion of visual designers, the dancer working within his or her stylistic constraints is considered creative and original in the fresh way in which he or she combines and recombines the choreographic elements. The movements dancers acquire from popular entertainers, for example, are Iranian movements. The movements that an individual acquires from an Indian or Egyptian film are those that can be remolded and reconfigured into an Iranian context. Except in a rare instance, the vast majority of dancers acquire their movement formulas from their immediate environment.

Typically, the dance performance, like the song composition, occurs rapidly and spontaneously. For instance, in a wedding, one does not know what *reng* (dance melody) the orchestra may play, thus the performance is spontaneous, and no two are alike. In my class, where I observe dancers like Marjan for many weeks, I use a variety of different musical sources, including those class members bring in to share. Each of the performances I observe is fresh and spontaneous. Perhaps the best example is the dance-play, *mojassameh* (statue), which is widely performed, at least in Iran and Afghanistan (where it is known as *Logari*), in which the musicians (or person at the sound equipment) stop playing and the dancers must "freeze" into a graceful pose. Those caught in movement must leave the floor until one is declared winner. This game was played at the final class party and Marjan won both times (December 8, 1995). The music was changed throughout the game, both the melody and tempo, to trip and confuse the dancers, and so they never knew which piece of music was coming and when it would stop, truly exhibiting the process of improvisation.

When Lord argues that the elements are "right," he alludes to what students in my class referred to as "natural," that is, movements that feel comfortable to them because they were learned in the same way they learned language, usually at a very young age. Marjan Haghnia, for example, could not remember learning her movements in a conscious way (personal interview December 8, 1995). I would question Lord's notion that they "seek no other," because Lord himself points out that each performer seeks to be unique. Perhaps it might be better to state that they do not seek new elements outside of the tradition, for within the tradition, as he correctly observes, the elements are flexible enough to provide an enormous storehouse of variation. I suggest that the performance of each movement allows a spontaneous generation of new ways in which to reinterpret or recompose a specific movement. For example, if Marjan performs her figure of drawing her hands in a bounded movement facing front, she may turn to one side to execute the same hand gesture, or change the pattern of her feet. She may kneel to emphasize the movement, this time with the hands held away from the body.

Necipoglu, through her study of the Topkapi scroll, stresses the point that improvisation also informs the creation of the visual arts, which in this way are connected to all forms of creative expression, both performative and visual:

> The scroll's ingenuously varied *girih* patterns testify to a standardized, repeatable, and flexible approach to design through simple geometric mutations arrived at by manipulating by-then-standard schemes made possible by a wide variety of intricate patterns, allowing the designer great scope for improvisation. (1996:52)

She continues to state that the individual patterns "do not provide clues as to how its individual patterns contained in discrete frames were related to one another..." (1995:52). I would suggest, as in music and dance, that the patterns represented formulae that were purposely left discrete to enable the creative individual familiar with them to combine

them as he or she wished. Necipoglu seems to agree with this assessment, for later she states:

> Geometric schemes in use since the eleventh century were
> transformed by the manipulation of their inherited gram-
> mar in terms of scale (successively fragmenting tradi-
> tional motifs into smaller elements or, conversely, magni-
> fying them in an unprecedented manner), composition,
> color scheme, material, technique, placement, surprising
> curvilinear patterns (vegetal, figural, or calligraphic) that
> expanded the set of designs to a virtually infinite number.
> (1995: 112)

Similarly, as Marjan has shown us, dancers create in a parallel manner
using movement practices learned in short, formulaic phrases as their
"design patterns" to create their expression through movement.

   Lord observes that the singer of tale's "art is not so much in repetition...as in that to compose and recompose the phrases...on the pattern
established on the basic formula" (1970:4). Thus Marjan's formula is
the "drawing" movement of the hands which she recomposes in a number of ways: moving slowly or rapidly, kneeling, turning, hands held
close to the torso, hands held extended away from the body, moving the
hands vertically or sagitally. Another formulaic movement that Marjan
performs is the movement, described above, in which she brings her
hands and arms from center high to side low by rotating the wrists and
forming a triangle.

   Lord adds, "what is important is not the oral performance but rather
the composition during oral performance." Marjan's dancing, widely
admired by all of the students, is also a masterpiece of composition, not
because she uses "new" movements, but rather in the always fresh manner of her performance, in which she uses the elements that she "just
allows to flow," in her own words (personal interview December 8,
1995). Using this rotating wrist movement, she might also elect to bring
one hand down, and then the other, successively rather than simultaneously. Or, she might choose to do a backbend, place one hand behind
her head, and bring the other down the length of her body with the rotating wrist movement just described. In a single performance, Marjan
used all of these variations.

   The manner of dance performance in the solo improvised dance at all
levels, both domestic and professional, is idiosyncratic; each individual
is conceived of, as is the case with classical musicians, as performing in
a unique fashion within a well known framework of movement and stylistic character.

   In sum, we can see that improvisation forms one of the most important aesthetic and performance elements in all Iranian performative expression, including the Iranian solo improvised dance form. I suggest

that the way in which these movements are utilized and combined can be best conceptualized by adapting Levi-Strauss' model of bricolage, along with Meyer's notion of "stylistic constraints," as a means of understanding the mechanism for performance, while the Lord-Parry theory and Necipoglu's penetrating analysis of the use of basic, formulaic visual design patterns provide a tool for demonstrating how the creativity of this dance form rests largely in the development of the detail of formulaic elements within the larger framework of the composition. Familiarity with the movement repertoire, its range and composition, and the process by which it is performed, will serve as a useful tool to, in part, enable the researcher to distinguish performances that are transgressive or perceived of as "out-of-control."

Aesthetic Connections with Other Expressive Forms
Links between Dance and Other Performative Expressions
Through Improvisation

In an Iranian or Iranian-American context, dance cannot be studied in isolation from other creative forms. In the opening essay of the monumental fourteen-volume reference work, *Survey of Persian Art*, the editor, Arthur Upham Pope, states:

> The peculiar genius of Persia found its most adequate embodiment in the so-called arts of decoration, those that depend for effect upon beauty of pattern and expressive design. In these Iran attained a mastery that scarcely faltered through the unequaled duration of her cultural history. As a people the Iranians seem to have thought decoratively, for the same canons of lucidity, precision, design, and rhythm are revealed in their poetry and music. (1964: vol I: 1)

This section seeks to establish connections and linkages with other forms of artistic and creative expression. First, I wish to connect forms such as the performative expressions of music, storytelling, and traditional improvised comic theatre through the use of improvisation. Second, I wish to link the visual arts of calligraphy and architecture and decorative arts such as architectural and book illumination and decoration, rug weaving and textile design, through the use of geometry. These connections and linkages demonstrate that dancing forms a part of a larger system of aesthetic and performative expression throughout the Iranian culture sphere and the Iranian diaspora.

> This parallelism among different media was also implied in the frequent use of craft metaphors by poets who likened themselves to practitioners of other crafts, metaphors rooted in shared processes of artistic conceptualization

and realization. (Necipoglu 1995:209)

Dance is linked to music, storytelling and traditional comic theatrical forms, such as *ru-howzi, siyah-bazi*, and the women's domestic plays, *bazi-ha-ye namayeshi,* through the use of improvisation. The Iranian dance movement has in common with music that, "Despite their usage well into the modern era the musical modes showed a remarkable capacity to resist the danger of ossification, allowing generations of musicians to improvise within their rhythmic cycles" (1995:209). This connection with improvisation was demonstrated in the previous section in some detail in regard to music and storytelling. In theatre this connection occurs more specifically in two ways: theatrical plays occur around the kernel of an idea, a motif that can be likened to a musical or choreographic phrase, and then, through improvisation, it is elaborated. As Ardavan Mofid stated, "if the price of bread went up ten cents, we do bread" (personal interview: April 4, 1994). This means that for the duration of an evening's performance, the actors of the *siyah bazi* create skits, jokes, sight gags, and plots based on the fact that the government allowed the price of bread to rise ten cents.

Thus, as Page describes for storytelling (1979), Farhat for improvisation in classical music (1965), Necipoglu for architectural decoration (1995), and Ardavan Mofid for theatrical practices (1994), what the students learn from the master is a set of formulae and the means of improvising on them. Page and Necipoglu described the uses of *tumar*, books or scrolls containing brief or partial motifs or formulae which are memorized and then developed and elaborated, while Farhat describes a similar process in classical music: the student of music learns short melodic phrases which he or she then learns how to develop, creating new interpretations from them. One of the projects of the previous subsection was to describe typical short choreographic phrases, which the skilled performer learns and then elaborates upon in an improvised performance. Unlike music, theatre, and storytelling, the learning of dance, as I described above, tends to be informally learned, although with classes such as those I conduct at the University of California, Riverside, and others advertised in the Iranian Yellow Pages, more formal means of learning this dance tradition are available and popular in the Iranian-American community of Southern California.

The second way in which dance and theatre are linked is that dance forms the movement practice for such theatrical forms: the performers dance during, between and after the plays, thus producing a blurred genre. Additionally, those persons who were called dancers (various terms such as *raqas* [dancer] or *bazigar* or *motreb* [entertainer], all of which carry negative connotations), often sang and acted as well. This is still true today, and such traditional-style performers may be seen or employed in current contexts in Los Angeles, and several are listed in the Iranian Yellow Pages. My own personal experiences with elderly professional performers in Bukhara, Khiva, Tashkent, and Tehran demonstrate that several individuals sang and danced at the same time. (I have recorded or acquired video cassettes of some of these performers.) In current Persian popular music contexts, seen frequently on Iranian television, most of the popular music vocalists in Southern California either themselves use dance movements from the solo improvised dance tradition or have dancers in the background, or both. Van Nieuwkerk describes the same situation as obtaining in Egypt until recent times, that is, performers exhibiting dance, vocal or instrumental music, acting, and acrobatics (1995: 62).

Links Between Dance and Visual Arts Through Geometry
In contrast to the linkages I have attempted to establish with other performance genres through similar uses of improvisation, in this section, I will establish the aesthetic link between dance and many of the visual arts such as calligraphy, architecture, and other decorative arts such as book illumination through their creative impulses, which derive from aspects of geometry. Rather than examine each of these forms separately, I will focus on calligraphy as a representative visual art form for comparison with dance, because it is both a beloved and highly esteemed art in an Iranian-Islamic context and because calligraphy epitomizes the elements I wish to stress in establishing linkages with movement. This selection also creates ambiguity since calligraphy is a highly esteemed, almost sacred art form, while dance is an earthy performative expression that is often perceived in a negative way. Thus dance and calligraphy provide true contrasts, and yet I wish to demonstrate how they are linked by geometric creative impulses.

Iranian life is permeated by geometrically informed decoration. One need only look at the details of Persian calligraphy, book decorations, fabrics, metal, stone, and woodwork, and decorative art in Islamic religious and civil architecture to see how paramount intricate geometric figures of stylized vegetal forms and arabesques are and then examine the movements of solo improvised dancing to see how this geometric conceptualization is translated into movement. In describing the effect of this conceptualization, Necipoglu notes that, "There is no doubt that they had fully internalized a sophisticated sensibility transmitted over the generations by scrolls and workshop practices" [that] "could not fail to aesthetically move even the most visually illiterate audience" (1995: 215).

Everywhere I find that calligraphy, as in all of the other decorative arts, is also described in terms of rhythm, movement and flow: "In most instances, Muslim decorators did not use sterile vegetal motives; they gave them constant movement, either by relating them to the flow of writing. . or by developing them in a kind of whirl of moving tendrils and leaves" (Hill and Grabar 1964: 82).

In describing a particularly cursive alphabet, *naskhi*, Pope et al. state that the curves "mark the beats in the rhythm of the movement which is an essential aesthetic quality of cursive inscriptions" (1964-65:1726). (See figures 25-30.)

Most books concerning calligraphy devote full chapters to the treatment of the geometric basis of this art form. (For examples see Khatibi and Sijelmassi 1976: 82-85; Frishman and Khan 1994: 51-71; Maheronnaqsh 1991 total work.) They also emphasize the "movement" and dynamism inherent in this art form, rather than any static quality that they might convey to the uninitiated observer. This art form is characterized by Hill and Grabar as "the fascination of the use of geometry in these designs…" (1964:82). In this section I wish to link these visual aesthetic elements with those employed in Iranian solo improvised dance, which I posit also has a geometric basis, and that this geometric aesthetic underlies virtually all Iranian and other Middle Eastern and Central Asian visual arts. Hill and Grabar describe how geometry informs calligraphy and the other visual arts and which geometric forms are utilized:

> A third theme of ornamentation was quite clearly geometry. The most common way in which geometry was used was in the creation of the basic patterns of design. At first glance, the tremendous variety of geometric shapes… all seem to show the most amazing imagination and inventiveness. A recent study on Central Asian ornaments has shown that practically all the geometric designs can be achieved simply with a ruler and with a compass and that almost all designs can be reduced to a series of comparatively simple geometric shapes.. The more significant facts about the geometric units used seem, however, to be, first, their constant mobility in time and space. (Hill and Grabar 1964:80-81)

To further clarify this discussion I use the term "geometry" as defined in the *American Heritage Dictionary* (1990 edition): "a branch of mathematics that deals with the measurement, properties, and relationships of points, lines, angles, surfaces and solids." I use the term "geometric" in relation to dance according to the third definition found in the same source: "A physical arrangement suggesting geometric forms or lines." The *Webster's New Collegiate Dictionary* (1977 edition) further refines and contributes to the meaning that I am using as: "of or pertaining to art based on simple geometric shapes." I posit the notion that in the positions of the body, arms and hands, and in the sculpting movements of the arms and hands, the dancer, too, is creating geometric shapes—circles, lines, and arabesques.

I do not wish to delve too deeply into the issue of which specific geometric or curvilinear forms, i.e., the spiral, the circle, the *girih* (knot), was predominant when or where for purposes of this study. Some art historians look to one or two forms as the basis of Islamic art. Islamic art historian Alexandre Papadopoulo, for example, claims that the use of the spiral and the arabesque form the geometric basis "which reveals itself only to those initiated into the secrets of composition of Muslim art, since, as is obvious, the spiral and arabesque are never given direct material form" (1979: 73, see illustration of dancers he uses, figure 6). By contrast, Necipoglu (1995) makes clear that each of these geometric forms, and many others, held ascendancy in different times and places. I wish to emphasize the general preoccupation that geometry, and its application in the visual arts, held for both theory and praxis for a wide variety of individuals in the Iranian world, which Necipoglu characterizes as "a general backdrop against which visual idioms were formulated and reformulated in specific historical contexts" (1995:186). She demonstrates that while the interest in geometric figures waned in large parts of the Islamic world after the medieval period (Egypt, Syria, and Ottoman Turkey, 1985 chapters Six and Seven), for Iran and Central Asia, the focus of this study, it has flourished into our own time. This holds true for the Iranian-American community as well. As an example, this community financially maintains the artistic output of several professional calligraphers in addition to other visual artists. The Iranian and Iranian-American world is filled with visual reminders of that geometric preoccupation in design, from monumental public buildings to restaurants, greeting cards, wedding invitations, and books.

> Widespread notions about the role of geometry as a bridge between the material and spiritual realms, coupled with the absolute beauty of its harmonious forms capable of purifying the mind, like music, must have made geometric abstraction a particularly appealing visual idiom. (Necipoglu 1995: 193)

The geometry of calligraphy, solo improvised dance, and all of the visual arts consist of two factors: proportion and forms. All of the Arabic alphabets utilize a geometric system of straight lines, curves, and dots, all in systematic relation to one another and for which rules have been formulated. For example, in any given form of an alphabet each letter will be exactly so many dots wide or tall. These rules are well-known to calligraphers and connoisseurs, of which there are many in the Islamic world, as well as in Southern California, where calligraphy is still a cherished art form, and many of these rules were developed a thousand years ago, as with the Kufic script. In Iran, the art of calligraphy "is like composing a Mozartian melody with its difficult resolutions, or playing a master's game of chess" (Pope et al. 1964-65: vol. iv: 1725).

Seyyed Hossein Nasr, a contemporary author of several works on Islam and mystical subjects, observes that:

> ...traditional calligraphy is based on a precise science of geometric forms and rhythms, each letter being formed from a number of points in a mathematical fashion differing in each major style but all based upon a *scientia* which possesses exact laws of its own...In fact the proportions of calligraphy are the key for the understanding of the proportions of Islamic architecture. (Nasr 1987:26)

And, again, I would add dance.

This is truly an ancient art. A thousand years ago, Ibn Moqla (d. 940 A.D.) formulated a set of twelve rules relating to the creation of calligraphy; these include his four principles of respect for the elements (*osul*), proportions (*nesbat*), composition (*tarkib*), and seating (*kursi,* i. e. proper placement). It is beyond the scope of this dissertation to explain these rules in detail, but briefly, the proportion of the dots which create the different letters (for example, the difference between *beh, peh*, and *teh* is that *beh* has one dot below a "dish-like" figure, while *peh* has three dots below, and *teh* two dots above the figure) hold a specific relationship to one another in both size and distance. In formal calligraphy these dots are rhomboid figures that are used as measures.

> ...so that an *alif* would be, according to the style, 5, 7, or 9 points high, a *ba'* 1 point high and 5 points long, and so on. This geometry of the letters, which was perfected by explaining the relations among the parts of letters in circles and semicircles, has remained binding for calligraphers to our day, and the perfection of a script is judged according to the relation of the letters to each other, not simply to their shape. (Schimmel 1984:18)

These rules have been expanded and elaborated through the centuries. They still resonate today in calligraphers' ateliers on Westwood Boulevard, in the West Los Angeles "Little Tehran" district.[9] Currently, both in Iran and Southern California, there is an enormous and exciting output of calligraphy as art, published in the form of small portfolios which include several plates, in which numerous calligraphers are pushing former boundaries and visual configurations of this esteemed form of expression.

I interviewed Masoud Valipour, a master calligrapher, and asked him if he could conceive of a link between dance and his art form. He was at first startled by the suggestion of linking a profane expression such as dance to a spiritual practice such as calligraphy, but nevertheless found it "intriguing and worth investigating since the movements of the hand while creating calligraphy could be characterized as dance-like, but until you asked, I always used 'dance' in the metaphorical sense: I tell my students I will teach their pens to dance" (personal interview in Persian: February 8, 1995). (The metaphor of dance in poetry stands for freedom and gracefulness of movement.)

Elsewhere, Golam [sic] Hosayn Yusofi characterizes one of the alphabets: "The fundamental characteristic of *tolt* (pronounced sols in Persian) is the predominance of 'round' components and the easy gentle movement of the pen, which is evident from the script. In writing *tolt* the pen moves so sinuously that it has been said to 'dance'" (1994: 691). Later, he also describes various alphabets in which "the letters and words may seem to dance" (1994:698). Most of the letters, with their sweeping strokes, are suggestive of movement and dance. I suggest as examples *sin, lam, beh*, and *he (jimi)*.

There are many ways in which a dancer can sculpt movements that duplicate the geometric forms found in calligraphy. For example, a dancer may place her right hand to the left side of her face at ear level, and with a downward sweeping movement, arc her hand to her right side at waist level, inscribing a *sin* or *nun* figure. I refer back to one of Marjan Haghnia's characteristic movements in which she raises both hands above her head and by rotating her wrists and hands outward (away from the body), she creates two lines moving diagonally down and to her sides, thus creating spirals with her wrists and circles with her hands, diagonal lines with her arms and a triangle with the full figure. It is also symmetrical, with the simultaneous movement of both arms and hands moving half the length of the body, and the timing of the movements of the two hands is equal. The proportion of the movements in the proficient dancer is in the style and carriage, the way in which he or she maintains the distance of the arms and hands in relation to each other and the body. In this way, we can establish that the dancer's movements are also created through the use of geometric elements of proportion, shape, and symmetry.

In sum, if I were to create a graph to represent the improvisational and geometric linkages with dance, it might look like this:

geometry	improvisation
solo improvised dance	
calligraphy	music
decorative arts	story-telling
architecture	comic theatre

This graph indicates relationships between dance and other forms of aesthetic expression, rather like the graphs created by linguists. Such illustrations indicate the grammatical and structural relationships of related languages, but omit the relative importance of a specific language as regards number of speakers, etc. Thus, a graph of Germanic languages might feature the Friesian language in such a way that, due to linguistic characteristics, it might appear in a more central position than English and not indicate the disparity in number of speakers, development of vocabulary and other features. In the same way, this graph indicates the link between dance and other forms of expression, but on a graph of social esteem within Iranian and Iranian-American societies it would be misleading. Such a hierarchical graph would perhaps appear as follows:

poetry
calligraphy
architecture   music
decorative arts

                        storytelling
                        comic theatre
                        dance

Some individual Iranians might give more weight to one or another of the forms of expression than I have indicated, but many would accept the hierarchy I have drawn.

Thus, I wish to establish dance as part of a larger aesthetic system in the Iranian culture sphere, rather than an isolated and marginalized performative practice. Its links through geometry establish dance as a performed and moving aspect of the visual arts, while its use and creativity in the practice of improvisation firmly link the process of its creation through the development of formulaic movement motifs with performative practices such as music, storytelling, and traditional improvised comic theatre, of which it is an integral part.

Chapter 2

Historical Aspects of Solo Improvised Dance

"Oh, miniatures! Sure sign of a petty mind."
line from the film "The Women"
Claire Booth Luce

Another thing I enjoyed very much was dancing. In my country there are traditional dances just as in America there are well-known songs and poems. Many of our dances tell stories: some are survivals from a very ancient time, like the Zoroastrian Dance of Fire. Some came from the Islamic influence. At first I used to dance just as I felt; but later I learned the traditional dances, blending my emotion with the emotion of the dance story. In our dancing the movement of the hands tells special things. There is a language of motion, and people who know this language can interpret the story as well as if it were in spoken words. People in America who have seen me dance say, "Your hands are so graceful!" Hands must be graceful in order to be talking hands.

Often when my mother had guests she would call me in to dance. In Persia one dances for a good cause—what you call in America a "benefit." It would not be appropriate for me to dance for money, to entertain strangers, to make a career. I know here in America entertainers are well thought of. Professional entertainers in my country are applauded but they do not belong to the upper classes.

Maybe one of our traditional dances will explain this. It is the story of a dancer who was loved by a prince. He could not marry her because she was a dancer, so she went away with a broken heart. Without her he could not be happy so he found her and told her that he would give up being a prince in order to marry her. If there were a choice between the kingdom and her, he had made that choice. But she knew that he must be a prince and later a king for the good of his people, so she told him that her broken heart had been healed by another and that she no

56

longer loved him.
    So I danced for my mother's guests, but I had not the
ambition to be a dancer. (Najafi 1953: 28-29)

Najmeh Najafi's colorful and highly fantastic characterization of Iranian
dance impels one to ask: What can we say about the history of this
dance tradition? Unfortunately, relatively little, especially if we compare the history of dance to the history of Persian literature, for example.
Najafi's description underscores the need to establish some kind of history, if only to demolish such orientalist and auto-exotic myths such as
hands that tell stories, Zoroastrian fire dances, and professional dancers
with hearts of gold. I must agree with anthropologist Joseph Alter, who
stated in his study of North Indian wrestling that "history must be integrated into a holistic understanding of institutions and groups. It is not
enough to make reference to the past without a critical evaluation of
how the history of an event is as much a reflection of current concerns
as it is an objective and impartial description, not an historical reconstruction" (1992:14). Alter's observation reflects the concerns of recent
attempts, such as those of Yaha Zoka' (1978-79) and Medjid Rezvani
(1962), to write a historical reconstruction, a chronological history of
dance in Iran. For this reason I must also state that Alter's assessment
concerning the possibility of writing some kind of complete and systematic history of Indian wrestling applies as well to constructing a systematic history of Iranian dance. Regarding the paucity of historical research material, Iranian dance is in a state similar to the Indian wrestling
tradition that Alter studied. For this reason he observes that with "the
paucity of historical accounts of wrestling...I do not believe that an adequate history can be written now..." (1992: 16). Therefore, although
some individuals might wish to create a history due to the lack of adequate historical evidence, they are instead reduced to speculating about
the history of dance and its meanings in the Iranian culture sphere.
    Historically, Iranians rarely, if ever, wrote about dance. Our evi-
dence of dance lies chiefly in the descriptions written by foreigners,
while the native view of dance is iconographic because in certain periods and in particular genres of art, dance was portrayed visually by Iranian artists. In this chapter I will chiefly look at the iconographic portrayal of dance. For those unfamiliar with Iranian artistic and aesthetic
practices it will be useful to present a detailed discussion of the problems of viewing art in an Iranian/Islamic context before I detail the evidence of dance left by each of the major historical periods.
    The motivation behind the attempts to write a history of dance seems
to be the need to imbue dance with a dignity that the various authors feel
Iranians do not accord it, and, in fact, to endow Iranian dance with a
history—a pedigree if you will. Historian Yaha Zoka's (1978) study of
pre-Islamic dance, for example, is an attempt to trace a chronological
history of dance. Zoka' notes that figures on vessels from archeological

sites depict people with their arms raised in the air, and assumes this pose represents praying, a questionable assumption about people who lived 6000 years ago and of whom we know little, including their religious beliefs or language. As historian John Curtis suggests,

> Modern Iran is composed of many diverse ethnic elements. In addition to Persians, who form the largest group, there are Turks, Kurds, Lurs, Baluchis and Arabs, as well as a number of ethnic minorities. This must also have been the situation in antiquity, with the country occupied by different groups with different backgrounds and speaking different languages. (1989:6)

Yet throughout his presentation, Zoka' attempts to demonstrate that dance was a part of religious observances of that time. Such an assertion cannot be proven since, as Curtis suggests, there were apparently many groups and many religious practices. Zoka' is unable to make any distinction between these groups based on his evidence. How could he? We know little of the various ethnic, linguistic, and religious identities of these people, and sources, such as the vessel figures, are unable to provide convincing details of specific religious rites.

Medjid Rezvani (1962), too, attempts to write a history of dance in order to prove the existence of a "classical" dance tradition with formal rules of performance and training (see especially 1962:150-159). Rezvani concludes that "...they are guarded, right up to our own times, the rules of the classical dance, even if a few old dancers are the only repositories of them" (159). Perhaps due to the paucity of accurate information and because Rezvani published his work through a reputable publisher of ethnomusicology studies, more than one scholar has taken seriously his suggestion that an Iranian classical dance form exists, with a codified vocabulary and movement system, and that it has somehow been secretly passed down from generation to generation. Ethnomusicologist Amnon Shiloah's work, citing Rezvani, provides a recent example: "From the scattered information we possess, however, it emerges that alongside non-professional dancing, a well-defined form of sophisticated dance did exist. The latter probably referred to the glorious preIslamic Iranian dance with its codified rules and aesthetics..." (1995:137). Thus, when one enters the tangled past in which glimpses of Iranian solo improvised dancing are tantalizingly viewed, it is tempting to "create" a history, but such a project still lies in the future, awaiting fuller documentation which may never be available.

This caveat having been issued, abundant iconographic evidence of solo improvised dance or a similar and related dance form exists, and attests to its presence for more than six thousand years. A seal carved on rock, dating from the middle of the third millennium B.C. and found at the important site of Shush (Susa), shows two female solo dancers

performing for two men in a banquet scene, the beginning of this historical odyssey of retrieving evidence for this movement practice. (Evidence of group dancing on several pottery vessels found at sites such as
Tepe Sialk, Tepe Giyan, and Susa date back even earlier, to before 5000
B.C.) The depictions of dancers in a wide variety of art forms confirm
the popularity of this dance practice. I am wary of speculation and of
reading possible interpretations into this data, for instance, that it has
religious or ceremonial import, that we cannot, at this point, comfortably
assert. Yet, some positive observations are in order.

Before delineating in chronological order the evidence that exists for
solo improvised dance, some remarks regarding those sources, and Iranian history in general, are necessary in order to understand the limited
evidence we possess. The Iranian world has been a central geographic
crossroads for the migrations of many peoples for thousands of years.
As geographer X. De Planhol notes, "The life of Iran is dominated
above all by the disparity between the nomadic peoples and those who
are settled" (1968:409). This historical theme is borne out by alternating periods of prosperity and devastation caused by the entry of new
nomadic groups who wrought wide-spread havoc and destruction, creating gaps not only in the history of dance, but lacunae in other expressive forms as well. An additional related note is that dancers are more
prominently shown at certain times and places, and they are visually
represented in certain types of art such as lustre ware from Kashan
(tenth-thirteenth century A.D.) and silver vessels from the Sasanian period (225-650 A.D.), while being almost absent during periods such as
the Achaemenid (550-330 B.C.).

Unfortunately, Iranians themselves did not write about dancing or
dancers except in a metaphorical way in Persian poetry. I argue that this
is largely due to the low social status of professional dancers and the
indignity of dancing, activities with which these writers did not wish to
be associated. Therefore we must rely primarily on two sources:
iconographic evidence, the only native source, and the writings of Westerners. Journals and reports of Europeans support these iconographic
depictions. These begin with the ancient Greek writers, and then after a
gap of time following the collapse of Rome, such writings resume with
the memoirs of Clavijo in 1404. The potential value of these writings,
samples of which I include in the following section under "the Safavids," is severely hampered by ethnocentricity. However, they are so
numerous that they tend to support one another as well as confirm or
contest practices depicted in the iconographic sources. Until the second
half of the twentieth century, the only existing, published texts on Iranian dancing had been written by Westerners. While these are relatively
numerous and certainly contain much useful information, almost without exception they are informed by a colonial gaze, and a hostile one at
that. That includes the writings of the ancient Greeks.

Limitations of Iranian Iconographic Sources for the Development of Historical Evidence of Iranian Dancing

Piecing together a history based on extant sources is an arduous task. The depictions of the art work and the literary references are considerably fragmented. Most of the works are not indexed by the subject depicted in the art, but rather, the focus of most studies has been on the technical aspects of the art. In this regard, art historian Richard Ettinghausen observes that "Comparatively little work has been done on other fruitful avenues of research, for instance, the exploration of the paintings, and for that matter, of other forms of figural representation as *documents of history*, particularly of social and cultural history" (1984: 713). Thus, in order to find pictorial or other references to dance activity, a researcher must spend many long hours combing through books and museums in order to piece together even the sketchiest historical record. The same applies to the writings of Westerners, since they are not generally indexed under "dance," and must be consulted individually, and these works are often long, such as the travel journals of Chardin, which appear in eight volumes, as well as several truncated editions. The latter source is, however, slightly easier to use since, with the exception of the ancient Greeks, European travel journals about Iran properly begin with the visit of the Spaniard Clavijo to the Timurid court in Samarqand in 1404.

Many choreographers, and even dance researchers, in the West and in the Iranian culture sphere attempt to utilize these iconographic sources, especially Persian miniature paintings, as if they were photographs, informative of a specific historic reality. Many orientalist productions have been based on such usage. Some observers, unfamiliar with the artistic conventions of Iranian art, erroneously conclude that what is seen in a Persian miniature is "real," by which one might mean an actual reproduction or representation of a specific historical happening or event, or a depiction of specific movements, which the artist actually saw and attempted to reconstruct pictorially. In fact, it would seem that Robert De Warren, the former director of the National Dance Ensemble of Iran (before it was disbanded by the Islamic Republic in 1979), certainly supported such a concept and acted upon it by creating a choreography based on miniatures.[1]

> Collections of his (the poet Nezami's) works...also contain a rich tapestry of miniatures...the representation of dance is very evident, the Safavid versions being the richest in movement and style. Not only has it been possible to trace actual dance movements, but also musical and percussion instruments that have long been lost...Each step and gesture is a reproduction of the real traditional painting. Choreographed after almost two years of research. (Mahalli Dancers of Iran 1976: n.p.)

De Warren points to the miniatures as a major source of his research and states that he was able to lay "twenty or so of them side by side" in order to recreate an authentic production of dances performed four centuries ago during the Safavid period (1501-1722) (1973:29). He does not, however, indicate in which order they were laid out to obtain his results. Dating many of these miniatures and determining their authorship still remain problematic to expert art historians such as Melikian-Chirvani (1985) and Oleg Grabar (1987). Art historians have never investigated the potential symbolism represented by dance in miniatures that include choreographic scenes.[2]

The miniatures and other pictorial art forms not only reflect highly idealized depictions of court life intended to be seen by only a few individuals, but they also require a deep study for their understanding. They cannot be considered as a source for recreating movement, as both Fermor (1987) and Lawler (1964) indicate in their respective studies of Italian Renaissance and ancient Greek dance. The dance figures are stylized and indicate only that dance is occurring, which underscores Strauss' (1978) contention that the most important use of such illustrative data is to ascertain poses rather than movement. Almost all of the dancers in the miniatures of this period, and the later ones as well, are depicted using the positions I mentioned earlier: 1) one arm up, bent at the elbow, the other arm held in the opposite, symmetrical position. 2) both arms held up and bent at the elbow, the torso bent, and 3) clappers being played in one of the above attitudes.

Rather than illustrating reality, except in the authentic details such as clothing and architectural forms, I suggest that this art form, like those investigated by Geertz (1983: Chapter Five), is informed by symbolism which is historically and ethnically specific. In addition to Geertz's notion of the need to see this art through what he terms the "period eye," I will also appropriate the idea proposed by Wolfgang Iser of the German Reception Theory school, that the viewer also creates meaning through blanks and negations. The artist omits much information which the viewer, with his or her specific cultural knowledge, supplies by filling the gaps (Holub 1984: 94-95). For example, since according to all the accounts of European visitors, dancers in the courts and elsewhere were public women, one must "read" this fact into the miniature, because the women who are shown dancing do not differ from other women in dress or other details, as prostitutes actually did.[3]

I argue that the symbol of the dancer and dancing represent vitality, happiness, celebration and the royal court at ease, enjoying itself—a highly political statement, since the opposite was often the case. In virtually hundreds of miniatures and other iconographic sources that have been located over the past several years, dancing almost exclusively appears in only two genres: weddings and fetes such as enthronements and banqueting scenes. The figures that populate miniatures from the

Iranian culture sphere constitute types rather than specific individuals. Persian figurative painting is peopled with character types: sultans and shahs, soldiers, older philosophers and dervishes, princesses, older maids-in-waiting, servants, courtiers, hunters and young lovers, as well as a variety of animals that represent particular cultural values. The scenes that are depicted most often are like stock scenarios: battles, hunting scenes, polo games, scenes of courtly love, enthronements, and what I call the "court at play," that is, scenes of revelry, all of which are designed to show the power residing in the royal court.

> As in literature, the image of people portrayed in the art of the miniature were created through the means of a synthesis of three processes: a highly conventional character, strict rules of etiquette, and realistic details. The painter, exactly the same as the poet, did not represent the world as he saw it, he represented it as it ought to have been following the ideas of his time. (Polyakova and Rahimova 1987:77)

In order to understand the contents of these miniatures it is also useful to look at Geertz's notion of art as a cultural system in which the members of the particular society and historical period are familiar with the artistic and symbolic conventions employed by the artists. In sum, this art form is replete with symbolism and meaning for artists and their tiny, privileged audiences at a particular time and place, all of whom knew the artistic conventions depicted; according to Geertz and Iser, they were culturally competent viewers. Depictions in Iranian art are often allegorical: layers of representation rendered in a painting or a piece of pottery need to be unpeeled and examined. It would then reasonably follow that the conventions of these art pieces were clear to the creators and their patrons. The problem for the modern researcher is finding that historical angle of vision.

> Representation follows two laws: it always conveys more than it intends; and it is never totalizing. The "excess" meaning conveyed by representation creates a supplement that makes multiple and resistant readings possible. Despite this excess, representation produces ruptures and gaps: it fails to reproduce the real exactly. (Phelan 1993: 2)

In spite of their limitations, I am convinced that iconographic and pictorial sources can provide us with certain kinds of valuable information on some aspects of dancing and dancers. That includes limited evidence of movement practices, clues regarding performative conventions, aesthetic canons, musical accompaniment, the social position of performers, clothing, issues of space, numbers of performers and circumstances of performance.

Issues in the Analysis of Islamic Visual Arts

Does Islamic art suggest or propose ways of viewing and perceiving that are essentially different from those in which other art forms are viewed and analyzed?

I question the oft-stated notion that Islam pervades all areas of human activity in the Islamic world. All observations indicate that certain art forms, such as figurative art, were produced for non-sacred contexts.

> The works discussed did not always have a specifically religious purpose, sometimes far from it, and the patrons and artists were not invariably good Muslims, and occasionally not Muslims at all." (Brend 1991:10)

One of the commonplace canons regarding Islamic and Iranian art from the Islamic period is that Islam prohibits the depiction of the human figure, and even animals, based on the notion that only God can create living things. It is probable that many, if not the majority of, Moslems believe that an injunction exists on the creation of figural art. "The axiom for Islam's essentially anaturalistic art was laid down in the teachings of the great Prophet Muhammad, in which he counseled against the representation of men and animals" (Du Ry 1970:7), is not an unusual point-blank statement that one encounters in books about the art of the Middle East.

> ..we must, I think, regard this invasion and the consequent conversion of Persia to Muhammadanism as a loss...Persia was destined to separate itself from the rest of the Mohammedan world, to establish its own specific variations of the Mohammedan doctrine, and to reject on the whole the ban on representations of the human figure and on the use of wine. (Fry 1931: xviii-xix)

It seems that only in the last decade has this notion of a ban on figurative art been seriously challenged by a new generation of art scholars, many of them from the countries of origin.

> Old misconceptions linger. The most persistent one is that figurative art in Islam was either banned or at best tolerated in a more or less "heretical" context. This mistaken idea owes a lot to the circumstances under which the art of the various Islamic cultural areas was discovered by the West...Thus figurative art in Islam came to be equated, wrongly, with Iranian painting...The Arab world

itself cultivated figurative art from the beginning on a
spectacular, monumental scale. A long-cherished view in
the West has it that calligraphy and abstract designs consisting of formal motifs developed in the East as a com-
pensation for the 'forbidden living image'...a glance at
Persian literature on painting and calligraphy is enough to
disprove the contention. (Melikian-Chirvani 1985:21-22)

There were, indeed, as has been previously stated, religious fundamen-
talists and zealous theologians who interpreted religious law in this
light, and certain rulers, such as Shah Tahmasb, who became a religious
bigot in his later years and closed down his atelier of art and book production. But this interpretation was not universally followed:

It is not precisely the case, as is sometimes stated, that the
Qur'an forbids representation. In the key passage in
surah v, 92—'O ye who believe, wine and games of
chance and idols and divining arrows are an abomination
of satan's handiwork; so avoid it and prosper'—it is
clearly the worship of idols which is condemned. An an-
tipathy to representation related to the Jewish prohibition
of graven images, seems to have been latent in early Islamic thought and to have hardened in the course of the
first century...The *hadiths*, traditions reporting the words
and actions of the Prophet, collected after his death and
sometimes at a considerable interval, tend to show him as
disapproving of images. The message, however, is not
absolute...Nevertheless, the doctrine eventually evolved
that the painter or sculptor was guilty of trying to usurp
the creative activity of God." (Brend 1991:19)

Were there an absolute ban on figural art, we would have no
iconographic art to study, but since such art exists, I maintain that it was
permissible in certain non-sacred contexts. Islamic art historian Gulru
Necipoglu puts this issue into a clearer context, which both acknowledges religious constraints and the continuous use of figural art in Islamic societies:

With its purely geometric vocabulary the *girih* (knot) was
only one of many abstract modes of design that flourished
in the medieval Islamic world in response to the constric-
tions placed on the scope of figural representation, which
from the very beginning was excluded from religious
monuments and illuminated Korans. Although figural
representation had a rich life of its own throughout Islamic history, it was consistently relegated to profane
contexts in architecture, the decorative arts, and miniature

painting. (1995:92)

Characteristics of Iranian Art

One of the major pitfalls in analyzing Iranian art, as I have tried to stress, is that reality resides in the details. Otherwise, the depictions are highly stylized and formal: the ideal is preferred to the real. According to art historian Soudavar, Persian figurative visual art is characterized by

> ...a distinct preference for the ideal over the real, for stylization over naturalistic representation." It was concerned, "not with objectivity or the reproduction of physical reality but with idealized and stylized representation. ...This preference, expressed in both literature and the visual arts, remained remarkably consistent over the centuries...A taste not concerned with objectivity or the reproduction of physical reality but with idealized and stylized representation. (1992: 14)

Iranian art is, for the most part, a royal and courtly art. This is because most art was expensive to produce and only the most wealthy and powerful could afford to subsidize it. Historically, Iranian artists did not utilize Renaissance perspective, and some claim they were unable to understand it; therefore, Iranian art never became 'adult' or 'mature.' Fermor and Lawler both indicate that depicting movement was a technical difficulty the painters and artists of the respective time periods they studied experienced, "a problem that they never solved," in Lawler's words. I think that this is a rather narrow Western viewpoint. In fact, Lentz points out that:

> Distinguished by the precision of its design, the artificial ordering of this space actively suppresses naturalism and three-dimensional perspective to produce an idealized, abstracted painting characterized by emotional and physical detachment. This artificial construct in the past has been characterized as charming but primitive because of its apparent lack of interest in physical reality. For the Timurids, however, its absence was intentional. While *there are* instances of three-dimensional perspective and illusionism in their painting, these options were mostly rejected in illustrative work. (Lentz 1989 : 171) (my emphases)

Iranian art, as we saw in Soudavar's estimation, shares with the art of ancient Greece certain characteristics:

> Greek art is often deliberately unrealistic, and is concerned with ideal beauty, design, balance, rhythm, linear

schemes, and stylization, rather than with an exact portrayal of what the artist saw in life." (Lawler 1964:17)
The following point made by Lawler is also important:
"The Greek vase painter often draws figures without a
'floor line'—a convention which has led some modern
interpreters to insert an imaginary 'floor line' of their own
in a given scene, and then to deduce from its position all
sorts of untenable conclusions, e.g., that the ancient
Greeks engaged in something like ballet, and even toe
dancing. Naturally, the observer must use great caution,
and avoid all such fantastic interpretations. (1964:21)

By fantastic interpretations, I presume she means the Persian version of
Revival Greek Urn Dancing, in which miniature *tableaux vivants*
"come to life," and the dancers, including the shah, dance. This type of
choreography was recently popular in Iran and currently survives in
Southern California as a staging technique for some local groups seen
on Iranian television and in formal concert settings. Robert De Warren,
the English choreographer of the Iranian State Dance Company, was
asked in an interview: "Do any of the court dances survive, because
there appear to be, in old Persian paintings and miniatures, considerable
suggestions of some kind of court dance?" To which he replied:

> In the miniatures one can find the best evidence of this.
> Even before the 15th century the earliest miniatures depict
> dance. When the Arabs invaded Iran and the Muslim re-
> ligion took over, it was against the religion to play music
> or to dance. Through centuries of Arab rule, Persians
> kept hidden their feeling for music and dance, but when
> they were eventually free of the caliphs, these arts imme-
> diately blossomed forth and the music really developed.
> Each shah would encourage artists to come and live in the
> court and, like they did in the French courts, create a na-
> tional tradition of art. Though, of course, they didn't go
> as far as establishing an academy or even a system of
> dance, but one can trace back to the musical rhythms of
> the period and from the miniatures, which are so clear, it
> is easy to compare the movement. If you place, say, 20
> miniatures side by side it's easy to see how the movement
> developed... (1976:30)

Believing that one can look at a series of miniature paintings and create
an exact replica of a dance form, De Warren in Iran, and several Iranian
dance groups in Southern California, have staged versions of miniatures
"coming to life" in which the dancers move from a "frozen" pose to begin dancing.[4] Whether or not the creators of these artful choreographies
believe that they can, in fact, reproduce actual historical and authentic

movements from studying miniatures, they certainly send this message to audiences, both Iranian and non-Iranian.[5]

Referring to Northern Italy in the fifteenth century, Sharon Fermor emphatically states, "...in spite of the apparent richness of paintings in this respect, the attempt to use them as a source of information for performance practice is a dangerous and highly unsatisfactory venture..." (1987:18). This is equally true for fifteenth-century Iran. She cites other problems as well:

> For the most part, in representing dance, painters relied on
> a set of established formulas, formulas which they knew
> their audience would recognize and which they them-
> selves could draw on without reference to real dance
> practice. These formulas probably bore only a very loose
> relationship to actual contemporary dance." (1987:18)

I conducted a survey of several iconographic Iranian sources which revealed that in most of the depictions, the dancers were shown in variations of three stylized positions, underscoring Fermor's observation.

And finally, as Fermor asks, "...how far is it possible either to represent or to reconstruct a particular step or movement from one specific pose?" (1987:30). This is, of course, the major objection to attempting to reproduce an exact replica of any historical dance. As Lawler concludes, "we shall never, in all probability, be able to restore any ancient dance in its entirety" (Lawler 1964:27).

Thus, visual arts must be employed for historical evidence of dance, since the native written texts are silent. Iranian and Islamic writers, in my opinion, do not describe or mention this activity, most probably because its professional practitioners of both sexes were often non-Moslems and associated with professional sexual activities as well. This placed them beyond the pale of the polite society they entertained and positioned their artistic and gymnastic activities beneath the notice of those in that society who wrote. I conjecture that had historians, political figures or literati written about dancers they would have lost status in society. For example,

> Some years later, around 1616, the official historian to the
> court of Shah 'Abbas, Eskandar Beyg-e Monshi, praised
> Aqa Reza son of 'Ali-Asghar of Kashan, as had Qazi
> Ahmad, and mentioned that Reza's love for wrestling and
> the wrestler's milieu (*ba an tabaqe* [with that class]) had
> alienated him from the company of artists. (Soudavar
> 1992:262)

Imagine how much more he would have been shunned had he taken up with professional entertainers! Wrestlers were, after all, a social step or two above them.

The first issue, then, is what is being portrayed in these works of art, for whom, and for what purpose? Even after years of living in Iran and among Iranians, seeing and admiring Iranian, and more specifically, Persian art in the form of miniatures and other pictorial forms, it was many years before I realized how Western my attitude toward viewing that art was. The contemporary Western city dweller does not realize how unique her or his life-style is in terms of the general availability of music and art compared to large groups of people in other periods of history. Today, performing and visual arts are ubiquitous in everyday life in a way that is unique in history. Music for any taste can be made instantly available by turning on a radio or playing a tape. Museum galleries, books, paintings, and even posters are everywhere, and people are used to visiting and owning them. In fact, in its present form, the viewing of art on the consumeristic and mass scale found in the Western world is almost a cultural given. In contrast, it was something of a shock to realize that in Iran, until recently, only the royal families and a few nobles ever saw figurative art as we know it, in the form of miniatures and pottery. The common people, at least in urban contexts, experienced art almost exclusively in the decorative elements of the mosques with their elaborate calligraphy, which is one reason they were so popular as gathering places. Large portrait paintings and other depictions of the human figure were almost never experienced in the lives of any but a few privileged individuals, until the advent of the Qajar period (1785-1925), when figurative murals began to appear in public buildings such as coffee houses. This is due both to popular religious perceptions regarding figural art as well as the exorbitant costs of its production.

> ...it is more surprising to discover to what extent the greatest works of painters and calligraphers have remained hidden from public view...The significance—and perfection—of the manuscript (*Shahnameh*) stands in comparison, in its own sphere, with that of the *Creation of Man* in the Sistine Chapel in the sphere of Italian Renaissance art. It was commissioned by a King, Shah Tahmasp of Iran, and executed by some of the greatest painters. The difference is that while millions of visitors have seen the Sistine Chapel, only a few thousand have set eyes on the miniatures from the Book of Kings and less than a hundred may have seen some of those now shown here. (Melikian-Chirvani 1985:20)

Cherished as treasures or offered as presents to kings and princes, luxury manuscripts were never widely circulated nor intended for popular reading, a relatively rare skill in the largely oral society of Timurid and Safavid Iran. Rulers shared the privilege of their production with a small circle of powerful and wealthy princes and amirs. In times of military defeat or retreat, manuscripts, and even painters and calligraphers, were often the few precious items rescued when princes were forced to abandon their treasuries. "Scribes, administrators, and historians were more familiar with calligraphy, which they used in their daily functions than with manuscript paintings, which were usually preserved in the treasury and relatively inaccessible" (Soudavar 1992:95).

Thus, part of the faulty idea of this modern perception of the general availability of art lies in the way that a wide variety of books of reproductions of Persian miniatures and other art forms have been made widely available to the public, creating a false notion of general availability within its own time frame.[6]

Chronological History of Evidence of Iranian Solo Improvised Dance
Pre-Islamic Iran
The dates that I give, although conventionally given in many historical works, do not reflect historical reality. Quite often, dynasties lasted longer than the dates assigned them in standard history books, if only at some diminished or local level. The historical periods I itemize below are important for historical information regarding dance.

Prehistoric Iran. In his four articles on dance in ancient Iran, Zoka' lays out much of the archeological iconographic evidence available. If one bypasses his speculative interpretations, his otherwise valuable work presents many of the extant archeological examples chronologically. These consist largely of dancing figures on pottery shards or almost fully reconstructed vessels. As Jean-Louis Huot points out, unlike in Greece and Egypt, "written records. . .are almost completely lacking in Iran" (1965: 11). This means "the material that sheds most light on the pre-Achaemenid period is the pottery" (1965: 79). In addition to pottery, Zoka' displays a stone carving and a set of three figures in metal.

The majority of the pieces show group dances in various postures and Zoka' interprets these in the light of present-day dance practices, as well as assigning meaning, such as the dancers are trying to get closer to heaven where the gods dwell, or five men are performing a "war" dance because they are holding one another's arms and shoulders tightly. In the depiction of the two solo dancers, which is difficult to discern because the stone has been rubbed heavily, he holds the opinion that the dancers are performing for warlords or strongmen (his terms), who also appear in the piece. At least one of the dancers appears to be unclad, a convention found in many Sasanian figurative representations as well (Zoka' 1979: part 2:2-3).

The arrival of the Iranians in their present homeland covered a long time span and largely took place outside the light of history. Of neces-

sity, accounts of timing vary. Historian Jim Hicks gives a historic range
of 2000-1800 B.C. as the time period for the "beginning of Aryan (Iranian) migration from the plains of southern Russia into the Near East"
(1975: 10). As historian Richard Frye notes, "the pottery and objects
uncovered by archaeologists have not been of great help in reconstructing the period of invasions of the Iranians" (1993: 24). Here we have
one of our first periods, over a thousand years, in which little evidence
of dance exists. By the seventh century B.C., the Iranian peoples such
as the Medes and Persians were settled in their present sites.

Historic Pre-Islamic Iran. Achaemenids (559-330 BC). As Zoka'
ruefully notes, "the remains and documents about dance in the historical
periods of the Medes, the Achaemenids, and Seleucids is rarer and almost nothing compared to the previous periods" (1978: part 3, 38). This
paucity of objects may be directly due to Alexander's conquest. As art
historian M. Roaf observes of the minor arts: "Before Alexander burnt
Persepolis he carried away all the immense treasure. Very few of these
objects have survived" (1989: 43). For the dance historian, Roaf's note
is important because dance is not shown in any of the numerous ceremonial depictions of the courtly history of this dynasty.

It is at this time that a few remarks concerning dance activities appear in the accounts of Greek historians. While these observations generally concern the dances of men, especially the pyrrhic dances (see
Shahbazi [1994: 640-641]), the historians occasionally make observations about solo dancing. Evidently, entertainers who sang and danced
were very numerous in the ancient Persian courts, for "when Parmenio,
the Greek general, took Damascus, he captured several hundreds of
them from the court of Darius III" (Farmer 1964: 2785). Most of the
pertinent citations for dance in pre-Islamic Iran may be found in
Shahbazi's brief article (1994:640-641).

Alexander the Great and the Seleucids (330 - 170 BC). Virtually
nothing other than the citation concerning Alexander and Roxane men-
tions dance. At a banquet held by Oxyartes, satrap of Sogdiana, for Alexander the Great, "thirty high-born maidens, including the satrap's
daughter Roxane, attended and participated in a dance" (Shahbazi 1994:
640).

The Parthians (170 BC - 224 AD). Little is known of Parthian art.
Art historian E. Keal details several reasons for this, not the least of
which is that "the majority of the 'name' sites...lie outside the boundaries of modern Iran" (1989: 49). Another major reason is that the Parthians did not develop an "imperial" art with an integrated style, but
rather developed local styles, reflecting the decentralized political arrangement that characterized these four centuries of Iranian history.
Nevertheless, depictions of dance appear more frequently during the
Parthian period than in the previous two periods, in banquet scenes on
painted walls, stucco, and terracotta figurines.

There is a depiction of a male dancer on a stucco relief from Qal'a-ye Yazdigird (Kurdistan), which is important because it shows the figure frontally with one arm up, bent at the elbow, and the opposite arm down, in a symmetrical opposition. This is one of the most typical, stylized poses of dancers throughout the history of Iranian art. The other popular stylized pose is depicted with the dancer holding two arms bent at the elbow, up at the sides and the torso bent at the waist. A third stylized depiction shows the dancers, usually in one of those two positions, carrying clappers or kerchiefs. Through these poses one can discern the dancer(s) in a crowded scene. According to Shahbazi, a terracotta figurine of a girl dancer was found in Dura Europus, an important Parthian archeological site (1994: 641).

The Sasanids (224-650 AD). Like the Achaemenids, the Sasanians devoted most of their efforts to the production of monumental art, excellently preserved remains of which can be seen throughout Iran. "Although Sasanian art was essentially the art of the monarch, and much of it was concerned with the representation of royal images" (Hermann 1989: 79), nevertheless we have a considerable quantity of depictions of dancers, a favorite subject for these art objects. The majority of these are found on the many silver vessels that were produced, even into the Islamic period (one can be seen in the Los Angeles County Museum of Art). Dozens of these Sasanian silver vessels can be found in a variety of historical studies (see especially Pope 1964; Ghirshman 1954, 1962; Harper 1981), which demonstrates how popular this dance form has been. I hazard the possibility that some of the figures might represent a goddess, perhaps Anahita, since they are carrying what appear to be votive items such as birds and flowers. Prudence Harper, a specialist in Sasanian silver, notes "a form of design appearing solely on the ewers and vases showing mythological or secular scenes including a number of dancing female figures holding specific objects or attributes" (an excellent example appears on a silver bowl with an enthronement scene) (Harper 1981:237 plate 36). The dancers are almost invariably portrayed as nude, or nearly so. Jahez, a contemporary historical writer, also describes Bahram Gur, a famous Sasanian emperor, as having a "keen interest in music, and having acquired singing and dancing girls" (Shahbazi: 1994: 641). Harper's keen insight into the specificity of dancers appearing in festive and celebratory events such as enthronements, weddings, and banquets will be echoed in the art of the Islamic period.

Islamic Iran (650 -). Given the destruction wrought by the invading Arabs, Mongols and Turks, which resulted in the massacre of tens of millions of Iranians and the destruction of populous cities that formed major culture centers, one might wonder that anything of value survived these onslaughts. Indeed, art historians Grube and Sims point out that "Much of the destruction of pre-14th-century Persian material culture was caused by Mongol armies before about 1260" (1989: 201). For this reason they assert, "Very little is known about painting in Persia during the first four centuries of the Islamic period" (1989: 200). Some of the destruction was also a result of religious bigotry when religious zealots wantonly destroyed manuscripts and illustrated books. There are periods in which barely any art production occurred. In the century following the arrival of the Arabs, that art which was produced, such as the Sasanian vessels described above, tended to be a continuation of previous styles and techniques. As one reads Harper's studies (1978, 1981), one understands that deciding the provenance of time and place of production forms a major question of inquiry. In other words, a Sasanian vessel might well have been produced during the Islamic period, with so little change from the pre-Islamic period, that even an expert such as Harper cannot always discern its period of origin. Thus, as was the case for pre-Islamic Iran, evidence for dance is of necessity skewed by what is available; one must grieve for all that has been lost and destroyed. It must also be stated, that while I have combed through well over one hundred volumes over the past twenty years, I have only managed to see a fraction of what must exist in libraries and museums throughout the world.

The Islamic period may be divided into several periods, with the understanding that these sometimes overlap. There are periods during which the entire nation was broken up into small rival political units, or simply existed in a state of political chaos.

Islamic Art historian Oleg Grabar makes the crucial point that a specifically Islamic art took at least two and a half centuries to form: "All works of art from the first two centuries of Islam were the result of a more or less conscious and successful filtering of past forms...Only in the ninth century did these individual operations finally reach a critical mass sufficient to create a style..." (1987:210). Three important cultural and artistic developments also mark this period, which covers most of the above time span: 1) The emergence of Modern Persian as a literary language in its present-day form. This process took three centuries, but the language began to reach its maturity of expression just prior to Ferdowsi, with the poetry of Rudaki (d. 940) (see Lazard 1974). 2) The gradual development of calligraphy as an art form. 3) The development of lustre ware pottery, which probably began in Iraq in the ninth century. Lustre ware, due to its elegant properties of shape, proportion and color, for the first time attracted the patronage of the wealthy to pottery; prior to this time, court and luxury vessels were created from metal. Lustre ware forms the most common surviving source of the iconographic depiction of dance from the tenth to the fourteenth century. (See especially Pope 1964: 1446-1666; Caiger-Smith 1985.) Not only does pottery from this era furnish our primary visual sources of dance activity, but Pope also points out that this pottery "throws indispensable

light, not only on ornament, but also on the evolution of Persian painting" (1964:1447). After the thirteenth century, up until 1925, painting
provides our chief iconographic source of dance. Not unsurprisingly, as
we near our own time, iconographic sources increase.

The Seljuqs (1037 - 1157) and the Il-Khanids (1220-1337). As
mentioned above, lustre ware pottery is our primary source of evidence
for dancing from this period. Pope observes that "Moreover, the theme
of dancers, an especial favourite with the Kashan decorators, appears on
several of the lustre plates" during this period (1964:1605). Painting,
according to art historians Grube and Sims, seems to have been a continuous activity during the Seljuq and Il-Khanid periods (1989: 200). In
spite of this, none of the paintings, mostly miniatures, that I have seen
from this period depicts dance.

The Timurids (1380 - 1506). After the initial destruction caused by
Timur (Tamarlane), the founder of this dynasty (and the Moguls of India), he and his descendants became remarkable patrons of the art. Beginning with this period, we are furnished both with plentiful
iconographic sources through a bounty of miniature production and the
first European journals.

From the poses, strikingly similar not only to contemporary dance
practices, but also to the figures, such as the boy dancer from the Parthian period, we might also speculate that the dances were possibly
similar to those seen today. However, we can say nothing certain about
the actual movements employed or the rhythms or tempos of the accompanying music. For example, we cannot say if the 6/8 rhythm that so
dominates this dance form in the twentieth century was played in antiquity, or even in the eighteenth century. We also know nothing of the
social position that dancers occupied. This is important to note because
other authors (De Warren, Rezvani, Miller and St. John) assert that prior
to Islam, dancers were honored individuals. I would suggest the opposite: that Islamic attitudes toward dancers may well have been formed
from pre-Islamic attitudes, since dancers, unlike musicians, are never
portrayed in official court or ritual scenes. Most often, dancers are depicted as part of court entertainments in the so-called minor arts, and
most of these forms of pictorial art of the period were created only for
the eyes of the elite.

Depictions of the dancers throughout the entire period, both pre- and
post-Islamic, show many of them carrying percussion instruments such
as metal, wooden or stone clappers or castanets, indicating that dynamic
rhythmic practices formed an important part of this dance tradition.
Indeed, such practice can still be found in certain areas of the Iranian
culture sphere. I witnessed a male dancer in a performance in Urgench,
Khorasmia, whose skills with stone clappers equaled the finest Spanish
castanet playing. Accompanied by a *tar* and *daireh*, he danced and
played a virtuoso collection of 6/8 rhythms (personal observation Octo-

ber 12, 1986).

Most of the depictions of dancing show a solo dancer, more rarely two, and one rare and very vividly executed painting shows a group of women performing this dance in a harem. From the very individual hand positions, it is clear that they are each performing in solo fashion within a group setting, a practice seen today.

The Safavids (1501 - 1722). In many ways, from the viewpoint of identifying sources for evidence of dance practices, the Safavid period is richer than the preceding ones. In addition to miniatures, which are relatively numerous, large wall murals such as those existing in Isfahan (see Grube and Sims ibid.) show several banqueting scenes with dancers. Textiles, now preserved in relatively large numbers, provide another source of evidence of dance. Ceramics also continue to provide depictions of dance activity.

It is this period, as well, for which large numbers of Western journals portray life at court, and, for the first time, the life of the common people. By Westerner, I mean the term in its widest sense, referring to historians and other commentators from ancient Greece, Rome, Byzantium, Western Europe, which culturally includes Russia (an important factor in the history of Central Asia, Afghanistan, and Iran), and later, America. These were travelers, military, political and mercantile, who wrote about dancing and dancers in the Iranian culture sphere in terms that are both ethnocentric and negative; thus, dance presents yet another demonstration of the perceived low moral tone and position of the Moslem natives. As Metin And observed of Europeans who described dancing in the Ottoman Empire:

> ...foreign travelers gave much attention to this topic in
> their books and, although they emphasized the slack mo-
> rality and obscene character of the dancing, they could not
> hide in their descriptions the breathless interest they took
> in these performances. (And 1976:138)

I will produce a few short excerpts to illustrate these attitudes:

> The dances, so far as I was able to judge, were by no
> means indecent, though they were often very lascivious.
> (Schuyler 1876:72)...In Central Asia, Mohammedan
> prudery prohibits the public dancing of women..., here
> boys and youths specially trained take the place of the
> dancing-girls of other countries. The moral tone of soci-
> ety is scarcely improved by the change. (ibid.:70)
> Dancing boys...more remarkable for acrobatic skill than
> for grace, at any rate according to our ideas. (Browne
> 1893:120)...His evolutions were characterized by agility
> and suppleness rather than grace and appeared to me

somewhat monotonous. (ibid.:320)

Interestingly, Browne was a Persophile, and wrote important studies of Persian literature, yet when it came to describing the dance, he could not restrain his European biases.

> The music did not play out of tune, but still the effect of the whole sounded not unlike a concert of cats. (Shoberl 1828:174)
>
> ... it is here too that the eyes and the ears which still retain some trace of shame are obliged to turn aside, being unable to sustain the indecency and lasciviousness of these last acts...(Chardin 1673-1677 quoted in Surieu 1967:130)
>
> While refreshments were being served, a number of the pretty, effeminately dressed boys attached to the establishment (a coffee house in Isfahan) came forward to give a display of dancing. The Spanish Ambassador was considerably shocked by the lascivious posturing of a Circassian and a Persian, who performed a competition dance. (quoted in Blunt 1966:100)

The travelers' journals rarely indicate any hint of artistry, gracefulness, or aesthetic content in either the dancing or the music. Occasional exceptions occur. For example, French traveler Gaspard Drouville, in Iran during the early Qajar period, 1812-13, observed that:

> They (the female dancers) are ordinarily very beautiful, and dance with a great deal of lightness; their attitudes are voluptuous but without indecence; they use the same castanettes as the men while (other) women sing while being accompanied on the guitar. This exercise fournishes them with the opportunity to use their arms with a good deal of grace. (quoted in Bier et al. 1987:259)

Virtually all of the Western observers make a connection between prostitution and dancing. For example, Sir Jean Chardin (in Iran 1673-1677) noted that "Dancing is reckon'd Dishonest or if you will, Infamous; and there are none but the Publick Women who Dance" (1988:207). Because of this association between prostitution and dancing, Moslem authorities pronounced that "musicians and dancers should not serve as witnesses at court" (Schimmel 1990:415). It should be pointed out that, in contrast, the iconographic depictions of the professional dancers give no hint of this, as both male and female dancers are dressed like other individuals. I suggest that the reason for this lies in the formulation of the idea of "negatives and blanks" posited by Wolfgang Iser, a scholar of the Reception Theory school as described by Robert C. Holub.

"Good literature, Iser implies, is characterized by the negation of specific elements and the subsequent search for a 'meaning' that is unformulated, but nevertheless intended in the text" (1984:94). "Negations and blanks, then, are the fundamental means by which communication takes place" (ibid: 95). Utilizing Geertz's notion of the "period eye," I suggest that messages of social class and other meanings can be "read" into these miniatures by the knowledgeable eye: "The work is full of 'indeterminacies,' elements which depend for their effect upon the reader's interpretation" (Eagleton 1983:76).

It is clear from most accounts that dancers were numerous in court entertainments of the Islamic period. Chardin reports that the king's (Abbas II) troupe "consists of twenty-four, who are the most famous courtesans in the country" (quoted in Surieu 1967:150). He also makes clear, despite De Warren's suggestions, that the dancers did not live at court, but were under the charge of a senior woman who saw to it that they were properly dressed and gathered them together when needed for appearances at court.

The value of European descriptions is that they fill in part of the "information" that is missing due to the gaps and indeterminacies of native depictions of dance, which are invariably oriented to showing the court in a favorable, idealized light. For example, in the iconographic evidence, the dancers are always young and beautiful. An illustration from a European journal serves as a corrective, showing a balding, middle-aged man as a dancer.[7] Travelers' journals indicate that dancers performed for the entertainment of all classes, appearing in urban coffeehouses and rural weddings. Iranian theatre historian Bahram Beiza'i (1965:167-170) claims that the traditional comic theatre gradually grew out of professional dance performances during the late Safavid and Zand periods (seventeenth century), when certain itinerant companies of dancers began to settle in major cities. In order to attract new audiences and hold the interest of their steady patrons, according to Beiza'i, they began to perform short comic skits, which became longer and longer until theatrical elements predominated. Dance still forms a basis of movement practice in the theatre.

The Qajars (1785-1925). Painting still forms our most common iconographic source, and the nature of painting changes. Large portrait style paintings largely replace miniatures, and dancers and entertainers are a favorite subject. Painting in the more realistic Qajar tradition is now found on many objects such as lacquer-ware pen cases and leather book covers. For the first time, folk versions of this painting style are found in books, on wall murals in coffee houses, and in other media, which indicates an audience beyond the elite.

Paintings of this period show dancers in a much wider variety of attitudes and poses, reflecting a more realistic view of their actual movements than the stylized, and static depictions of previous periods. The

Safavid miniatures and paintings do not depict the dancers performing acrobatic movements, but the travelers' accounts, such as those of Chardin, do describe such movements. The dancers often balanced or manipulated in highly acrobatic fashion such items as tea cups, saucers, candles and daggers. The Qajar period paintings often show dancers, both male and female, balanced on one hand which is holding a dagger plunged into the floor. Dancers also wrote the names of patrons on the floor using rice or wheat flour during the course of the dance (Khaleqi 1974: 474).

From the middle of this period, beginning in the 1860s and 1870s, photography provides an extra source of information (See Najmi 1988). However, due to the slow speed of the shutter, movement could not be captured and the dancers are carefully posed. These photographs are useful for learning about details of clothing and sex and gender (since there were transvestite performances), make-up, musical instruments and the ages and numbers of entertainers in the different groups, rather than as documents of movement practices. Photographic evidence also demonstrates that itinerant bands of entertainers plied their trade in the countryside and were hired to perform in rural festivities as well. This practice continued into the Pahlavi period.

The Pahlavis (1925-1979). For the purposes of this study, the corresponding period in the areas of the Iranian culture sphere within the Soviet Union, some of which was under the rule of the Qajar and other Islamic regimes, was the Soviet period. In this period, particularly after World War II, new venues of performance appeared in the USSR, Iran, and Afghanistan. National companies were founded, European-style theatres served as new venues of performance, and research on regional folk dance was conducted. Solo improvised dance, in its traditional setting, became somewhat of an embarrassment to the respective Ministries of Culture and Fine Arts. The attitudes of the Iranian and Soviet governments were strikingly similar toward traditional performance: they ignored and marginalized it, and virtually all of the available publications reflect this view. Attitudes were negative, which was the tenor of almost all of the observations, both in the Russian and (later) Soviet and non-Soviet spheres of this vast region. For example, Tkachenko (1954:12) stated in the section under Tajikistan that the "feudal" period featured dances that were "unhealthy," performed exclusively by professional dancers who had now disappeared (Tkachenko 1954:436). Both in Iran and the former USSR, highly sanitized performances were supported by the state for both foreign and domestic consumption.

An additional source of evidence for this dance form in Iran is films of the 1960s and 1970s. Not only do these films show the movements in a largely transgressive fashion, they also reveal social attitudes that dancers are fallen women. One of the best ways to understand social attitudes toward dancers is to view musical films made in Tehran during this period. A typical plot: aristocrat's son meets dancer and falls in love. The father discovers this affair and exhibits distaste and disapproval. The father, with the lure of wealth and money, attempts to seduce the dancer, who repels his advances indignantly. The father reluctantly accepts the fact that this particular girl is virtuous, *even if she is a dancer*. Son marries dancer amid songs and dance with the Father smiling benignly. Thus, although the audience understands that dancers in general are women of loose morals and easy virtue, this one is an exception. The worst fate that could befall a family, as the film makes abundantly clear, is that a son would marry a dancer, a public woman, recalling Taj Al-Saltaneh's previous remark from the early twentieth century that Abdi-jan, being a dancer, was worthy of no one's love.

Conclusions
From all of these sources several facts emerge: 1) Dancing and prostitution were associated with one another and this connection of ill-repute largely contributes to the ambiguity with which Iranians regard dance. The primary source for evidence of this linkage is found in Western journals; the iconographic evidence, except for the films from the period 1950-1978, does not overtly indicate this. 2) Dance is depicted almost exclusively as entertainment rather than as ritual or serious art. Its scenes are depicted in banquets and revels. As previously stated, the iconographic sources for dance, particularly in the pre-Islamic period, are found in the so-called minor arts, not on the huge stone reliefs associated with the Sasanians and Achaemenids, which depict political and religious ritual and ceremony. This suggests that dance was an activity for enjoyment and festive occasions rather than an activity of a serious or ritual nature. 3) Historically, the dances were often highly acrobatic and required enormous physical strength. Until the Qajar period, dancers were primarily depicted, at least in the court, in a stylized, frozen fashion. Occasional outdoor scenes depict boys performing handstands. During the Qajar period, paintings depict the dancers in a wide variety of poses, including acrobatic ones, thus conforming to the European accounts of dancing as highly athletic. 4) Both males and females danced and both sexes are shown in the iconographic sources, photographs, and travelers' accounts. 5) Although most iconographic sources until the twentieth century focus exclusively on court activities, Western sources extending back to the Safavid period indicate that dancing was very popular as a form of entertainment among all classes, and 6) The geometry alluded to earlier is shown throughout the Timurid and Safavid periods by the iconographic evidence, which depicts the dancers in poses indicating that symmetry and balance typify the activity of solo dancing.

The iconographic evidence cannot convey the specific movements in a dance performance, and neither source provides evidence of improvisational practices. Although discussing the literary analysis of a novel, Terry Eagleton's advice also applies in using the historical resources I have outlined: "The work's insights, are deeply related to its blindnesses: what it does not say, and *how* it does not say it, may be as important as what it articulates; what seems absent, marginal or ambivalent about it may provide a central clue to its meanings" (1983: 178).

For these reasons, dance is often perceived negatively. Nonetheless, dancers are frequently depicted dancing romantically in an idyllic setting in some miniatures, producing a positive symbol expressing joy, youth, and spring. Thus, although dance can serve as either a positive symbol in a metaphorical sense, such as that found in poetry, more commonly, dance forms a negative symbol, creating some ambiguity. In sum, with the iconographic sources and supporting evidence of travelers' journals, we possess a sufficient body of material to prove the existence of this dance tradition, but have little information regarding the dancers themselves, the specific movements they used, or the music that accompanied the dance.

As Alter (1992) pointed out, there is a need to establish some historical background, if only because the performers themselves feel such a connection. With the collapse of the Pahlavi dynasty and the resultant formation of a sizable diaspora community outside Iran, venues and contexts for the performance of solo improvised dance have, to some degree, changed and altered, although these contexts are largely adaptations of past practices in a new environment. I posit that opportunities for viewing and performing dance are currently greater than they were in Iran under the Pahlavis, and, of course, it is currently banned by the Islamic regime, which seems to result in a "forbidden fruit" syndrome, enticing more individuals to dance.[8]

Chapter 3

Dance and Other Movement Activities in An Iranian-Islamic Context[1]

After the conquest of the Arabs,
the Iranians, bent under the yoke, were forced
to endure the rigorous laws of Islam and
were forced to assume an appearance
of scorn toward the dance which they had
always adored. (Rezvani 1962: 148)

*O*ne of the major objectives of this study is to demonstrate the contemporary ambivalence with which dance is regarded in societies within the Iranian culture sphere. Such ambivalent and negative attitudes emerge from historical, cultural and religious contexts and as the data I present shows, similar reactions resonate strongly within the large Iranian-American community in which I carried out the most recent research for this study. In this chapter I argue for the viewpoint that dance scholars need to consider native categories when identifying and analyzing what constitutes dance and other kinds of patterned movement in Iranian-Islamic society, rather than relying upon the working definitions of dance scholars unfamiliar with this society. This is because dance is such a potentially emotionally-charged activity in both Iranian and Iranian-American contexts, that culturally competent individuals clearly distinguish between the categories of which activities constitute dance and which do not. I follow that usage because it best aids my analysis of the ambivalence toward dance which characterizes the Iranian-American community. In this chapter I address two important auxiliary questions: 1) What role, if any, does Islam, as a belief system, play in the negative and ambivalent views of dance in the Iranian/Islamic environment? 2) What other forms of patterned movement, which are not considered dance by Iranians, exist in the Iranian culture sphere? The former topic requires attention because many writers have singled out "Islam" as a monolithic and totalizing reason for negative attitudes regarding dance in Islamic/Iranian contexts. Alongside this often unsubstantiated "Islamic" hypothesis one finds the accompanying proposition that in pre-Islamic Iran, dancers were "honored" artists. (See for example De Warren 1973, La Meri 1961, and Rezvani 1962.) Both positions, that a simplistic, single reason such as "Islam" serves as an all-encompassing explanation for negative feelings, as well as the concomitant notion that dance was an honored or highly esteemed art prior to Islam, need to be questioned. The entire issue of dance and non-dance in Islamic contexts is addressed because several writers have variously called different rhythmic, patterned movement activities in that context "dancing," even though native viewpoints differ sharply from such characterizations.

Certain dance ethnologists have pointed out that in some societies there exists no separate word for "dance," in contrast to other movement or musical activities. As dance ethnologist Adrienne L. Kaeppler observes, "In many societies, however, there is no indigenous concept that can adequately be translated as "dance" (1985:92). This is not true in Iranian and Iranian-American society. Dance, its contexts and its environments, have clear parameters, and culturally competent Iranians recognize them clearly.

While dance, and a word to denote that activity, exists in Iranian society, and we can perhaps come to an agreement over what dance is, an even more crucial issue is what dance *is not* in an Islamic environment. This latter issue is an important one because many activities in which participants perform patterned movements are devotional or spiritual in the view of the participants. Some observers from outside, and sometimes inside, the society unquestioningly term this type of activity as dance because it is patterned, rhythmical movement and because music and/or rhythm accompany it. I strongly support Kaeppler's assertion that:

> Western notions tend to classify all such movement dimensions together as "dance," but culturally it would seem more appropriate to analyze them more objectively as movement dimensions of separate activities. The concept 'dance' may be masking the importance and usefulness of analyzing human movement systems by introducing a Western category. (1985:92)

None of the definitions that I have encountered takes into account dance and dance events in societies such as those of the Islamic areas of the Middle East, Central Asia, and North Africa where the term for dance (usually *raqs*, a word of Arabic origin) frequently has powerful negative or ambiguous connotations. This conflation of dance and non-dance activities carries the implication that all movement activity labeled "dance" is condemned in Islamic societies, whereas movement activities such as those of the *zur-khaneh* are highly esteemed by many individuals who would not accord such a positive attitude toward dance.

> The concept 'dance' appears to be an unsatisfactory cate-
> gory imposed from a Western point of view because it
> tends to group together diverse activities that should be
> culturally separated...What is it that we have in our heads
> when we decide if something is dancing or not? I have
> not yet found a definition of dance that satisfies me.
> (Kaeppler 1985:93)

Dancing and dance events in what I will term "choreophobic" societies,
such as many Islamic areas of the Middle East, North Africa, Central
Asia, and their diaspora communities in North America, have, to date,
received little scholarly attention, although this is changing. My strat-
egy is to look at dance and other patterned movement activities from the
viewpoint of the people in those societies, because they have created
clear categories of what constitutes "dance" and other rhythmic, patterned activities which they would not consider "dance." This will, in
part, counter the trend of writers who, in their attempts to analyze and
describe Iranian dance, subsume all patterned and rhythmic movement
activity as dance.

Many definitions containing most of the elements noted by numerous dance scholars have been summed up by Anya Peterson Royce.
Royce asserts:

> We must have an adequate working definition of dance
> about which there is a measure of agreement. In other
> words, it should be the minimal definition necessary to
> allow us to agree on phenomena that occur in the middle
> of the category "dance"...Basic to all definitions of the
> dance is the concept of rhythmic or patterned movement.
> Obviously this is not sufficient to distinguish dance from
> many other kinds of rhythmic activities: swimming,
> working, playing tennis, hollowing out a canoe, to name a
> few...A streamlined definition, but one which still in-
> cludes the two concepts basic to almost all definition of
> dance, would be one which defines dance as "patterned
> movement performed as an end in itself." (1977:7-8)

In addition to demonstrating that the boundary between dance and non–
dance is difficult to draw in Western contexts, I wish to echo Royce and
others in the need to establish how the participants themselves define
which movement activities constitute dance and which they consider
non-dance activities.

...But there are two levels of understanding: one between analysts and another that has significance for natives. As scholars of the dance, we may create more and more sophisticated definitions of the dance, but they are only useful as analytic devices in that they may not correspond to definitions of dance that are meaningful to those engaged in the particular dance form. (Royce 1977:8)

Following Royce, I wish to emphasize the point that it is crucial that native viewpoints and categories be recognized for these activities as they relate to the Middle East, North Africa, Central Asia, and among their diasporas. The dance ethnographer or serious researcher who labels as "dance" those activities which the participants themselves regard as religious or as non–dance, simply because they fit a particular academic description, perpetuates a kind of cultural imperialism. Many native participants would be deeply shocked and distressed to discover that someone had defined the activity in which they participated as "dance." In this study I privilege Iranian native categories and concepts because they are clear concerning what constitutes dance and what does not.

I argue that what separates dance from other types of patterned, rhythmic movement activity is the *intent* of the person who enters the dance. When a person in Iranian society dances, then dancing, not martial arts or spiritual activity, is his or her intent.

Dance in an Islamic Context
Every researcher of dance or music in the Middle East, Central Asia, or North Africa is soon confronted with the ambiguity and even hostility with which music, and even more, dance, are regarded. Dance is seen by most Moslems as the least of the arts, if indeed as an art form at all. Many writers comment on this negative view of dance without elucidating the sources for their statements. Thus we find passages like the following: "The austerity and rigidity of Islam did much to discourage music and dance and waged a relentless war against them" (And 1959:13).[2]

Because dance has historically been beneath the attention of most Moslem scholars, most of the learned commentary within the Islamic world concerns the permissibility and propriety of music. Since music accompanies most dance, one may assume that the strictures mentioned apply to dance as well. The second Moslem caliph, 'Umar, "was always very hard when he referred to dancing girls and always mentioned dancing girls with music" (Choudhury 1957:73). This is especially true since there is a serious category of art music that has a spiritual or philosophical aspect, as well as purely light, secular music for entertainment. It is the latter which Islamic authorities often condemn. Dancing is not a usual aspect of serious music performances, and, in my own personal experience, many classical musicians avoid any professional connection with dance performance as demeaning to their own serious art. Even books that address general historical subjects often comment on the Islamic view of music. Albert Hourani, in his authoritative *History of the Arab Peoples,* states that:

> Court music was associated with the worldliness of court life and the music of the people, too, might be an accompaniment of worldly celebrations. The men of religion disapproved of it, but they could not condemn music altogether since it soon came to play a part in religious practice: the call to prayer had its own rhythm, the Qur'an was chanted in formal ways, and the *dhikr*, the solemn ritual of the repetition of the name of God, was accompanied by music, and even by bodily movements, in some of the Sufi brotherhoods. It was important therefore for those writing within the legal tradition to define the conditions on which performing and listening to music were permitted. (Hourani 1991:198-199)

Hourani's thoughtful explanation of the care with which medieval Arab scholars discussed the propriety of music and dance has not been heeded by modern scholars, who tend to oversimplify this crucial issue and give no proof for their assertions. Farhat states, "At the outset, Islamic religious leaders had assumed a hostile attitude towards music, and regarded it as a corrupting frivolity" (Farhat 1965:6). La Meri observed, incorrectly, that:

> The Koran indicted the secular written word and the pictorial image of living things so in olden days, the dancer and musician were important to the people as purveyors of news. Later Mohammed himself banned music and dance, and the arts withered. But somehow they managed to keep alive. (La Meri 1961:44)

The Quran contains no definitive statements concerning music or dance, nor does it overtly place any prohibitions on them. According to Islamic historian M. L. Roy Choudhury, "The Qur'an has not made it (music) either *haram* nor *halal*, i.e., neither condemned nor permitted" (Choudhury 1957:5).

Thus, Islamic attitudes toward dance and music are more complex than And, La Meri, Farhat, and Rezvani (quoted at the beginning of the chapter) would have us believe. If the Prophet Muhammad had indeed explicitly forbidden music and dance, or had there been a clear statement to this effect in the Quran, then the issue would have been long ago resolved and these performing arts would not exist. Clearly, this is

not the case. Indeed, some clergy members do not regard music negatively. In a recent broadcast on Radio Seda-ye Iran (August 27, 1996),
Ayatollah Haeri stated that he was not against dance or music. "Music
is the food of the soul (*ghaza-ye ruh*)," he declared. However, Haeri
would seem particularly "liberal" since Mrs. Foruhar, editor of the Iranian exile journal, *Liberasion*, interviewed by Hossein Mohri on the
same radio station that same evening, claimed that when a woman athlete recently attempted to open an aerobics class in Tehran, the Sisters of
Zeinab (a zealous, quasi state-sponsored group of women charged with
countering any activities they regard as anti- Islamic) attacked her, saying that "she was opening a house of prostitution through her dancing."

Since neither the Quran nor the *shari'ah* directly addresses the permissibility of music and/or dance, the *hadith* are turned to as a source of
their propriety in light of what the prophet said or did about their performance. Because the interpretation of the *hadith* can be ambiguous
and sometimes contradictory (there are several schools of interpretation), and the possibility of bogus *hadith* exists, so, too, are the attitudes
of Muslims often at variance with one another.

According to Choudhury's detailed study of music in Islam, which
also includes a few citations for dancing, the *hadith* have been interpreted differently by various individuals. Thus, those against music and
dance, such the Taliban of Afghanistan, who are widely reported to have
forbidden both (*The News Hour with Jim Lehrer*, October 7, 1996,
showed the destruction of cassette tapes), as well as those who approve
of them, cite those *hadith* which are congenial to their causes. For example, Choudhury cites a well-known anecdote utilized by those who
support music:

> Once an Abyssinian musician appeared in presence of the
> Prophet on the occasion of 'Id (festival). The Prophet
> asked 'Ayisha (his favorite wife) if she would like to en-
> joy music. On 'Ayisha giving assent, the Abyssinian was
> called in. The place of performance was the Prophet's
> own house. The mosque of the Prophet was adjacent to
> his house. The courtyard of the house of the Prophet and
> that of his mosque was the same. In fact, the performance
> took place in a sacred place-*hareem*. The Abyssinian ac-
> robat sang and danced. 'Ayisha enjoyed it for a pretty
> length of time. (1957:69)

On the other hand, Choudhury also notes that the forces which oppose
music turn to *hadith* like the following:

> The traditions of the early days of Islam refer to innumer-
> able narrations regarding singing girls, instruments of mu-
> sic and dance. The Prophet is said to have told: "I have

> been sent and commanded to destroy music vocal and
> manual (instrumental). (1957: 72)

Given such contradictory evidence, Choudhury details the many learned
opinions regarding the propriety of dancing and music in various Islamic contexts. Such opinions are by no means uniform.

It can be seen from these sources that the ambiguity toward music is
amplified in regard to dance because of the social class of the professional performers and the often erotic and/or grotesque content of their
performances. Whereas in the Iranian culture sphere there has always
existed a classical form of music that may have a philosophic and spiritual component, there is no corresponding genre of dance prior to the
recent attempts to develop a serious classical dance form during the Soviet period in Uzbekistan and Tajikistan. While many important historical and contemporary studies exist concerning music, dance is rarely
mentioned. I posit that a major reason for the lack of serious studies of
dance in this vast area, and one of the reasons I call it choreophobic, is
the avoidance of the topic of dance and dancers due to their associations
with prostitution in public contexts and with other low and unsavory
elements of society. In fact, Choudhury points out that the "notoriety of
the singing girls of the taverns had brought forth such terms as *Mughan-
niya* (female musicians), *Sannaja* (female *sanj* [cymbals] player), *Zam-
mara* (female *Zamr* player) becoming synonyms for courtesans and
adulteresses" (ibid 72). Islamic historian Clifford Edmund Bosworth, in
his important analysis of the medieval Islamic underworld, the Banu
Sasan, included individuals who were entertainers as well as the "fully
criminal ones" as part of the underworld classes (1976: 1).

A solid reason for this ambiguity toward music and dance is Choudhury's proposition, which lies in the attitudes of pre–Islamic Arabia attitudes:

> Singing girls were employed in the taverns for the enter-
> tainment of visitors. Pre–Islamic literature is full of refer-
> ences to these tavern girls. Arabic literature is full of
> praise of these singing girls of taverns, and their flowing
> cups, alluring harps, and delightful cheers. Their influ-
> ence was utilized by enemies of Islam against the early
> Muslims to seduce people by singing satires, reproaches,
> and invectives. That is why in the early days of Islam,
> there are so many references against singing girls, their
> teaching and professions, and their instruments.
> (1957:55)

These women directly and negatively affected the Prophet Muhammad's
mission; the behavior of the singing girls constituted both a threat and
an insult to him and his mission of spreading the fledgling Islamic faith.

Some writers imply that when Islamic authorities attempt to ban or restrict dance they are reacting to ancient, pre-Islamic religious practices of the Middle East. For example, Hanna states that under Islam, "Heterosexual dancing has been banned in an attempt to eradicate goddess worship…" (1988:48). This reference to unnamed goddesses forms a common theme advanced by writers like Wendy Buonavenura (1990), a belly dance devotee, and Judith Lynne Hanna, who both seem to superimpose modern historical thought on the attitudes of both the medieval and contemporary populations of the Islamic world. But their grasp of history is tenuous, for as Lewis observes, "The pre-Islamic history of Arabia is little known and is encrusted with all kinds of myths and legends" (1995:141).

Clearly, Islam as a belief system, and Islamic thought *per se*, cannot be posited as the sole reason for regarding dance as a negative activity, although some individual Moslems, such as Ayatollah Ruhollah Khomeini, may attempt to ban or restrict dance and music activities by turning to Islamic sources such as specific *hadith* citations to bolster such decisions. In his famous *Kashf ol-asrar* (Discovery of Secrets), Khomeini, later spiritual and temporal ruler of Iran, proclaimed that "Music which encourages the spirit of passion and love among the youth is forbidden in the *shariat* and should be taken out of school programs" (1971: 313-14). Parvin Paidar, a scholar of Middle Eastern women's studies, observes that "Khomeini criticized Reza Shah (father of Muhammad Reza Pahlavi, the last ruler of the Pahlavi dynasty) and Ataturk as 'idiotic dictators' (for) spreading 'the means of pleasure,' and preoccupying people with unveiling, European clothes, cinema, theatre, music and dance" (1995: 121).

"The intensity of their objections" and opposition of large segments of the population to dance, and indeed other activities, such as listening to radio and television, according to political scientist Mehrzad Bouroujerdi, "varied according to their class backgrounds, levels of education, and bonds to various social groups" (1996:97). Historic, pre-Islamic, social attitudes, whose origins we may never know, may also play a part in shaping contemporary attitudes.

Non-Dance in an Islamic Context

In general, both Western and native writers who attempt to broaden the category of dance in an Islamic context often include spiritual practices within Islam (that timeless, frozen, spiritual site, in Said's terms) which incorporate movement. I wish to focus especially on the movement activities of the Mevlevi dervishes, who are Sufi mystics and often called "whirling" or "dancing" dervishes, because of the salient position they occupy among the writings and descriptions of Western observers.

Iranians state almost universally that dance is found only on happy occasions, whereas spiritual or religious contexts are serious. I argue, however, that it is the intention of the participant or the knowledgeable observer which must determine whether an activity can be called "dance" or not.

Boualem Bousseloub, a Moslem informant, stated regarding the Mevlevi dervish ritual that:

> When a Moslem performs ablutions and prepares himself
> to pray, he mentally announces his intention to pray and
> to address God. In all of this the intention is important
> and one says this silently. Intention is everything, and
> must be followed by action. Clearly, their [the dervishes]
> intent is to use turning to communicate with God, not to
> dance. The word dance can not be used in religious or
> holy terms, except perhaps in quotation marks. (personal
> interview February 12,1993)

Another informant, Jamal, insists that any activity, no matter how rhythmic or musical, in which the participants are:

> ...sending *salavat* (a type of religious incantation calling
> on God) or where the participants repeat the terms "Al-
> lah" or "'Ali" (Hazrat [saint] Ali was the fourth caliph,
> and, after the Prophet Muhammad is the most revered fig-
> ure in Shi'i Islam) cannot be called dance—the intent is
> religious. (Jamal: personal interview February 12, 1993)

Moslem prayers follow synchronized, patterned movement, but few dance researchers would call it dancing. Unfortunately the same cannot be said of the movements of the so–called "whirling dervishes," which is the term often applied to the Sufis of the Mevlevi brotherhood. It must be stressed that the Mevlevi brotherhood constitutes only one, al- beit the most famous in the West, of many Sufi brotherhoods and orders, and thus their movement practices are not characteristic of all Sufi asso- ciations. Many Westerners and Western–educated native scholars call these circular movements practiced by Mevlevi adepts "dancing" be- cause the movements might be called so in non–sacred circumstances. But this practice needs to be questioned because the intent is similar to that of prayer: God is being invoked. Several of the works cited have called this dancing, or have included it in descriptions of dance. (See And 1959, 1976, Bourguignon 1968, Friedlander 1992, Friend 1994, Hamada 1978, Rezvani 1962.)

The word *sama'* (or sama"), which applies to Sufi ceremonies, is a term variously applied to both the ritual and the music which accompa- nies it. The word comes from the Arabic word *sama'a,* to hear, and can refer to spiritual music and may or may not imply movement. In *Haim's Shorter Persian English Dictionary,* the definition of *sama'* is singing, song, music, hearing. Movement is not mentioned.

Whirling or circular motions are well known for helping to bring about the dizziness or a condition of disassociation that is characteristic of some trance states. In the Sufi brotherhood of the Mevlevi this is practiced for years and the initiates are taught to gain control over this state. The music and the context aid the devotee in his quest for a state of religious and spiritual ecstasy.

Katib Celebi, a seventeenth-century scholar (cited in And), in referring to the Sufis stated:

> The Orthodox Ulema have classed those whirlings as "dancing" and have pronounced it forbidden, branding as infidels those who hold it permissible. The Sufis begin by saying that the definitions of dance is not applicable to it. They continue thus: The cyclic motion is a form distinct from dancing and for the good of mankind. (Celebi 1609–1657) quoted in And 1959:13)

Thus, as Celebi stated, many Sufis do not regard their patterned movements as dance and some have expressed outrage at this suggestion. This was, in fact, no small matter, for such accusations could result in charges of heresy that were punishable in some cases by agonizing death. One of the foremost scholars of Islamic history, Marshall Hodgson, observes that "the more Shari'ah-minded came actively to distrust the Sufis and were inclined to persecute the less cautious of them for heresy" (1974, volume 1: 402). If the Sufis do not wish their sacred practices to be thought of in terms of dance, how, then, can the uninitiated do so?

Specific Dance and Other Movement Activities
Dance in an Islamic-Iranian Context

It was a pleasant, warm spring day in Tehran in 1959 and I was seated in the courtyard of a girls' high school in a middle class neighborhood in the midst of a crowd of parents and friends waiting for the end-of-the-year program with which many Iranian high schools closed their school year. Music and dance were to be featured in the program along with the usual declamations and poetry recitals. In order to ward off the sun, I, like many present, was sitting in the shade of the dome of a large mosque that loomed above the courtyard adjoining the school. Minutes before the program was scheduled to begin, rumors began to circulate through the crowd that it was to be canceled. The principal of the school, Shahla, was a friend and had invited me to the program because she knew of my interest in dance. She mounted the podium with great dignity and announced to the disappointed crowd that the authorities of the neighboring mosque had objected to the scheduled musical and dance portions, that the school authorities had complied rather than

*create an incident with the religious authorities, and she was not able to
prevent the cancellation. The girls tearfully filed out of the school
building to their disappointed parents, and crestfallen, they all left,
leaving an air of unfulfilled promises. Shahla asked me, "I must hand in
my resignation, how can I continue in this atmosphere?"*

The common, everyday term for dance throughout this region which
I call the Iranian culture sphere is *raqs,* or some variant of this word,
which is of Arabic origin, and *raqsidan* means "to dance" in Persian.[3]
Among the large Turkic-speaking groups such as the Uzbeks and Azerbaijanis, some version of *oyun,* meaning "game" or "dance" is used, but
raqs or some version of it is also found (see And 1973:23, Hasanov
1988). The terms for dancer, *raqqas* for male and *raqqaseh* for female,
can be pejoratives with more than a hint of ill–repute attached. (This is
also the case in Turkey, according to And, 1976:145.)[4] Even more
common is the term *motreb,* applied to any professional entertainer, musician or dancer (*motreb* "one who gladdens" from the Arabic root *ta-
raba* "to make happy"), which is also found in Turkey and Azerbaijan,
and can apply to either sex. All of these terms are for professional entertainers and are dreaded insults if applied to any serious concert or
performing artist. The term *luti* is used in Iran for a street performer and
may also carry very negative connotations.[5] Local terms such as *almah,
shlluh,* and *ghawazi* abound in the Arab world, as well as others in the
Iranian and Turkish linguistic areas, to denote professional dancers.
(For further information consult And 1959, 1976, Hasanov 1988, Karimova 1977, Mo'in 1992, Moran 1945, Rezvani 1962.)

Non-Dance Movement Activities in Islamic Iran

Many individuals in the Iranian cultural sphere participate in a number
of patterned movement activities that differ from those in other Islamic
areas. Because of the influence of Shi'ism in much of this region, this
section is devoted to those specific activities. Also, as several informants insisted, "dance in an Iranian context is only for happy occasions,
never for solemn or sad events" (Azad; Jamali; Valipour: personal
communication, 1993)[6]. In this section I briefly describe some of the
more familiar of these activities, which have unproblematically been
subsumed under the category "dance" by various authors. However, no
two writers include the same activities. Rezvani, for example, cites
'aza-dari as "nothing but dance" (1962: 168); Friend and Hamada do
not mention this activity. While all three of these authors touch on the
movements of the Mevlevi dervishes' (who are chiefly resident in Turkey not Iran) under the context of "dance", Hamada, unlike the other
two authors, does not touch upon the *zur-khaneh.* Thus, some need for
clarification would seem to be in order.

I review these activities to show not only how they differ from
dance, but how, in the eyes of native observers and participants, the no-

tion of categorizing such activities as "dance" becomes surprising and naive. These activities, some of which I briefly describe below, fall into two general categories: spiritual and martial arts, which can also carry spiritual connotations. The following listing may serve as an introduction and an aid to clarify these various activities:

1) Patterned, rhythmic activities found in spiritual or religious contexts:
   a. *aza-dari*—the rhythmic striking of the body in a ritual manifestation of grief for the martyrdom of Imam Hosein and his followers at Karbala.
   b. *zekr*—a ritual in which the name of God is repeated over and over rhythmically. This ritual often includes movements (which vary in the different Sufi or dervish orders). The actual meaning of *zekr* is to recite, to mention.
   c. *zur-khaneh* (house of strength)—A martial arts activity which is steeped in spiritual and religious meaning.
   d. *zar* (also called *jenn-giri*—the capturing of the *jenn* [genie], a type of malevolent spirit)—A healing rite of exorcism found in the Iranian districts adjacent to the Persian Gulf. Variants of this ritual are found on the East coast of Africa, in Egypt, the Arabian peninsula, and southern Iran. In Iran, these rituals are often conducted by individuals who are locally recognized as religious or spiritual personages.

2) Patterned, rhythmic non-spiritual activities:
   chub-bazi (stick play)—A martial arts form performed widely among the tribes of southwestern Iran. Another type of *chub-bazi* with short sticks is found in Eastern Iran, but this form is truly a dance, and the sticks are used for rhythmic accompaniment. (See Hamada 1978 for a description and analysis of an example of this type of dance.)
   b. sword and shield activities. This category contains both dance and non-dance activities. In the former, the dancers often dance alone and brandish the weapon, while in the latter, as in the *chub-bazi*, actual combat between two individuals occurs.

I assert that each instance of movement activity needs to be examined by researchers to determine if the observers and participants consider themselves as dancing or engaging in a sport, martial arts, or a ritual—a project awaiting further study.

In sum, I have briefly described some of the movement systems that exist in an Iranian and Iranian-American context which have been variously subsumed by various writers under the rubric "dance." In an Islamic context, where dance has ambiguous and negative connotations, I feel that it is most profitable to observe native distinctions as to what

constitutes dance activity and to find appropriate terminology and categories for other kinds of patterned movement activity, particularly those
that are conducted in a spiritual or religious context. Native categories
for dance and non-dance serve as a potential guide for the dance scholar
who wishes to analyze movement practices in this region. Kaeppler
states, "Every society has cultural forms in which human bodies are manipulated in time and space. How these forms are regarded by the society itself seems a crucial question for an understanding of that society"
(1985: 93). To date, each of those who has looked seriously at Iranian
dancing or dancing in Islamic societies has chosen some of these events
or movements to call dance, while excluding others. This is because, as
in the practice of the Mevlevi dervishes, the movements such as whirling or circling that one sees in a particular ceremony seem to fit comfortably into the category of dance established by some academician far
removed from the Islamic world, while such activities as prayer, no
matter how rhythmic, are clearly not dance. I think that it is important
that all types of patterned movement, both those considered as dance
and those not considered as dance, be investigated and researched.
These movement practices form a body of material that 1) tells us about
communication of the human body, 2) aids the scholar in determining
native categories, functions, and relationships between the various contexts in which these practices are performed, and 3) identifies which
activities constitute dance, which are considered patterned movement
but not dance and what connections exist between them. If, as Rezvani
claims, all of these movement practices are dance in all but name, that
distinction becomes an important area of inquiry. Indeed, the way in
which participants in these various activities use their bodies, postures,
gestures, and movements will be a fruitful area of future research in a
choreophobic area which has had scant serious attention.

Chapter 4

The Iranian American Community

*The exilic experience has
fostered a strong devotion to
the homeland among many
Iranians in Los Angeles*
(Kelley et al. 1993:76)

*I*n this chapter, I wish to introduce the historical and geographical
background which have, to a large degree, shaped the people
whose dance tradition I am investigating. History looms large in the
minds of many Iranians, for they recognize and celebrate the antiquity
of their heritage. After giving a general background of the Iranian culture sphere, I will undertake a specific overview of the focus population
I am investigating, the Iranian-American community of Southern California, the largest outside of Iran. Since dance serves as the prism
through which I wish to look at this society, the presentation of social,
cultural, political, historical, and aesthetic points will be introduced for
the purpose of elucidating conditions under which dance is performed
and evaluated.

One of the major purposes of this study is to determine ways in
which dance will illuminate social and religious attitudes in Iranian society. It will be the intention of this study to establish what Stanley Fish
refers to as an "interpretive community" (1980). The establishment of
such a community always carries the inherent risk of totalizing, and
therefore the ideas of other theoreticians, such as Robert C. Holub, a
scholar of literary criticism (1984), and dance historian Susan Manning's observation of a dance performance (1995), will be invoked to
account for the issue of individual reactions and attitudes within larger
communities, as well as how aesthetic expression is perceived by a
range of individuals within a single society. Clearly, it is impossible to
account for all individual attitudes within any society, and yet all individuals are raised within a specific society, with a specific language(s),
at a set period, all of which, to some degree, shape individual reactions
and attitudes.

> That three participant-observers had three such different
> experiences of the same event underscores that interpre-
> tation is not monolithic or even subject to predictable
> variation. Social, political, economic, and institutional
> contexts surely inform the relations of ideology and form,
> but so too does the unpredictable range of spectator-
> ship...my model could not do justice to the variability,
> much less the range, of possible responses to perform-
> ance. (Manning: 1995:174)

Because Iranian solo improvised dance forms a highly idiosyncratic and
individual performative practice within a culturally stylistic framework
which, nevertheless, all culturally competent Iranians (a concept I develop from Stanley Fish's notion of literary competence, 1980:4-5; 13-
16), recognize as "their" dance tradition, I sought theoretical frameworks that would constantly refer to the issue of individual behaviors
and attitudes within specific cultural parameters. Such theoretical viewpoints, to some degree, enable the researcher to account for the individual performance, reaction, or attitude within what I call the "generality
of performances and attitudes." This theoretical concern tries to make
sense of the question: to what degree does an individual act within or act
independently of cultural constraints? The theorizing of individual
agency within cultural and social constraints is a question still unre-
solved, that is, how to account for independent individual agency within
a general cultural structure and determine how much emphasis each aspect should receive on a theoretical level. In this study I attempt to account for and acknowledge both aspects of this issue.

The concept of an interpretive community is useful in determining
the extent of ambiguous Iranian attitudes toward dancing, and how these
negative or ambiguous reactions might be limited to specific situations.
This is because texts, including dance, "mean anything at all only when
they are read, and what they mean depends entirely on the shared values
of those reading them" (Shepherd 1989:97).

In this context, folklorist Dr. Robert Georges, like Susan Manning,
offered the important notion that within a Greek story-telling session all
of those present were familiar with the tales and the attitudes and morals
presented in the stories, but not everyone believed or accepted them to
the same degree, and thus there exists a range of possible attitudes and
reactions within a single cultural group (1969). Literary scholar Stanley
Fish notes that "whether the reader likes or dislikes the experience of
Faulkner's delays, he will, in common with every other reader, experience them" (1980:5). While Fish assumes that I, as the reader of his
study, understand who his reader might be, I make no such assumption
in this study: my interpretive community is the present-day Iranian and
Iranian-American community, within which a wide range of reactions to

dance and performances exists. An added note: these attitudes are dynamic, not static, and an individual's attitudes and reactions may alter through personal experiences. This study will attempt to account for both the group attitudes and the ranges of individual differences within that community.[1] For this reason, it is important to look at both the present-day Iranian diaspora community and its historical antecedents in order to define the interpretive community and to elicit and characterize what Jauss terms the group's "horizons of expectations" (Holub 1984: 15). Holub characterizes Jauss' notion: "When we read a text (or dance) we are continuously evaluating and perceiving events with regard to our expectations for the future and against the background of the past" (1984:90). Thus, I am attempting to identify attitudes of this focus group as well as create and account for examples of individual variations within that group.

One additional point worthy of note stems from the construction of the "Iranian-American" individual for purposes of this study. Naficy cautions that in constructing "the spectator" in the Iranian case we cannot, "...nor should we universalize the Western psychic structure, which is based on a strongly individuated self" (1993b: 106). In contrast, "The Iranian is theorized to be different from the American-Western self in that it is not completely individuated, rather it is a communal, familial self that involves significant others" (1993b:146). This communal tendency helps in establishing a specific Iranian interpretive community.

Iranian Culture Sphere

In this study, I lay out in some detail the cultural, ethnic, and geographic parameters of the Iranian culture sphere. This introduction to the Iranian culture sphere is intended to demonstrate how the long-term cultural and historical identity formation of the Iranian peoples in this large region provided the environment for the development of this dance form, as well as other expressive and creative forms such as music, visual arts and architecture. I argue that there are two important components that have contributed to the formation of the Iranian/Islamic identity. The first element is a historical, Iranian consciousness that stretches back into at least Sasanian times (224-650 A.D.). I emphasize that identity or consciousness is not to be confused with twentieth-century nationalistic or patriotic feelings; what constitutes *Iraniyyat* (Iranian cultural consciousness or "Iranian-ness") has most likely changed and mutated through time. The second element is that for over a thousand years this Iranian identity has been embedded in a larger Islamic identity. The Islamic and Iranian aspects of life in the Iranian culture sphere often create tensions. As historian Juan Cole pointed out, this intellectual concern was being articulated in the nineteenth century by Iranian intellectuals such as Mirza Fath Ali Akhundzadeh, who "signaled the two major and ultimately competing intellectual preoccupations of the later culture of Iranian national identity—ancient Zoroastrianism and Shi'ite Islam" (1996:38). Such concerns have an impact on this study because the perception of these two identities forms a salient dialogue in Iranian society. Iranian historian Mohammad Tavakoli-Targhi observes that, "In the political struggle between Islamists and secularists in the twentieth century, the allegorical meanings of ancient history figured into the competing rhetorics of cultural authenticity" (1996:175). Thus, assumptions such as that made by Robert De Warren (1973), former director of the Iranian State Dance Ensemble, the Mahalli Dancers, and others, that dancers were honored artists in pre-Islamic Iran, loom large within this discourse.

Although scholars in such fields as Persian language, literature and visual arts do not always specifically refer to these domains as a single cultural unit, they demonstrate their points with examples originating throughout this geographical and cultural region, implicitly assuming the existence of the culture sphere I wish to define. This broad region forms the cultural and geographic scope of the *Encyclopaedia Iranica*. It has not, unfortunately, been used by dance scholars, who have instead used the narrower parameters of the nation-state of Iran, which often produces unsatisfactory conclusions.

At this point it is important that I identify what I mean by "Iranian." To some observers the use of this term may seem to be self-evident. It is not. Furthermore, the term is often used interchangeably with "Persian," and while the categories of "Persian" and "Iranian" may overlap in some usages, they are not synonyms. To further confuse this issue, many Iranians and Persians themselves use these terms interchangeably in English. (In Persian language usage, *Farsi* is the language, while *Irani* is the person or adjective.)[2]

Currently, the term "Iranian" has two meanings: 1) Any person who is a citizen of the nation-state of Iran. It may also be used as an adjective, as in "the Iranian government" or "the Iranian people." 2) A group of related languages, including Kurdish, Baluchi, Pashtu (Pakhtun), Persian, Ossetian, and several other smaller linguistic communities from the Caucasus to Western China. Of the Iranian languages, Persian is spoken by the largest number of people. It has several variants, a word I choose carefully, such as Dari and Tajik, spoken in Afghanistan and Tajikistan, respectively. Sometimes, for cultural, political, or emotional reasons, some individuals maintain that these are separate languages; however, Central Asian historian Karl H. Menges observes: "Tajik is a modern Persian dialect, digressing from the literary language only in insignificant features" (1995: 64).

The term "Persian" has meanings other than "Iranian." A Persian is a native speaker of Persian (Farsi). This is particularly important in contemporary usage, because Persians make up only slightly more than half of the population of the nation-state of Iran (some claim fewer than

half). Several million speakers of the Dari and Tajik variants live in
Afghanistan and Tajikistan and form a significant population in Uzbekistan, particularly in the ancient (and highly contested) cities of Samarqand and Bukhara. Thus, while all of those living in the nation-state of
Iran and holding citizenship there are Iranians, only those who speak
Persian as their native language can be considered as Persian in a strictly
technical sense.

"Persian" is also widely used to denote historical aspects of Iranian
history, particularly the pre-Islamic Achaemenid (550 - 330 B.C.) and
Sasanian (220 - 642 A.D.) empires. One can perhaps make a case for
this usage because these two empires arose in Fars (from which the
word for Persian [Farsi] derives) in Southwestern Iran. Some scholars
use the word "Persianate" to describe this area or its cultural aspects.

This terminology becomes important because previous dance studies
in this vast region used narrow, national borders and unproblematized
terminologies that created incomplete, even erroneous impressions. As
a recent example, I turn to Robyn Friend's (1994) article, "Modern Persian Dance."

Friend, a scholar of Iranian linguistics, entitles her article on dance in
the *Encyclopaedia Iranica* "Modern Persian Dance" (1994: 641). This
is surely incorrect. The contents of the article show that her intention is
to describe dance activity within the current political borders of the nation-state of Iran, as opposed to the wider Iranian culture sphere. For
example, she describes the dances of the Baluchis and Kurds, both Iranian peoples by virtue of the languages they speak and also because
Friend primarily refers to the dance activities of those populations resident in Iran (in contrast to those living in adjacent political jurisdic-
tions). In addition, Friend describes the dance activities of Turkmen,
Azerbaijanis, and members of the Qashqa'i tribe. These are all Turkic
language speakers who are "Iranian" by virtue of their citizenship, but in
no way can they be considered "Persian."   More importantly, I argue
that there is no specifically "Persian" dance, that is, a dance form that is
performed exclusively by the Persian-speaking population in contrast to
other Iranians.

Thus, while it is possible to designate as "Persian Literature" that
literature which is written in Persian (but not only by Persians, since
non-Persian, non-Iranian individuals in the Ottoman and Mughal Empires, as well as other Iranians, such as Kurds or Azerbaijanis, have
composed literary works in Persian), by contrast, "Persian Dance" does
not exist as a separate category.

Thus, for purposes of this discussion I will use "Iranian" to encom-
pass the cultural and aesthetic expression of the wide Central Asian region that I detailed earlier: the Caucasus, Iran, Afghanistan, and Muslim
areas of the former Soviet Union, such as Uzbekistan and Tajikistan. In
other words, this constitutes an area much greater than the contemporary

nation-state of Iran.   In order to fully understand the solo improvised
dancing that occurs and was developed in this region, the concept of the
Iranian culture sphere will enable us to look beyond the narrow borders
of the nation-state of Iran, which forms only one site for this practice, as
well as provide important historical contexts.

Iranian Identity
The identity formation for Iranians has covered a span of centuries.
Within this process, I argue that what "Iranian" signifies in terms of ethnicity has changed through time and so we cannot assume that a twentieth-century nationalistic identity has historical depth, although it may
have historical roots.

> Ethnicity is a modern concept occasioned by the rise of
> nation-states from the late 18th century onward. Before
> this time, national feeling was in most parts of the world
> subordinate to other forces--fealty to a particular king or
> leader, adherence to a common religious tradition, alli-
> ances based on political convenience or economic neces-
> sity, or conquest of one group by another. A few of the
> world's peoples had a clear sense of their own ethnic
> identity in ancient times: the Japanese, Chinese, ancient
> Egyptians, Arabs and Iranians.   (William O. Beeman
> 1995:86)

In more recent reassessments of ethnicity, other scholars, like John
Hutchinson and Anthony Smith, point out "the relative neglect of the
deeper historical roots of ethnicity. A longer-term perspective reveals
the significance of ethnic ties and sentiments in every period of recorded
history..." (1996:v), revealing a variety of ethnic identities and consciousness as existing for a longer period than current research suggests.
(For a discussion of the ancient origins of ethnic identity, see Smith
[1986].)
      I am uncertain to what degree this "Iranian-ness" was articulated
prior to the Islamic invasion of the Arabs and subsequent invasions by
Turkic groups. A clue to that question is provided by religion and humanities studies scholar Bruce Lincoln, who cites a passage from the
Middle Persian (Sasanian era) apocalyptic epic, the *Jamasp Namag*,
which includes the following: "All Iran falls to the hand of the enemy,
and Iranian and non-Iranian mix together such that non-Iranian-ness is
indistinguishable from Iranian-ness, and Iranian becomes like non-
Iranian" (1989: 43).[3] I argue that the way in which that Iranian identity
was articulated after Islam was largely based on the need of Iranians to
favorably and distinctively position themselves as a separate and unique
ethnicity in contrast to the Arabs and Turks, who for over a thousand
years (650 - 1900 A.D.) held military, and thus, economic, power over

them.

To some extent, the question of what characterized Iranian identity through various periods may never be known. That such an identity existed is beyond question, since Ferdowsi worked from a long pre-Islamic literary and oral epic tradition (laid out very well by Persian literature scholar Gilbert Lazard in Frye 1974: Chapter 19), which demonstrates the consciousness of an Iranian identity. "Persian epic, which is completely unique in type, consists of the recital in verse of the whole of the history, factual or imaginary, of Iran from the creation of the world to the end of the Sasanian dynasty" (Lazard 1974: 624).

As further examples of Iranian identity awareness I will cite two of the most important literati: Hafez (1326-1390), one of the greatest Iranian poets, who makes references to a Persian identity in contrast to a Turkish one. (See for example 1994: 75, *ghazal* 5.) A century earlier, Jalal Ad-din Rumi (1207 - 1273), Iran's most celebrated mystical poet, also refers to "*Parsai-ye mara*," "my Persian-ness" (Shiva 1995:58).

Some scholars, such as Roy Mottahedeh, have suggested that this identity may have been shared only by an elite and he would "emphasize that we are talking only about educated Iranians who could record their opinions, not about peasants whose feelings of group identity are lost to history" (1976: 181). In contrast, I would suggest that the long-standing art of *nagqali* and *shah-nameh-khani*, in which story-tellers recite and enact the episodes of the *Shah-nameh* with which their often illiterate audiences are very familiar, would indicate an Iranian identity that is widely shared among several classes of the urban milieu at least, if not the peasantry. The art of *naqqali* can be traced to the *gosan* [bards] of Sasanian times, and it has traditionally been recited in coffee-houses and other public spaces, not just in the palace. Ardavan Mofid, a well-known *naqqal*, is in demand throughout the Iranian diaspora to recite and perform the *Shah-nameh*. Such values as honor, loyalty, and bravery, recurring themes in the *Shah-nameh*, resonate with audiences of Iranians in the diaspora today just as they did a thousand years ago. The idea that literary sources must be written rather than oral is a modern conceit. In Iran, as in other places, such as ancient Greece, oral and written literature coexisted.

In this study I emphasize this Iranian identity as exemplified in Persian literature, an identity that many contemporary Iranians utilize to set themselves apart from Arabs, with whom they share the Islamic religion, even though they feel strong cultural differences, through both scholarly works and references in Persian literature. This identity is also expressed through unique visual, literary, musical and choreographic expressions.

Islamic Identity [4]

In the previous section I attempted to show that an Iranian ethnic consciousness existed at a relatively early period. I also attempted to show certain non-religious elements of this complex ethnic consciousness, such as awareness of dynastic loyalties and language and literature, with their accompanying specific historical and cultural values. Now I turn to the salient characteristics of the Moslem identity in which this Iranian identity is embedded, not always comfortably. After the advent of Islam, as Iran gradually became a primarily Moslem territory, Islam became an integral part of the identity of most Iranians.

I wish to destabilize the notion of a monolithic Islam. Multiple Islams exist on a number of levels, and can perhaps be illustrated through the example of Sufism, a mystical quest for union with God, as an alternative to Shi'i and Sunni beliefs. There are many brotherhoods of Sufis, just as there are followers of various schools of jurisprudence, such as the Hanafi, all of which indicates a fragmentation of the Islamic community. These schisms began shortly after Muhammad's death in 623 and are detailed in Marshal Hodgson's monumental study of Islam (1974). One might think that the unanimity of belief and practice many scholars and Moslems themselves profess would weld this vast group of believers into one monolithic community, and so they are often presented on both popular and scholarly levels. With the division between Sunni and Shi'i, one can see that, like the Protestant-Catholic division in Christianity, and all of the bloodshed and animosity that conflict implies, Islam, too, is a divided house.

Islam is often applied as the basic element in all Middle Eastern and Central Asian identities, even by the people themselves, in an unexamined fashion. I do not intend to question that the overwhelming population of this vast region professes Islamic beliefs or to say that Islamic cultural traditions such as art and architecture do not exist, but rather to point out, following Eickelman (1995), that there are many Islams with multiple local expressions. Islamic scholar John Esposito offers a useful corrective to the monolithic notion of Islamic fraternal unity and equality and shows that ethnicity, as well as religion, is an important factor:

> Muslims say that commitment to Islam supplants ties of ethnicity, the way in which individuals and groups characterize themselves on the basis of shared language, culture, descent, place of origin, and history. Yet from the first Muslim conquests in seventh-century Arabia, as Muslim armies spread forth from the Arabian Peninsula to peoples who neither spoke Arabic nor could claim Arab descent, such concerns frequently surfaced in practice. (Esposito 1995: 448)

Many scholars point out that Iranians formed a uniquely Iranian Shi'ite version of Islam. This is manifest in certain Iranian performative practices, such as *rowzeh-khani* (the recitation of the martyrdom of Ali's son, Imam Hosein, at Karbala), and the *ta'ziyeh* (the dramatic recreation of those same events). Regarded by Iranians as Islamic, these performative practices are unique to Iran and, in my opinion, have direct roots to the related and corresponding non-sacred practices of *shah-nameh-khani, naqqali,* and *siyah-bazi* theatre. In other words, these are uniquely Iranian expressive forms embedded in an Islamic context. The content of the former is Islamic, and the latter Iranian, but the performative aspects are almost identical in the use of elements such as improvisation. (See Chelkowski 1979 for a full study of *ta'ziyeh* and *rowzeh-khani.*)

It might be useful to cite one further example in which Iranian and Islamic identities are inextricably enmeshed: the *zur-khaneh*. The *zur-khaneh* is a form of martial arts specific to certain urban centers of the Iranian culture sphere. The area in which the athletes perform their co-ordinated exercises is known as the *god-e moqqadas*, the sacred pit, and Islamic prayers close and open the sessions. However, during most sessions, the leader (*morshed*) recites verses from the *Shah nameh,* which extols pre-Islamic values and heroes. The rhythmic declamation of the verses provides accompaniment to the exercises. Iranian history scholar Houchang Chehabi says about the *zur-khaneh*: "As a cultural institution, the *zurkhanehs* reflect Iran's dual Iranian and Islamic, especially Shi'i, heritage" (1995:50).

Thus, the intertwining of Iranian and Islamic identities in Iranian society is complex. I would argue that one of the most basic elements for many individuals in the Iranian culture sphere is his or her religious identification as a Moslem. I also suggest, however, that it is only one identity element in a complex mixture of identity markers. Others include historical and literary, as well as local—clan, family, and *mahal-leh* (quarter or neighborhood of the city) – identities, which are still salient today.

I would also like to challenge the notion, held by many scholars, that there was a sharp break with the past after the advent of Islam. Many scholars treat the two periods as if one night in 650 A.D., the lights were all turned off and the next day Islam dawned and everything was changed; or alternatively, as if the transition between the two periods was smooth. The reason that I state that an Iranian identity is embedded in an Islamic one is because the two have always been inextricably intertwined. Tension exists between these two identities and symbols of Islamic and Iranian identities clash and co-exist both in Iran and in the diaspora. This can be viewed in television programs, both those made in the United States and those from Iran: minarets and the Peacock throne, turban and crown, No-ruz and Islamic prayers, Persian poetry and Quranic recitation collide and contest with one another in daily life.

Dance, too, struggles for space within these identity tensions, and it is these tensions which create the ambiguities surrounding dance prac-

tices in an Iranian/Islamic context, not only in Iran, but also in the diaspora. *"How can you dance tonight of all nights?"* the mother of one of
my dancers queried her daughter, whom she was bringing to rehearsal,
"it is Ashura-Tesua *[the commemoration of the martyrdom of Imam
Hosein]. "I don't care about all of that,"* the daughter replied. *She
danced and the mother left to join the growing crowds gathering to
mark Shi'i religious observances.*

The Iranian Revolution of 1979 illustrates the tensions of the Ira-
nian/Islamic identities. One of the major reasons for the passion the
Revolution generated (among other myriad reasons) was that the Islamic
clergy perceived a threat to Islamic identity from the pre-Islamic, Iranian identity and its values, espoused by the Pahlavi regime and many
intellectuals. "In the late 1970s a significant (if improbable) rumor circulated to the effect that the shah would soon reveal himself a Zoroastrian and would proclaim Iran once more to be a Zoroastrian nation"
(Lincoln 1989: 33). In 1976, the Shah's regime revised the calendar "so
that time was no longer to be measured from Muhammad's hegira, but
rather from Cyrus's accession" (1989: 32), which touched off widespread public demonstrations. Sociologist Mansoor Moaddel confirms
that during the Pahlavi period "the importance of Islam was down-
played, while the Shah's ideologues glorified the pre-Islamic Iranian
kingship and culture" (1993: 11). Further, "the Shah's glorification of
pre-Islamic kingship and ancient history was basically an attempt to
overlook and undermine the influence of Islam in society...This insen-
sitive policy contributed to the shaping of Iran's Islamic opposition"
(1993: 194). Many members of the group characterized by Moaddel as
the "dependent bourgeoisie" who were "staunch supporters of the mon-
archy-centered nationalist discourse, strongly pro-West, and highly
critical of the traditional Iranian lifestyle" (1993: 68), came to the
United States. Thus, while an Iranian identity is embedded within a
larger Islamic one for many Iranians, the fit is not always a comfortable
nor an easy one. Such tensions are manifest in the Iranian diaspora.

Southern California Diaspora: A Focus Population
A local television talk host inquired of one of the local Iranian dancers,
who directs a "pick-up" group staffed by a changing group of young
American women which performs in local Iranian television ads and
videos, weddings and cabarets, *"Why are there no Iranian girls in your
group?" "Would you send me* your *daughters? I would love to teach
them,"* the dancer replied. The television host from Jaam-e Jam *quickly
changed the subject.* (Jaam-e Jam, *Iranian television interview program, March 19, 1996).*

The Iranian community in Southern California is complex on ethnic,
religious, and economic levels. Adding to this complexity is the important fact that this is a new community still largely in the process of

forming, and new individuals are added on a daily basis. This community formed largely in response to the Islamic Revolution of 1978-1979. Prior to this date no more than a few thousand Iranians or Afghans lived outside of the Middle East. Because so many of the newly arrived were political refugees who wished to return following misplaced hopes of a quick collapse of the Islamic Regime, they differed from economic refugees who came to make a new home and life and remain. Even today, one may listen to the call-in programs on Iranian radio and understand that many individuals partly exist in the Old World Iranian culture sphere I characterized above, while others have begun to establish roots here, particularly in the past decade. The Iranian community maintains close ties with the old country because of extensive travel activities and the ease of communication facilities. I wish to also emphasize that today, many members of the Iranian diaspora community visit Iran regularly, and Iranians also come here, so it is easy to keep abreast of events in Iran. Thus, while the research population of this study is focused on the Iranians resident in Southern California, that focus must be viewed within the larger context of on-going events in Iran, Afghanistan, Azerbaijan, and Central Asia. This characterization of the Iranian-American community is crucial to the shaping of this study.

The history of the Iranian-American community, or perhaps more accurately, communities, may be best apprehended in two parts: from the end of World War II to 1978, and after the 1978/79 Revolution. The latter period almost exclusively forms the subject of the many recent scholarly studies profiling the Iranian exile population. Scholars associated with the Center for Near Eastern Studies at UCLA, in particular, have conducted extensive research on the post-1979 Iranian population of Southern California. A series of presentations of data and analysis of all aspects of the Iranian-American community is currently in the process of being researched, analyzed, and published in the form of books and scholarly papers by an outstanding group of social scientists.[5] The profile in this presentation is intended for purposes of background information for aspects of the dance genre that forms the topic of this study. Thus, the background information provided in this section is relevant to issues of dance practices and attitudes toward dance and those who dance. These attitudes and reactions, however, may well have implications that relate to other aspects of Iranian life both in the United States and in the larger Iranian culture sphere.

The difficulty in establishing what characterizes the Iranian community is further complicated because they do not live in any single area in large numbers. To a large degree they embody Benedict Anderson's notion of the "imagined community," integrated not by the literal fact of speaking (or living) together but, "it is imagined because the members of even the smallest nation will never know most of their fellow members, meet them, or even hear of them, yet in the minds of each lives the

image of their communion" (1983:6). One often hears radio and television personalities addressing "Iranians, wherever they are" (*Iranian
harja'i ke hastand*). Naficy suggests that they are a unique community
shaped by, constructed and held together largely by media, particularly
the radio and television, and thus in many ways they are an electronic,
truly imagined, community. Naficy's notion is underscored by the fact
that the most popular broadcasts seem to be call-in shows, which further
allows the community the illusion that they are communicating directly
with one another. Because of this, Naficy observes that "outsiders,
sometimes even insiders, will have difficulty recognizing these boundaries because of their abstract, simulacral nature and their dispersal across
many media" (1993b:34).

Although Naficy, Sabagh and Bozorgmehr and other scholars identify crucial differences between exiles and immigrants, i. e., those who
were forced out by political and religious circumstances, and those who
left of their own accord for economic, professional or personal better-
ment, these differences do not appear to affect the way in which dance is
apprehended.[6]

One further note needs to be sounded, and that is the overwhelming
role of poetry in Iranian society, wherever it is located. While one
might argue that poetry is enjoyable and important to people in many
cultures, I have never experienced a society in which poetry plays such a
pervasive role. To one not familiar with this society, the place of the
Persian language and its expression in poetry is unimaginable. For Iranians and Iranian-Americans, poetry makes life both bearable and enjoyable; it permeates every aspect of life. Poetry readings, featuring
classical poetry and the efforts of local poets, constitute an important
feature of Iranian society. This kind of get-together, known as *shab-e
sh'er* (poetry evening), is held in private homes and public venues such
as restaurants, which may advertise a particular evening for the occasion. The featured personality of such an evening might be either a poet
of some note or an individual well-known for his or her reading, recitation, and analytical skills. Both high-flown political and everyday mun-
dane speech are peppered with quotations from poetry. Virtually without exception, every radio and television announcer opens his or her
program with a poetic reading. Poetry can be used to elevate or demean
events and personalities. In the most informal social gatherings, everyone begs the talented to recite. In his portrait of the Iranian exile community of Southern California, Naficy observes:

> For Iranians, it is poetry, especially Sufi poetry that pro-
> vides the paradigmatic world view and language of exile,
> embodying many journeys, returns, and unifications.
> Such an assertion may seem implausible to readers unfa-
> miliar with Iranian culture...As historians, anthropolo-
> gists, literary critics, and any number of Iranians can at-

test, however, theirs is a culture suffused by poetry and
shaped by the citation of canonical, classical (and at times
contemporary) poets in daily life; rich and poor can and
do cite Ferdowsi, Sa'adi, Hafez, Rumi, and Khayyam.
(1993:148)

Naficy does not overstate the case. The privileging of poetry within this
society overshadows all other forms of expression. Vocal music, because of its association with and use of poetry, to some degree shares in
this focus—many classical art songs utilize the poetry of the classical
poets mentioned above.

I raise this point because not only does the overarching importance
of poetry suffuse every element of society, but for the presentation of
dance, which is "the least of the arts" (Khosrow Jamali personal interview: 1994), if an art form at all in the eyes of many Iranians, it is crucial. Many presenters of this dance tradition, Iranian and non-Iranian,
attempt to utilize staging strategies that are informed by stories or
themes gleaned from well-known classical poetic sources, which fet-
ishize the Iranian past, to lend credibility and respectability to dance as a
legitimate form of expression. "This nostalgic past is itself ideological
in that, as Said writes in *Orientalism* (1979:55), it has become an
'imaginary geography,' a construction created by exilic narratives"
(Naficy 1993:151). These are the poetic images so important to the Iranian public that are invoked, along with orientalist costumes and sets, to
create the romantic images that I will discuss in detail in Chapter Six. It
is important to always retain the concept of how poetry dominates, and
has always dominated, Iranian life.

*The a small   local group appeared on the UCLA Student Union
stage, the choreographer and artistic director of the group clad in
clothing that was designed to be reminiscent of thirteenth-century Iran,
but in reality more closely approximated a Hollywood misconception of
that fashion. He choreographically enacted the role of Hafez, the most
important lyrical poet of Iran. Moving to modern movie music, he
walked and posed eloquently, as if formulating the composition of timeless poetry. Surrounding him were a bevy of women dressed in garments that were distinctly designed with* Kismet *in mind: coin bras,
never worn west of the Suez canal, were of such visual proportions that
the harem pants, veils and bare midriffs paled by comparison. These
costumes, with their exposed flesh, elicited several negative comments
from the overwhelmingly Iranian audience, which, nevertheless, cheered
for the performance with its emotionally-charged poetic theme.*

Pre-1978
*In the 1950's and 1960's, Iranian male students throughout the United
States, including Southern California, outnumbered female students by
at least 25 to one. It was a very unusual family that allowed a girl to*

come to America, and those who were here almost always lived with family members. Unlike the vast majority of male students, the young women students sometimes appeared in public performances, and some of them were extremely careful about the context, movement vocabulary and costumes in which they danced. Their performances were usually in an international student talent show or a similar event that did not carry any negative connotation. In the 1950's Nahid (pseudonym), my first teacher, Homa, Leili, and Shahla (pseudonyms), all appeared in various performances and performance spaces, some more respectable than others in the eyes of the Iranian students. It is of interest to note that the costumes and the movements of the four young women varied greatly. Two of them wore costumes with bare midriffs, an element from Hollywood movies, rather than Persia, in which actresses such as Maria Montez and Hedy Lamar, among other "exotic" types, parodied oriental dancing. The American interest in and demand for the exotic was not lost on these women students, each of whom represented Iranian dancing in various ways. Appropriating costumes that were created in Western orientalist productions such as "Kismet" is one example.

Nahid, who was invariably accompanied by a family member, usually her mother, and who also sang, was the only one of the four who had professional-level talent. Homa was a proficient amateur dancer, but constantly worried that she would never find a husband and that her family would be most displeased to discover her dancing in public, no matter how decorously. The other two young women had other plans: Leili wanted to be in movies, and indeed, she landed a bit part in a Hitchcock film, but a successful movie career was not forthcoming, and Shahla wanted to make money. Iranian students at that time were outraged at the appearances of Shahla and Leili in costumes that were obviously not Iranian in provenance. It was even rumored that Shahla danced nude at private parties, certainly an unusual claim in the 1950's. She did go on to own a nightclub in Hollywood in the 1970's, that was famous for its nude dancers.

Demographics for Iranians of all periods are of questionable accuracy, and in any case, the overwhelming number of Iranians at that time held highly-prized student visas. According to INS records, only 35,000 immigrants entered the United States from 1950 - 1977. According to Bozorgmehr et al, figures for an Iranian category do not exist before this time and I do not think more than a handful was resident in American colleges and universities before that time. France was the preferred foreign destination for Iranian students before 1950 (Bozorgmehr, Sabagh, and Der-Martirosian 1993: 65). For this reason my personal accounts, as well as those of several long-time residents, serve as the basis for the following, brief profile.

My first memories of Iranians in the United States date back to 1954, when the majority of Iranians in the United States were students from more-or-less privileged backgrounds whose original plans, upon arrival, were to obtain an education and eventually return to Iran. In many cases, they harbored altruistic plans to better the lives of their less-fortunate countrymen and women. For this reason "the vast majority majored in engineering, engineering, and engineering" (Khosrow Jamali, personal interview: June 22, 1996).

In March 1955, the date of my first No-Ruz (Iranian New Year Celebration), the Iranians resident in Los Angeles could fit in one medium-sized recreation room in a student center on the University of Southern California campus and could be readily counted; I knew most of them by sight as well as by name. That year they probably numbered about 100-200 individuals. Most of the Iranians gathered together that evening were young and males probably formed 95% of the group in that salon, partaking of a potluck dinner with foods, music, dance, and language that were new and exotic to a wide-eyed young American. At that time, the only formal organization for Iranians of which I was aware was the Iranian Students' Association, which was national in scope, government-sponsored and supervised by a government official assigned specifically to student affairs from the Iranian embassy in Washington, D. C. (I attended the national conventions of this organization in 1957 and 1958). Even in that relatively early period, the Iranian government was aware of, and feared, a brain drain, as well as being sensitive to the political activism that soon accelerated throughout the next two decades. So important was this issue that the Iranian government stationed another student advisor at the Iranian consulate in San Francisco to attend to student affairs in California. Then, in 1955, and for the next few years, many members of the Iranian community knew one another by sight, and most interactions were among small, informal groups of close friends, who were often cousins and brothers as well. The degree of interaction, of course, varied. Some individuals rarely saw other Iranians, while others formed their most important social networks among their countrymen. At this period, Iranian students were more evenly distributed throughout the colleges and universities of the United States. Students also changed colleges and universities, particularly after they had successfully gained sophisticated English skills, and therefore there existed a certain fluidity and impermanence among the Iranian students. Certain smaller, Mid-Western private colleges met tight budgets by issuing student visas and teaching these students English. After acquiring the requisite linguistic skills, many of these students headed to schools like UCLA and Berkeley, Harvard and Princeton. The great population concentrations that currently characterize the contemporary Iranian communities in large cities like Los Angeles, New York, Washington, D.C., Houston, and Seattle did not then exist. A few Iranian government officials and their families could be found in New York and Washington, D.C., but other non-student individuals were extremely rare.

It was also clear in that period that there were some individuals who planned not to return to Iran. The reasons for this were several, but important among them were: 1) The acquisition of a non-Iranian, generally American, spouse who had no desire to move to the Middle East (Iran was depicted as highly turbulent under the Mossadegh regime and widely publicized in the American press of the time). 2) Political dissidents, rare at that time, but dramatically increasing in the 1960's and 1970's, became a powerful political force whose activities had an immense impact on the fall of the Shah's regime in 1979. Their activism publicized human rights abuses under the Pahlavi regime to the general American and Western public, which caused the American government to distance itself and withdraw support from the Shah's regime. The number of students began to swell in the late 1960's and throughout the 1970's due to the increased financial abilities of the growing middle class in Iran, shown by the growing demographic figures (Bozorgmehr 1993: 65). I saw more Iranian students on the campuses of Southern California such as USC, UCLA, and Pepperdine College. (I frequently interacted with these students in the production of concerts.) 3) Personal reasons also motivated some to stay. For example, some individuals acquired skills such as costume or set designing, became professional dancers and painters, or found similar opportunities in the field of film and the arts. These promising professional activities, in their infancy or nonexistent in Iran, encouraged some individuals to stay. I can cite as examples several successful individuals in the field of opera, costume design, art history, and similar fields. Other exceptional individuals acquired such specialized and advanced skills in scientific fields such as physics, astronomy and aeronautics, social sciences and psychology, that there existed no professional slot in the Iran of that period into which they could fit. A few Armenians, Assyrians, Baha'is and Jews with bitter personal experiences of religious discrimination did not wish to return to a homeland where they formed a part of a despised minority group (see Menashri 1986). (Others in those groups prospered in pre-1979 Iran and moved in social and educational circles where they escaped such discrimination.) Those whose sexual orientation or other private and personal proclivities might cause problems in the family-oriented environment of Iran often opted to stay as well.

In the late 1970s a few individuals, sensing the coming potential personal disaster facing them should the Pahlavi regime collapse, made their way here.

Thus, slowly, from the mid-1950s until the 1979 Revolution, some individuals, often with non-Iranian spouses, for economic, career, religious, personal or political motives, began to stay in the United States. Once they had obtained residency cards or citizenship, these individuals often arranged for family members to come as immigrants, accounting for a large portion of the figure of 35,000 mentioned above. A few rare Iranian male students in that period received Iranian brides, sometimes arranged for by their families.

This disparate group of individuals grew throughout the 1960s and 1970s to the point that their numbers could support one or two restaurants in the Los Angeles area.[7] "In the pre-Revolution all of these establishments struggled because the patrons were more interested in politics than shish kabab," claims former Iranian restaurant owner Khosrow Jamali, "but now the restaurants have an easier time because people today are more interested in shish kabab than politics" (personal interview: June 24, 1996).

This group of individual Iranians could not have been considered a community, for there was no formal, or even informal, structure to bind them together. Even politics did not engender the formation of large groups; to do so would have invited the attention of SAVAK (Pahlavi regime's secret police), and everyone suspected that any student was potentially a paid agent. Rather, as individuals, some of them went to these restaurants simply to indulge in Iranian cuisine in an Iranian atmosphere. The first of these restaurants, Patoq, also served "American" food in a separate room in order to survive. There were no specialty stores as there are today, in which one can purchase Iranian food items, spices, and pastries, music, books, art, calligraphy, and other specifically Iranian-made products. No communications systems, such as the numerous Iranian yellow pages or radio and television programs, exile theatre and cinema, popular and classical music concerts, that currently link those in the Iranian community who are interested, were available, even on a limited basis.

It was during the 1960's that the first tentative differences began to become apparent among Iranians resident in the United States, and these were largely political. There were three main groups: the pro-Shah supporters, the anti-Shah dissidents (further subdivided along the left to right political axis), and the apolitical. Increasingly, every public gathering, such as the annual No-Ruz celebration, which was held in a large hotel to accommodate the increased numbers of people, and often featuring programs of local dance (essentially my company) as well as an important vocalist from Iran such as Marzieh, Ellaheh, or Gougoush, became highly politicized, with raucous scenes filled with shouts of *"zendeh bad shah"* (long live the king) and *"mordeh bad shah"* (down with the king) and ending in shouting matches or fisticuffs. The politically-oriented groups, right and left, began to hold separate functions. The apolitical increasingly stayed away.

In the opinion of many of the anti-regime groups, any celebration of Iranian culture supported the Pahlavi regime, and they understood it to be their duty to seize any opportunity to protest and make public their grievances against it. *This series of protests in Los Angeles culminated dramatically during an official visit by the Iranian National Dance Company, the Mahalli Dancers, in 1976 on the USC campus. Outside the theatre, opposition students, many in masks, attired themselves in a dramatic way and confronted the police, who were clad in full riot gear, posed surrealistically in choreographed lines. The police appeared more like extras in a science fiction film than a viable force useful for purposes of practical crowd control. That night the campus was fraught with tension and a sinister feeling filled the late spring night. In spite of all the security in the auditorium, the students managed to dramatically unfurl large signs from the balconies, and one jumped down on the stage and attacked the choreographer, Robert De Warren, an Englishman.* Dramatic scuffles between the opposition and the police ensued before the program continued, a symbolic prelude to events soon to be staged in the streets of Iran.

The Islamic Revolution of 1979, which many did not expect, began shortly after this tumultuous visit. The small group of Iranians, mostly students and many with leftist political leanings, was suddenly overwhelmed by a flood of refugees. Hundreds of thousands of political and religious exiles reached Southern California, forever changing the profile of the Iranian-American community. Many of the more radical students returned to Iran, only to be devoured by the revolution, which turned upon them. (See especially Abrahamian 1989).

Post-1979 Iranian Diaspora
While the first Iranians entering the United States had arrived primarily as students, the wave of people who now arrived were political, religious, and economic refugees fleeing from the chaos emanating from the revolutionary upheavals of the Islamic Revolution.[8] Many of these cherished the hope that the Islamic government would collapse under its own weight, American intervention, or through means of the Iraqi invasion. Many, but by no means all, of this group of people were financially well-off, including hundreds of multimillionaires. As a group of immigrants they were also well-educated, many having received higher education in the United States, Europe, and Iran. In this way they more resembled well-heeled Chinese and Korean immigrants than the more unfortunate political and economic refugees of Mexico and Central America. However, there were also those who arrived nearly destitute. (See Kelley 1993.)

For this wave of exiles, demographic data does exist, but much of it is suspect. "The number of Iranians in Los Angeles is a subject of intense controversy. Iranians themselves continually speculate about their numbers" (Bozorgmehr, Sabagh, and Der-Martirosian 1993:70). As one can readily see, there is no accurate count of Iranians resident in the United States or Southern California. Various estimates among Iranian sources, both from the media and individual claims, run from one-half to two million individuals in Southern California. (See also Kelley 1993; Fathi 1991.)

Many of the recent arrivals could not speak English, and there were those who seized upon the moment and began opening a series of businesses oriented to the needs of this vast number of newcomers. The largest and best-known Iranian area in Los Angeles, known as Little Tehran, is located on Westwood Boulevard between Wilshire and Olympic Boulevards and typifies the types of services and goods offered to this ethnic community. These range from restaurants, book and music stores, calligraphers, beauty parlors, grocery stores, gift shops, pastry shops, travel agencies, photography studios, and myriad professional services. In addition, large concentrations of Iranian establishments are found in downtown Los Angeles, where Iranians, particularly members of the Jewish community, dominate many areas of garment manufacture and sales and jewelry sales.

In Southern California, one must speak in terms of Iranian communities, rather than community. These divisions are determined by differences in religion, ethnicity, class, and politics. Prior to 1979, Iranians of all backgrounds gathered together, at least occasionally, to celebrate No Ruz. Currently in Los Angeles, there exist communities based on 1) Religion: Moslem, Jewish, Armenian and Assyrian Christian, Zoroastrian, and Baha'i. 2) Language and Ethnicity: Azerbaijani and Kurdish, Armenian and Assyrian, all of whom maintain their own organizations. 3) Politics: Pro-Shah, pro-Khomeini, and apolitical—political rallies still attract hundreds, sometimes thousands of individuals. With the growing realization that they will not be soon returning, many people are shifting their energies to domestic concerns rather than focusing on events in Iran as they used to do. Nevertheless, pro- and anti-Islamic government rallies still occur on a regular basis. 4) Socio-economic class. When one attends a wedding or other social event, it becomes clear that these events are segregated to a large degree by class. It should come as no surprise that marriages are, more often than not, arranged by income, religion, and social class. Young Iranian students who pump gas and park cars are not encouraged to marry young ladies from families who were once known as the "Thousand Families" (*hezar famil*).

However, these communities are also characterized by permeability. Some groups, particularly those with cultural, business or scholarly orientations, encourage participation by individuals of all religious and ethnic backgrounds who share a particular common interest. This inclusiveness is often stated publicly. Since 1979, many groups and associations, such as NIPOC (The businessmen's [and women's] association of Orange County), and countless others have formed on this basis. Most of these groups focus largely on cultural activities. For example, a recent Iranian Festival (August 17-18, 1996) sponsored by the Iranian Students of UCLA prominently featured booths and entertainment fea-

turing all Iranian ethnic and religious groups. Staffs of radio and television are particularly ecumenical, and I am acquainted with Armenians,
Moslems, Jews, Baha'is, and Assyrians who continuously interact together in the media world.

I wish to stress that in no way can the community of Iranians in
Southern California be considered a parallel of the general population in
Iran, for a number of reasons. First, the ratio of Moslems to non-
Moslems is not representative of the homeland, particularly since many
minority individuals specifically left Iran because of the religious and
political strategies employed against them by the Islamic Regime. Second, the people living in Southern California were overwhelmingly
middle and upper class residents of Tehran, and virtually no representatives of the peasant or urban proletariat population exists here, while in
Iran millions of people live in villages and the underclass areas of cities.
Thus, the population that made its way to Los Angeles is overwhelmingly literate in contrast to the high illiteracy figures which exist in Iran
(*Statesmen's Yearbook* 1994-95 lists 54% of the population of Iran as
literate in 1990). Thirdly, the Moslems themselves form a group that is
more highly educated and areligious than that of the general population
of Iran. For example, Bozorgmehr, Sabagh, and Der-Martirosian report
from their intensive study that "almost 80 percent of Muslims never
follow the Islamic practices of daily prayers, fasting during Ramadan,
and so forth, partly because of their secular background and partly because of disenchantment with the role of Islam in Iran." Additionally,
their report shows "a mere two percent of Muslims...always observe
their religious practices" (1993:76). The implication of this finding is
that one may encounter more events in Southern California in which
dance occurs than one might find in Iran, although dance occurs in Iran
even under the threat of severe governmental punishment. Conservative
Moslems comprise a tiny fraction of the Iranians resident in Southern
California, which suggests that those persons who feel free to dance, and
individuals and families who hold events in which dance occurs, statisti-
cally outnumber such groups in Iran or Afghanistan, even if official
laws in those countries did not exist. The other non-Islamic religious
groups do not labor under religious strictures that frown on the performance of dance. I will show in the next chapter that negative views of
dance proceed from a variety of social, economic, and other factors as
much as from religion.

Within the new and developing Iranian-American community, I turn
to the specific sites and contexts in which solo improvised dance is performed.

Contemporary Contexts for Solo Improvised Dance

I suggest that the current contexts for the performance of this dance tradition in Southern California, in most cases, seem to be adaptations of

past practices. In the Iranian culture sphere just prior to the Revolution of 1979, dance occurred in private events in extended family gatherings such as weddings or parties and public venues such as nightclubs, restaurants, state and private-sponsored public concerts, and films. Historically, at the turn of the century and before, dance occurred in private events, generally organized around the extended family, in gender-separated celebrations, and in public venues such as coffee houses or street shows frequented almost exclusively by men.[9] Women entertained themselves separately in their own quarters, or, on special occasions, hired groups of female professional entertainers. The difference between the Qajar (1785-1925) and the Pahlavi dynasties (1925-1979) was that the Pahlavis dropped patronage of traditional dancing to encourage Western forms such as classical ballet, and later, Western style stagings of folk dance. A second change that occurred under the Pahlavis was that family gatherings, at least among the educated classes, became mixed, a direct result of Pahlavi social engineering with its emphasis on Western-style mingling of the sexes. The import for the study of this dance tradition among the diaspora is that it is the educated, Western-oriented classes that overwhelmingly make up this community. It is important to note that during the 1970's, turn-of-the-century dancing again became popular and several nightclubs and restaurants with Qajar-period themes opened to appeal to this nostalgia (personal observation October 1976). Jamal stated that the nostalgia "movement" was very conscious and that it continues today in theatrical and other productions (personal interview Dec. 12, 1995).

In the diaspora community, what might appear as new practices and venues are, in fact, adaptations of older practices. The main context for the performance of dance remains family-oriented events such as weddings and other celebratory gatherings of family and friends. That was historically true for the Iranian culture sphere, and it remains true for the diaspora community as well (personal observations and numerous interviews). I note this fact because for children, this is the site of the primary learning experience of this dance form.

For many young adults, discotheques such as Club X and Chaos and restaurants such as Darya also provide venues for dance performance on a social level. A music industry with a constant churning out of pop tunes with a 6/8 rhythm, the favored beat for this dance, has sprung up in Southern California (Zinder 1992:32-37). The current vocalists give frequent concerts in which the singer and his or her musicians, and perhaps backup dancers, perform or sketch movements from this tradition. The audience frequently dances and the most common space for the audience is a dance floor rather than an auditorium with seats. Such concerts are no longer permitted in Iran.[10]

These types of performances are also a staple of numerous Iranian emigre television programs. The popular music industry creates MTV-

type musical videos, some approaching the elaborateness and expense
found in a Michael Jackson video production, which are widely available both on television programing and in Iranian music stores.

> Recent sexist videos by male Iranian singers feature white
> leggy dark-haired Anglo female dancers who try to pass
> as Iranian, using their physical similarity to Iranian
> women as well as imitations of the Iranian dancing style.
> If the former qualities favor their inscription as Iranian
> women, the inexactness and exaggeration of their imita-
> tions give away their "inauthenticity." (Naficy 1993:
> 180)

A third venue for domestic style dancing (*majlesi*) is public celebrations
of Iranian holidays such as those of Mehregan or No-Ruz. These are
generally held in large open spaces such as parks, and both spontaneous
domestic dancing, as well as prepared performances, may be experienced. A frequent, related type of occasion is one in which the community is encouraged to participate and show their dances, music, costumes, food, and other arts. Such occasions are different and more organized by community than they were in Iran, and they have taken on a
symbolic meaning of nationalism. People who would never have considered donning a peasant or tribal costume in Iran, happily and proudly
do so here as a patriotic duty—a departure from practices in Iran. For
example, community organizations such as the Iranian Businessmen's
Association of Orange County (NIPOC) or the Rotary Club of West Los
Angeles sponsor frequent large public events to profile the Iranian-
American community in a positive way.

Professional dancing may be seen in concerts of such local ensembles. In Iran, such performances are banned by the Islamic regime, but
previously such large-scale performances were generally officially or
semi-officially sponsored by the Ministry of Fine Arts, as were demonstrations by peasant and tribal groups. In the diaspora, these concerts
and performances are privately sponsored; the sponsors range from organizations such as women's clubs and Iranian students' organizations
on the various Southern California campuses, to private individuals
wishing for entertainment at weddings, circumcisions, and bar- and bat-
mitzvahs. To keep a perspective on the relative importance of aesthetic
expression in an Iranian-American environment, it must be stressed that
among Iranians in Southern California, dance is less important than
singing. For a wedding or other social event to receive a true cachet, it
is far more important to secure the services of a noted vocalist than to
have dancers.

Nightclubs, now banned in Iran, also feature professional dancers,
usually soloists, but they are incidental to the featured vocalists. Some
of the performers in these venues also sing and perform comic skits,

reflecting a continuation of the traditional style of performance. (These performers generally call themselves actors [*honarpisheh*] or artists [*honarmand*] rather than "dancer.") These locales most approximate the up-scale end of those formerly found in Tehran and other cities. Many of the current nightclubs are often family-oriented, a change from the largely male-only clientele found formerly in most night spots in Tehran. From medieval times until the present century, the coffeehouse was also a context for public dances, storytelling and other activities, and in Afghanistan they still served as a venue for these activities until just before the Soviet invasion (personal observation, November, 1976).

A final venue for viewing professional and participatory dancing is weddings and other celebratory parties held in private residences. Such performances also offer a stimulus to spontaneous domestic dancing by the guests. Both iconographic sources and travelers' accounts show that the custom of hiring professional entertainers goes back for centuries. It is well-known that one must have dancing at weddings, but one often despises the performers, thus creating ambiguity.

In sum, with the arrival of hundreds of thousands of Iranians in a new environment, contexts for dance performance of all kinds have changed to some degree, both in Southern California and in the Iranian culture sphere. However, as I have shown, the alterations may be more accurately characterized as adaptations of older patterns than as new ones. These venues characterize the spaces and contexts for the dance events that I will investigate.

Chapter 5

Solo Improvised Dance in Social Contexts

Among Middle Eastern audiences, if
people are especially moved by a
performance, they may well jump up and
join a dancer on stage. (Buonaventura 1989: 185)

How and when is an individual potentially perceived as transgressive or out-of-control through the performance of solo
improvised dance? This is one of the core questions of my study. I
cover the topic in detail in this chapter, in which I lay out the research
findings of what constitutes such behavior. As an example, I will describe a party I attended at which dancing that was considered transgressive and out-of-control was observed. I will then construct and establish
a generic Iranian-American dance event. This "anatomy of an Iranian
dance event" derives from a compendium of elements that I viewed in
dance events over a period of several years, from which I have extracted
the elements that I describe for this presentation. My description of this
"typical" event reflects not only the past few years, but in many ways
includes virtually all of the basic elements of the dance events that I
have witnessed and in which I have participated for more than forty
years. I then turn to specific events in order to furnish the most important and basic elements and their variables, which together comprise the
categories of "normative," "transgressive," and "out-of-control" behavior in dancing and how these categories elicit the reactions that I term
choreophobic. Jumping on stage with a professional dancer, as the
quote at the beginning of the chapter suggests, can be considered normative, transgressive, or out-of-control depending on a constellation of
elements, which I present in an Iranian context in this chapter. I later
compare these terms with the categories of "effectiveness" and "appropriateness" that William O. Beeman outlined in his study of Iranian verbal communication. I conclude with a comparison of Jane K. Cowan's
important study of dance events in Northern Greece as a contrast to this
study of Iranian events.

The party began sedately enough. It was on a warm Sunday afternoon, with about fifty guests, several of them dancers from AVAZ (May 5, 1996). Wine and other convivial beverages flowed freely, which perhaps accounted, at least in part, for what followed. People were seated in small groups on the patio, which was well-screened from the neighbors. Dance music was played and eventually the host, a supporter of AVAZ, managed to encourage one of the AVAZ dancers to begin dancing by dancing with her.[1] Soon, many of the company dancers, as well as several Iranian women, were encouraged to join in. The dancing had been standard and normative up until this point.[2] In a pause during the music, those who had been dancing sat, and the host played a new selection. Two women, Nazi and Jaleh, the latter a well-known performer, cheerfully, and somewhat loudly, critiqued the dancing, saying that it was not "sexy" enough to be "real" Iranian dancing. At that point, Nazi, an elderly woman whom I had known for many years, and who was generally known for her publicly correct, even prim, behavior, began to dance in what was, for her, a rather transgressive manner. She moved her hips and facial features as if to show the young non-Iranian girls how a "real" Iranian dancer ought to look. Her dance movements were actually minimal: she picked up a man's hat that the host had provided to perform *shateri*, and placed it on her head. This use of the hat announced something different from her usual style of dancing. Presently, she picked up the hat and held it in both hands above her head while she swiveled her head from side to side. Her small, slight hip movements were initiated by stepping on the ball of one foot and pivoting on the foot while straightening her knee, rather than initiating the movement from the pelvis. At one point, with a roguish grin, she threw imaginary breasts in the air like a male dancer, considerably startling some of the non-Iranian guests. This gesture was sketched in a subtle but unmistakable fashion. Her husband looked utterly astonished and blushed in embarrassment, shaking his head in disbelief. A woman seated next to me, who was well acquainted with Nazi, leaned over and said, "I never knew Nazi had it in her!" Everyone, with the possible exception of Nazi's husband, began to enjoy the spectacle of this prim, elderly lady dancing with such relative abandon and they clapped and laughed to encourage Nazi in her memorable performance.

After some minutes of Nazi's performance, Jaleh, a younger woman in her forties who had come to the party with her husband, who was well-known in the Iranian community, stood up dramatically and began to dance with even more abandon than Nazi. In the back-lighting of the setting sun, it was apparent that she wore little or nothing under her thin summer dress. With piercing, smoldering gazes at several of the men, she began to move about the dance space, first moving her pelvis in an overtly sexual manner, thrusting it forward in time to the music, and then alternatively moving side to side by thrusting her pelvis in a series of rapid movements. These pelvic movements were initiated from the hips, unlike Nazi's, which were initiated from the feet. In Persian, such movements are called *gheir* and are a hallmark of transgressive and out-of-control behavior.[3] Consequently, Jaleh's movements were larger, more determined and overt. Jamal, one of the guests, leaned over and whispered, "she's on something." Whereas Nazi's dance had been mildly transgressive and fun, Jaleh's dance was, in the view of everyone present, including her red-faced, but seemingly amused, husband, "out-of-control." People who had known Jaleh, usually a picture of rectitude, for many years had never before seen her dance in this fashion. Some were genuinely shocked or at least very surprised. Jamal gave the opinion that "she was trying to out-do Nazi, and 'lost it'."

Significantly, each husband, aware that I was writing on Iranian dance, later sought me out separately and shamefacedly protested that he "did not know what had gotten into my wife," to dance in this totally unexpected fashion. Nazi came over to Jamal and me later and said in Persian, "I have never danced this way. I don't know what happened."

In this case, all of the people with whom I spoke felt that Nazi had indeed danced in a delightfully transgressive fashion, but she certainly did not exhibit out-of-control behavior. Her performance was judged to be transgressive, in part, because Nazi simply had never performed that way at the several parties and weddings where I and others had observed her. Her husband smiled indulgently, if a trifle woodenly, when some individuals congratulated him on having such "a good dancer" for a wife. Nevertheless, he is, in his own words, "old-fashioned" and likes to observe the proprieties in public, and in an aside he told me that he was less than pleased that his wife had made a "public spectacle" of herself. On the other hand, everyone agreed that Jaleh's performance was, in the words of different witnesses, "surprising," "out-of-control," and "out-of-hand." In reply to my question, "what made her performance out-of-control to you?," people variously identified three specific aspects of her performance as being out-of-control: 1) the way in which she focused on certain male on-lookers during the dance, seeming to direct her movements toward them 2) her clothing and 3) her pelvic movements, which three or four individuals said "looked like belly dancing." "She looked like she was trying to belly dance, but she really doesn't know how," scornfully observed one individual. This event, and her dancing, formed a topic of conversation for some days to come.

The Anatomy of an Iranian Dance Event
Whether Iranian or non-Iranian, one's first experience of solo improvisational dance is usually in a social setting: a small party or perhaps a large wedding. More recently, it may be encountered in some form in a formal performance, or it may be seen in its most modern manifestation on Persian television shows accompanying the latest pop videos. The distinctive music, in a rich array of six-eight rhythms (called mother's

milk, *shir-e madar*, in Persian), is put on and the hostess begins her round of encouraging her guests to dance. Eventually, if she is successful, the music and the urge to dance call dancer after dancer to rise and move. The movements, especially in the beginning, may be simple, shy. The arms are held out at shoulder level, the hands moving in graceful, circular motions rotating from the wrist, as the performer moves about the dance space; he or she may be unconsciously sensual, or even overtly sexual in the performance. You, too, will be expected to get up and perform, and if you feel you can not, that you are awkward (and chances are you will be), your efforts will provide your Iranian hosts with much amusement. Perhaps during the course of the evening a woman of considerable talent will take the floor and perform elaborate filigreed movements of arms, hands, and fingers, deft and unusual movements of the head, and sensuous and openly sexual movements of the hips, lips, and the eyebrows. In a men's party, the dance will feel very different: a grotesque miming of an infirm old man in which the dancer pushes a recalcitrant knee only to have the opposite one collapse; coquettish, suggestive and rakish twitchings of the buttocks, throwing imaginary breasts in the air, slipping the head from side-to-side on an immobile neck, quivering lips, eyebrows made to move and dance by themselves—all for comic effect. Still later, you may see these movements at the traditional theatre as a comic display—but nevertheless, they belong to the same dance tradition that can be seen from China to Turkey, as well as in the United States, in a startling rainbow of moods and colors. Rich expressions of mood and attitude are more important than creating original movements in these social settings. This is not rural, peasant dancing done in colorful costumes in lines and groups, this is the dance of the urban world, performed by ingenue and professional prostitute, state-employed dancer of a national company or actor in the traditional theatre, housewife or grandmother, worker from the southern slums or upper-class landowner in his cups at a wedding. This is the dance banned by the Islamic Republic, but still performed behind closed doors and curtained windows in houses in Tehran and on buses on rural highways.

Historically, as we have seen, dancing was almost invariably included in travelers' narratives and Persian miniatures in which a marriage ceremony, a court entertainment, or some joyful event is portrayed and described. Today, Iranians enjoy many social gatherings where dancing may occur. Like the historical events, these are joyful, celebratory occasions such as weddings. The frequency of dancing depends on the relative enjoyment it provides for the hosts and their guests. Many Iranian hostesses (for it is generally the wife who is responsible for this aspect of the party), feel that dancing enlivens their function and is, therefore, highly desirable. For weddings and engagement parties, dancing is almost universal, and is an appropriate means to express happiness and celebration. Musicians or a professional deejay are almost always hired for these larger formal celebrations. Professional dancers are also often brought in, especially for large weddings, which are more structured, elaborate events than the more informal social gatherings which I will describe. In the Iranian Jewish community, where Bar Mitzvahs and Bat Mitzvahs can be almost as elaborate as weddings, professional dancers and musicians are common. The *Iranian Yellow Pages* (1995) lists nine individual dancers or dance groups (1995:1039), three disc jockeys (1995:1037), and 59 "entertainers" (1995: 1036), all of whom are available for weddings and other celebratory events, indicating how extensive the market for such activities is.[4]

Iranians often form quasi-formal groups known as *dowreh* (circle), in which they frequent one another's social events.[5] The concept of *dowreh* includes the notion of circulating through social events in a chain-like fashion, moving from one home to the next. These get-togethers and parties are often held on a regular weekly or monthly basis. More commonly than Americans, many Iranians maintain close social ties with extended family members who may be part of a *dowreh*. In Southern California and other areas of the diaspora, however, because many individuals were uprooted by the Revolution, family members have been replaced, through necessity, by close friends. The *dowreh* can also be web-like, in that an individual may belong to more than one social set. Different *dowreh* groups feature different activities depending on the composition of the *dowreh* members: some play cards, others hold poetry evenings, while yet others may converse or play or listen to music, among other activities. Men in an all-male *dowreh* might play the ever-popular backgammon (*takht-e nard*), while women may entertain themselves by participating in the *bazi-ha-ye namayeshi* (women's theatre games described in the next chapter), although sex-segregated *dowreh* groups are less common in America than in Iran, and their activities are often held in the day rather than evening hours.

Being an excellent host (*mehman-navaz*) constitutes a major cultural value in Iranian society. In order to embody this cultural attribute, *dowreh* members often engage in fierce competition, manifested in the elaborateness of food, drink, and entertainment provided and the number of guests invited, particularly if a luminary poet, artist, or other figure graces the event and can be prevailed upon to perform by reciting a poem or singing, thus providing the host family with a social coup. Iranians, as a group, host more social events than their American counterparts. Having friends and family around one is the greatest joy, one enthusiastic hostess informed me. Those Iranians that I know well, unless they are in mourning or observing solemn religious holidays, host weekly dinners, and larger parties at least once a month. The social round is completed when they appear as guests. A sharp eye is kept out at such events for likely marriage candidates for the single, and business affairs are discreetly conducted.

In Iranian society, dancing generally occurs at weddings. At a large wedding or hotel party, where hundreds of guests sometimes attend, there may be some initial hesitation when the orchestra plays, but usually one or two women, or in the past decades, a mixed couple, soon take to the dance floor, where they are then joined by many others. In this way, large events differ from the smaller informal events at which the hostess must work hard to induce the first dancer or two to rise and perform.

When and if dancing occurs at these more informal parties, which may have in excess of one hundred guests, it is generally near the end of the evening. This is for several reasons. First and foremost, there must be a critical mass of guests present, and it is fashionable, and a stock joke among Iranians, that everyone attempts to arrive last, a not unfamiliar feature of American celebrity events as well.

Second, the uniquely Iranian element of *ta'arof* (an elaborate system of politesse) reigns in Iranian social interactions, as William O. Beeman masterfully observes (1986). No guest at this type of event would begin to dance without specific and numerous entreaties by the senior hostess, who generally begins the dancing herself, although, in order not to intimidate guests with superior dancing skill, she generally sketches the movements. The hostess seems to begin the process of inducing guests to dance when she feels a lull in the event, or when she intuits that the time to dance has arrived. To dance without several entreaties by the hostess would be truly out-of-control and considered *jelf* (vulgar) or *sabok* (frivolous). In fact, it is the skill of the hostess at encouraging a sufficient number of her guests to come into the dance area that determines whether there will be dancing, and whether it will be general or peter out after a few attempts. If she wishes to have dancing to enliven her party, she invites individuals that she knows love to dance and are good at it.

Jamal stated, "no matter how much a person may tell you they cannot or do not know how to dance, virtually every one in Iran can at least sketch out the movements of this dance" (December 12, 1993). Morteza Varzi, a prominent musician in the Southern California Iranian-American community, observes that:

> At the end of the musical performance, a dance piece would be played to bring the audience back to the present reality and to "break the spell"...They love dance and song. But, although some of them are very good at these performing arts, customarily they deny their skill, or even their knowledge of these things. They must be pushed into performance. But soon, they would get carried away with the dance music, and it would become difficult to stop them. At this stage everybody, skillful or clumsy,

> would be dragged into the dancing. This dancing would
> help them to release the emotional tension built up by the
> music, and would prepare them for the main
> meal...(1986:8)

Other observers also notice the ambiguity which people exhibit when
called upon to dance:

> Dancing is perhaps more common today at the *bazm* (a
> type of evening social event with music) than was for-
> merly the case. However, the traditional attitudes that
> music is to be preferred over dance, and that "nice girls
> don't dance," persist. A girl or woman still must be given
> considerable urging before she will dance, even if she
> truly wants to do so. In any case, this is social dancing,
> not a professional entertainment. (Friend and Siegel
> 1986:10)

This passage, however, seems to indicate that Friend and Siegel, while
aware of choreophobic attitudes, are not familiar with the rigors of
ta'arof. I would contend that in Los Angeles, people are hesitant to
dance more because of transgressing the unspoken rules of *ta'arof* than
fear of being labeled a "naughty girl."

Third, *ta'arof* dictates that there is a long period as the guests arrive
during which they are plied with tea and refreshments, which ensures
that the hosts enact their cultural roles as skillful *mehman-navaz*.
Guests are taken around and introduced, particularly if they are not familiar to the members of the *dowreh*, and are not left alone by a member
of the family until someone is found among the guests who can comfortably chat with the newcomer(s). Young adults are trained carefully
to make guests feel at home, a skill most of them ably enact from the
time they first emerge into polite society. This period of warming up
the party is important in creating a friendly and welcoming atmosphere.

At this point, it is not uncommon to ask one of the guests to sing,
play an instrument, or recite a poem. This is generally a son or daughter, or an honored guest of senior years—in any case, someone the hostess can count upon to perform and break the ice after the niceties of
ta'arof have been properly observed. If an instrumentalist is present, he
or she, at the behest of the hostess, might begin a dance melody (*reng*).
The hostess will perform a few simple movements and move toward her
female guests. It is usually necessary to approach three or four individuals, since to jump up and begin dancing first would be a breach of
ta'arof. Often, the first few women invited state that they are unable to
dance: "Believe me, by God, I can not dance or I do not know how to
dance." These women, who truly protest too much, are generally among
the finest dancers, which the hostess knows well. She also knows that

they love to dance. If the hostess is successful, soon the dancing will be general and will last for some time. Unlike other ethnic groups, where such dancing might continue for long hours, an Iranian event is often interrupted at midnight for a large supper, as elaborate as possible, and generally served as a buffet. It is difficult to re-establish a mood for dancing after a heavy meal, and Iranians, who admire excellent conversation, generally end the evening in this way. Farewell taking and thanking the hosts for a lovely time can also be a lengthy affair under the unwritten rules of *ta'arof.*

If the party is fairly elaborate and alcoholic beverages are served, children are generally excluded. I know of families as rigorous as British Victorian and Regency society in observing the proper age for a young adult to appear at adult events, for these can serve as a means of identifying potential mates for children and close relatives. Families that I know well adhere strictly to these conventions. Children do, however, generally attend wedding parties and other large celebrations.

Choreophobia in Practice
How and where, then, can an individual be considered out-of-control or transgressive? To some degree, this depends upon the individual and the context. The first clue is when an individual uses overtly sexual or sensual movements not proper to their age, class, or gender. Certain pieces of music, such as *baba keram* or *shateri*, are known to symbolize, signal, or suggest such transgressive movement practices, and some young women avoid dancing when such selections are played, while others, more daring, perform happily.

The party was in full swing in the den and drinks were being liberally consumed when the deejay put on a recording of *bandari*, a dance genre from the Persian Gulf with heavy African influences in both the rhythmic patterns and dance movements. I could see the guests slowly parting and forming a circle to make room for a perspiring man in his shirt sleeves and loosened necktie who gyrated his hips and shimmied with startling expertise to the pounding rhythms. The guests, not knowing what to expect next, nervously watched and clapped, while the host, who was standing next to me, muttered, "he's drunk," and signaled quietly to the deejay to change the dance selection, thus diplomatically bringing the problematic performance to an end.

A second way of potentially incurring unfavorable comment is to dance in what appears to be a sexually provocative fashion in the view of spectators, especially unrelated male strangers. Strict Moslems observe conventions regarding the mixing of male and female members of society. (For a full discussion of this topic see Mernissi 1987, and for Iran, see Haeri 1989.) In such households, women do not appear before men who are not related in highly specific ways, such as husband or father-in-law. Echoes of such conventions continue to resonate even in the homes of the most Westernized families, where gender mixing began in the 1930s under the social engineering initiated by Reza Shah (1925-1941). For purposes of this study, I will conclude that such conventions are observed by some individuals, but in a looser fashion. That is to say, extremely close male friends of the family, especially older and middle aged men, are sometimes regarded as family, and the strict kinship relationships laid out by Haeri (1989) are observed in a more lax manner by most families in Southern California.

Dancing before strangers can be deemed inappropriate by conservative individuals and can occasionally cause some degree of scandal. Such choreophobic reactions by family members have caused several young Iranian women to withdraw from AVAZ. Censorious views can be modified or quelled, however, if the individual is able to turn such a performance into humor, which Iranians enjoy immensely. Most young women who are unmarried or recently married prudently avoid dancing in a transgressive manner unless among close intimates of the same sex, whereas, as in many other societies in which the behavior of young women is closely monitored, older women have some degree of freedom, which a few are not loathe to exercise, as I will show.

One young woman informed me that she, as a feminist, refused to dance in front of men "who just want to look at my body," while her sister declared, "I don't care. Let them look, I love to dance" (Personal interview February 2, 1996).

Iranian attitudes regarding the propriety of dancing do not seem to differ widely between Moslems and non-Moslems. Choreophobic views concerning dance were demonstrated in a largely Jewish gathering a few weeks following the first event I described earlier.

At a recent party, attended by several members of the Iranian Jewish community of Los Angeles, as well as a few Moslems, the hostess called upon several of her guests to perform, a situation I had experienced often in such gatherings. The guests included men and women, young and old—all dressed in the height of fashion to match the elegance of this Beverly Hills penthouse. The clothing worn ranged from formal evening dresses to the ubiquitous, but chic and expensively-cut black suits favored by many Iranian women to eliminate the expense of wearing a new gown to each of the numerous parties they attend, consisting of coat and skirt (rarely pants), with expensive jewelry to match. Iranian women often own extensive jewelry collections, featuring genuine emeralds, rubies, pearls, and turquoises set in elaborate 24 carat gold. When I lived in Iran, I was struck by the size and extent of such collections, but in Southern California, for reasons of security and changing tastes, women wear more discreet jewelry in public.

To establish a convivial ambience, the hostess turned out the lights, lighted several candles and recited a piece of well-known classical poetry which everyone warmly applauded as her contribution to the evening's entertainment. She then turned to a chicly dressed woman, well into her eighties, deferring to her advanced age and social position and expecting her to recite some well-known sonnet. The elderly guest, however, instead began to recite quietly from the *bazi-ha-ye namayeshi* (women's theatre games), and as she warmed up, the verses and body language grew increasingly earthy and bawdy. This unexpected turn from classical poetry to a more earthy form clearly startled the hostess, but the other guests were delighted and enthusiastically encouraged the senior performer to grow bolder by clapping to the rhythm and serving as a response chorus. The hostess, noting my presence and clearly worried about what kind of impression such a performance was going to create, sat next to the elderly performer and attempted to restrain her by, as politely as possible, firmly placing her hands on the performer's shoulders. The elderly lady, thoroughly enjoying the sensation she was creating, shrugged off the hands of the agitated hostess, and with a roguish gleam in her eyes, secure in her position as a very senior personage of impeccable social standing, grew even more outrageous. She moved her shoulders alternately back and forth, gestured coquettishly with her hands, made her eyebrows dance, and mimed some of the verses (see Shay 1995b). The more we all laughed, clapped, and responded, the more the performer recited, and the more expansive and bold the movements grew, seen especially in her facial expressions with raised eyebrows and picturesque and arch moues. Such behavior in a younger, socially less-secure individual would have been immediately deemed out-of-control by many of the same audience members who were frankly enjoying this highly transgressive performance, which it surely was for the highly embarrassed hostess, whose efforts to suppress it came to naught. (Lest the reader assume that I am describing some kind of general prudery, I might add that it was not long after several of us had contributed a song or performance on the piano or *tar*, that many of the elegantly attired guests, seemingly less musically inclined, contributed to the jollity of the evening by telling many explicit and raw jokes with detailed physical references to sex, that would have been considered outrageous in a similar evening at a similar American gathering. This was by no means the first party at which this occurred. [Personal observation: August 17, 1996]. The movements of the elderly performer were actually minimal, and performed seated, but the reaction of the hostess indicated, that in her opinion that in this context, they constituted potentially out-of-control behavior. Nevertheless, in my opinion, the elderly performer, who exploited her high social position and advanced age, performed in what was clearly, for both herself and the highly-delighted onlookers, a highly transgressive and outrageous fashion.

A third event I recently attended was an Iranian senior citizen's gathering in Irvine, California, to which I had been invited as a guest speaker (Sept. 18, 1996). Among the more than two hundred smartly-dressed attendees, women outnumbered men by about two to one. The recreation room which they had secured for their monthly gatherings in a senior citizen's center, was very large and the crowd sat around tables that each seated eight to ten individuals. The hostess had told me that the attendees entertain themselves and that generally a considerable amount of dancing, singing, and other forms of diverting activity occur. I was not disappointed, for on this evening, in addition to the de rigueur poetry recitals, the dancing was plentiful and diverse in individual styles. (These women danced in the manner I laid out in Chapter One, within many idiosyncratic stylistic frameworks.) Several women were enticed onto the floor by the hostess more than once during the evening.

Even in such large gatherings, *ta'arof* is generally observed, as it was on this occasion. The hostess busied herself keeping the program running with the aid of the well-known and brilliant actor. He introduced the guests and performers, while the hostess darted about the room encouraging people to dance. Her efforts were aimed almost entirely at the female portion of the audience. Several women were enticed onto the floor and performed in a generally normative and pleasant manner. This consisted largely of the graceful use of hands and arms, as well as the foot work which I detailed in Chapter One. None of these dancers utilized provocative movements of the torso, such as *gheir* (see footnote 4).

Stylistically, watching these senior women dance confirmed that the older generation uses torso articulation (*gheir*) far less than younger dancers. Their movements of the hips resulted from the movements of knees and feet. The older women concentrated on intricate arm, hand, finger, and shoulder gestures, maintaining the torso largely immobile. Jamal observed that this stylistic difference is not merely a matter of generational differences, but also class difference, and women who wish to avoid being labeled *jelf* (vulgar) or *sabok* (light) shun public display of overt pelvic and torso movements and concentrate on hands and arms (September 22, 1996). I feel that the generational differences may also be reflected in the varied experiences younger women have in Southern California, where many, but by no means all, of them feel that they may act more freely because of their dance experiences in discotheques and school functions. Unlike the younger women, the dancing experiences of the majority of women over 50 has been generally confined to private contexts. Certainly, Western popular dance styles have, to some degree, had some impact on the way in which many young, and a few older, Iranian-Americans dance. Egyptian belly dancing, seen at parties, in films, and cafes, has also had some influence on individual dancers, although attempts at imitation are not deep, since the dancers rarely receive formal training in that specific technique. Iranian night clubs in Southern California often feature belly dancers.

There seems to be an almost unwritten rule that the better the dancer's ability, the more she will protest that she can not dance. Two or three individuals required little encouragement, one of whom was one of the most inept movers I have ever seen at an Iranian gathering. She moved aimlessly, her arm and hand gestures were not clearly articulated; and she seemed unable to rotate her hands or wrists in even the most elemental manner—a rarity among Iranians, who learn this basic movement as they learn their language. Instead of the use of energy demonstrated by a skillful performer, she moved her hands and arms in a listless, unfocused fashion, her gestures without geometric or aesthetic substance. She danced almost throughout the evening, oblivious to being pointedly ignored by the audience. She turned slowly and without purpose, moving in a manner that suggested a psychologically disturbed person. I was seated with a former judge who wryly observed that "she did not dance well," to which I replied, as diplomatically as possible, that she showed "great enthusiasm" to stay so long on the dance floor. Among the several dancers at this same event, there were two other interesting dancers from the perspective of this study: one transgressive, one verging on out-of-control.

The latter woman, unlike the majority, who wore fashionable suits, and some of the even more conservative, who were dressed in head scarves, wore a see-through, short dress of chiffon-like material, well above her knees, which visually placed her apart from the others because her attire was perceived as inappropriate for a woman of her advanced years. While the inept lady had jumped out on the floor first, this woman, requiring no prompting from the hostess, danced out from the other side of the large room. She picked up her short skirt in both hands and began flipping it up in the air—a gesture I had never seen in the social dancing of this dance genre. Such a movement seemed more appropriate to a professional dancer from one of the former establishments of the Lalezar district of Tehran. People tittered, and reacted nervously because they seemed uncertain about how high she would lift her skirt and if they whether they would see her underwear. This was a gathering of the elderly, and although they were generally indulgent with their age mates, this woman clearly made many people distinctly uncomfortable.

The transgressive dancer, on the other hand, delighted the audience. She was an outstanding dancer, Mrs. Elaheh (pseudonym), whom I estimated to be in her fifties. She performed very transgressively, to everyone's delight: *shateri, majlesi,* and witty imitations of Indian classical dance, Egyptian belly dance, and Kurdish dance, the last three without music. The actor, acting as master of ceremonies and well-known in his own right, danced the male-associated dance, *shateri,* with her, and provided her with the props of a man's hat, coat, and large kerchief supplied by audience members. During this *shateri* dance, wearing an ele-

gant evening dress of heavy ivory colored satin, she performed outrageous, super-macho movements, such as flexing arm muscles and slap-
ping her hand on her chest, that had the crowd cheering and clapping.
She called out several vulgar expressions common to lower class men,
pulled on an imaginary moustache, and threw several naughty asides to
the delighted onlookers. In contrast to the first woman I described, Mrs.
Elaheh's movements were forceful, energetic, and focused. When she
danced in a female style, between her selections, her hands sculpted intricate, geometric figures, holding her audience spellbound. Several
audience members made a point of coming up to me to extol Mrs. Elaheh's obvious choreographic excellence, an opinion with which I enthusiastically concurred.

Her professionalism (she later told me that she teaches Iranian folk
and solo improvised dance in Europe, where she lives) demonstrated the
difference between potentially out-of-control and transgressive: the
audience was comfortable with what they could expect to happen. Each
transgressive movement was, to a large extent, predictable, while the
woman in the see-through dress, whose movements were considerably
more minimal, made many people uneasy because they had no idea
what she might do next, creating considerable tension in the gathering.

Generally, in each of these three events, elderly women seemed able
to negotiate the currents of choreophobia successfully, although the elderly woman in the short dress and Jaleh, a much younger woman described in the first event, were unable to do so. Reactions ranged from
amused to outraged, but there is no question that Jaleh's performance
created a minor sensation, causing some individuals to view her in a
new and unflattering light. As is the case with many societies, in Iranian-American society, senior women are allowed more latitude than
younger, still sexually available women. Senior women are not perceived as sexually threatening, whereas younger women, in the eyes of
Moslem society, may tear the fabric of society by overt sexual display,
for which dancing provides a unique opportunity. In Islam, both men
and women are believed to possess powerful, potentially out-of-control
sexuality, which is legitimate in legally sanctioned relationships such as
marriage arrangements of various sorts. Sexual segregation is considered the best means of controlling this powerful force, which has the
power to destroy an improperly regulated society. Thus, the behavior of
younger women, because it is considered potentially more dangerous
than that of senior women, is more carefully scrutinized and regulated
by family and society.[6]

Elements and Variables of Choreophobia
When considering how behavior might be regarded as transgressive or
out-of-control, I earlier referred to its complexity. At this point it would
be useful to look at some of those elements that I assert can contribute to

choreophobia and their variables. These are, among possible others, gender, age, social class, religion, context, and a last variable and random element, which I can only describe as "individual." I now discuss each of these elements and variables and their effect on how an individual might be regarded as dancing in a transgressive or out-of-control fashion. Often, several elements must be considered together, because, for example, the element of age sometimes mitigates that of class. Thus, the compound of different elements can aid the researcher in understanding how a specific dance performance might be considered transgressive or out-of-control.

To be perceived as transgressive or out-of-control, an individual must possess at least the minimal choreographic skills to commit such an act. The movements which I detailed in Chapter One and which most competent dancers have acquired, are secondary to the elements I detail below. It is important to remind the reader that while dance is often perceived in a negative way, many individuals are also highly attracted to perform and/or watch it in the right circumstances and contexts, thus complicating the description and analysis I present. Poets extol its virtues and grace by comparing the movement of flowers in the wind to dance, but it still may not be acceptable for that same poet's daughter to dance publicly.

Gender. The findings of this study show that women are more readily perceived than men as transgressive or out-of-control. This not only reflects their social status vis-a-vis men, but also the fact that, in my experience, they dance more readily than men. As I mentioned earlier, Islam recognizes female sexuality as equal to that of the male; however, in a society where a female's physical virginity is expected and prized upon marriage, women's behavior is far more scrutinized than male behavior and for a far longer time. As in many societies in which a double standard obtains, gender is only one element, and Iranian women possess a range of freedom depending on the individual. To universally depict them as downtrodden chattel is a highly orientalist cliché. The reality of sexual inequality is far more complex, and as I demonstrate, is colored by elements such as age, social class, context, and individual character traits.

Dancing that makes a young woman appear *sabok* (light) or *jelf* (vulgar), that is executed in a manner perceived as sexually overt in mixed company, potentially damages her reputation, often making it more difficult for her to find a suitable husband. Transgressive dancing symbolizes a woman who is out-of-control and brings dishonor to her family, examples of which are available in many Iranian films. Overtly sexual movements by women or girls in the prime of sexuality can be perceived as out-of-control. Most of the situations that I present in this study in which individuals were considered by those around them to be transgressive or out-of-control involved women, although men, such as

the one I described who had had too much to drink, can also be perceived as out-of-control. Several young, unmarried women and their
parents expressed considerable trepidation regarding dancing in certain
contexts, particularly in public performances, for fear that "they would
never find a proper husband." Therefore, women's dancing is always
closer to the potentially out-of-control end of the normative-
transgressive-out-of-control continuum that I theorize. While this study
focuses on negative images found in solo improvised dance, I must also
emphasize that dancing which is perceived as especially beautiful,
graceful, and modest can be positively apprehended, and may, to some
degree, enhance a woman or girl's image.

When men perform the dance, as long as their movements are not
effeminate, or if effeminate, are grotesquely humorous, or in a manner
similar to that which Cowan makes clear in her study of gender and
dance in Northern Greece, in which the movements are expressive of a
super machismo, safely satirizing the feminine by performing female
identified-movements with no tarnish left on their own unquestionably
masculine bodies, they are admired and encouraged and their performance is enjoyed by both observers and participants (Cowan 1990:
Chapter Six and elsewhere). Nevertheless, the danger of being labeled
effeminate deters many young men from dancing "too gracefully." At
least three male public performers in Southern California create gossip
regarding their sexuality because of their dancing and performance
styles, which are characterized and condemned by many as "*jelf*" (vulgar). Cowan characterizes the dance in Northern Greece as "ambivalent
in a distinctly gender-specific way" (1990:188). A similar situation pre-
vails in Iranian society, but even so, certain individuals in the Iranian-
American community, both male and female, can also perform this
dance and be impervious to criticism (personal observation). The young
woman from AVAZ who performed a transgressive movement, which I
described earlier, escaped censure because of her obvious innocence,
and because of the context: she was among close friends who knew her
spotless reputation well. Had she performed in this manner in a more
public context, eyebrows would have been raised.

In 1992, I planned to stage the women's theatrical plays, *bazi-ha-ye
namayeshi*, which can become earthy and transgressive, qualities I
wished to convey in these performances. I offered one of the roles to a
young Iranian woman in my company. At first she seemed pleased, but
then her face fell and she wailed, "If I do that in public, I'll never get a
husband!" Indeed, her fears of being perceived in this way were soon
borne out, for during one of the performances (August 21,1993), an irate
Iranian woman came backstage to wrathfully demand that I inform the
audience that "not all Iranian women do that."

Age. The element of age often mitigates other elements, such as
gender or class. In Iranian society, elders are generally highly respected,

regarded as wise and deferred to in many ways. For this reason they carry a certain authority, and while an elderly individual may dance in a transgressive way, they are rarely considered to be out-of-control. The very young and very old, those perceived of as pre- or post sexual, do not pose a threat of potentially out-of-control sexuality. Individuals of both sexes, but particularly females, seem to relish dancing when they are considered, in Peirce's term, "post-sexual" (1993:23), which permits them the opportunity to kick over the traces. In my observations, many of those who cast discretion to the winds and performed in a transgressive manner, some more overtly than others, were elderly women: in these cases there was no fear of not finding a husband or being considered *sabok* or *jelf*. These performances were considered fun by most of the observers. Older men rarely danced in any public context, although some danced in "safe" contexts or showed me their choreographic abilities in private. For many older men, dancing holds connotations of undignified and unseemly behavior.

Social Class. A third element that enters into the discussion of transgressive and out-of-control behavior is social class. Generally, the higher the social class, the more readily an individual who dances in a manner beyond the normative is determined to be transgressive. For example, a shah, despite orientalist choreographic depictions to the contrary, may under no circumstances dance.[7]

Briefly, because a thorough analysis is beyond the scope of this study, social class in Iranian society is complex and resists easy characterization, and Western models are not applicable to the Iranian case, where numerous urban socio-economic strata commingle with tribal and rural sedentary groups, each with its own special socioeconomic categories and niches. These so-called classes were always highly fluid, to some degree, which reflected the widening educational, economic, and professional opportunities that characterized post World War II Iran. The old, dismissive saw that "there are only the rich and poor," which I have often heard regarding Middle East countries, will simply not characterize Iranian society. As an example, in pre-Revolutionary Iran, one found the old landed gentry (*zamindar*) class, the bazaar merchants (*to-jar-e bazar* or *bazari-ha*), and the *nouveaux riches* (*tazeh be douran rasideh*), as three general rich, upper classes. Each of these classes had its own ethos and life styles. But I also knew famous artists, intellectuals, and literati who did not comfortably fit into any of the social and economic niches described in the numerous studies of Iranian society. Abrahamian (1989) demonstrates how class played a role in the composition of the revolutionary cadres that brought down the Pahlavi dynasty. (Other works detailing the social structure of Iran and the Iranians of Southern California are: Fathi 1991, Kelley et al. 1993, Moaddel 1993, Parsa 1989, Paidar 1995.)

Many of the old landed gentry and *nouveaux riches*, as well as numerous individuals from upper-middle and middle class professional, entrepreneurial, bureaucratic, military, literary, communications, and artistic occupations and groupings, form the majority of Iranian immigrants in Southern California. Bazaar merchants, rural populations, and urban underclasses are not represented in the Southern California community in any significant number. Furthermore, class differences are increasingly blurred in Southern California because educational opportunities and expanded professional and economic advantages for women allow more individuals to move into higher economic brackets. More and more frequently, young people are making their own marital choices, which include non-Iranians, further breaking down old socio-economic barriers. Also, some families and individuals were forced to leave Iran with nothing or very little and had to start afresh. These individuals, like many immigrant groups before them, proudly assert how they became "self-made" successes because they have achieved wealthy or upper-middle class status in the United States.

As a general rule, the higher the social position, the more difficult it is for a man or a woman to dance in an improper context. In a recent party in Los Angeles, a woman of high social status who performed *shateri* was not condemned because she danced in any overt style, but because of her social class. A woman guest at the party asked wonderingly, "why did she have to do that? She's a dentist!" (Personal interview: March 30, 1995).

In 1996 rumors were spread, and it briefly became a topic on the radio, that the pretender to the throne was seen dancing at the wedding of his cousin. Even though this was a private affair, several people calling in to the radio considered it unseemly, undignified, or even scandalous that the future shah should conduct himself in such a fashion, while others expressed the opinion that it was his right to dance as a celebration of his cousin's future happiness, and especially since it occurred in a private venue.[8]

My experience has demonstrated that men of high social standing in particular consider it déclassé and "dangerous" to be seen dancing in a public place. Women of high social status seem more relaxed, but nevertheless many feel that there is a loss of dignity involved in dancing in the wrong contexts. This suggests that women are held to somewhat different standards than men, and they are also generally more relaxed about dancing in contexts they regard as safe.

Religiosity. Highly religious people often deem dance as improper or sinful for Moslems. As I pointed out in Chapter Three, Ayatollah Khomeini, among others, condemned it. The famous composer/musician Hossein Alizadeh, during a talk in which he extolled the Islamic regime's support of serious Iranian classical music, was asked by an Iranian woman audience member, "What is the situation with dance?" The first time she asked the question, he ignored her. The questioner, however, was persistent and asked the question again, to which he replied, "It's there, but," he said firmly and coldly, "I am here to discuss music."

Nevertheless, in certain contexts, even a pious individual may dance. Jamal recalls an aunt who prayed five times a day, but she could not resist participating in the women's *bazi-ha*, even while chiding those around her for being ungodly. (See Shay 1995b.) "The mentality with some of these people is that if they cover one eye with their *chador* (veil) and watch the dancing it is less sinful, and so they watch, and enjoy, the dancing in this way" (December 10, 1996). This point was underscored by the presence of a young student who wore *hejab* (proper Islamic covering) and attended my class to watch her friends, but never danced herself.

Since this study addresses the issue of choreophobia in Southern California, where the vast majority of people are not practicing or strict Moslems, I briefly mention this as an element, one that I am aware of in wider Iranian society, but not one which I encounter often in the diaspora community. If one goes to Little Tehran, one occasionally encounters women who wear *ru-sari* (head scarf) or *hejab*, and who are, presumably, devout to some degree, and therefore such an element can not be totally discounted. However, I have only interviewed two such individuals, one of whom I helped with a homework assignment, and who would not shake hands with me (because I was a non-related male), but both came to our concert and loved it. "I may be religious (*mazhabi*) but that does not mean that I am fanatic (*ta'sob*)," (Maryam [pseudonym] personal communication: March 2, 1997). This merely serves to emphasize that the investigator may not essentialize all practicing Moslems, non-practicing Moslems, or any other group, as perceiving dance in a unified fashion.

Context. The context of a dance event forms an important element in the consideration of transgression. These contexts range from very small intimate, private all-female, all-male or family social gatherings, to large picnics with thousands of people in attendance. In between these contexts, one can attend a party with thirty guests with family and some close friends, a larger party with one hundred guests, a wedding with a thousand guests, or a picnic with a few hundred individuals. The more private, en famille, the event, the "safer" it is considered. I have seen many individuals dance within a small "safe" atmosphere among close friends and/or family who would not dance in any public context such as a picnic. Clearly, the late shah's son considered himself protected from criticism by his "private" environment, i.e., an intimate wedding party. Young unmarried women happily dance in my class or in a family gathering, but will not appear on the stage, no matter how decorous or proper the circumstances. The same is true in Iran, although conservative individuals are often censorious, and an upper class individual could lose face if he or she performs in the wrong context.

Individual Characteristics. Individual character is a random dynamic in any analysis of how a particular dance performance is perceived. I have often noticed that no matter how an investigator, including myself, wishes to lay out clear parameters for a study like this, there exist certain individuals whose personalities contain characteristics that are often difficult to assess that permit them to trespass all of the observer's "rules" and carry off the most transgressive style of dancing without incurring social censure. This issue of individual variance, or agency, is one that many social scientists appear to grapple with in peeling away layers of human behavior for purposes of analysis. For example, Bennett M. Berger, sociology scholar, notes wryly:

> Now if this image of more or less probablisitically determined individual choosers offends you, don't cry reductionism or oversimplification and moan about deterministic efforts to reduce human complexity. Look for sustenance to the people who fall into the categories of unexplained variance, and who therefore may be regarded as having outwitted—at least so far—the voracity of social structure. (Berger 1995:138)

In other words, I am attempting to account for individual variance without reducing all behavior to what Berger labels "micro-interatctions," instead of factoring these variables into a "macro-system" of choreophobia (Berger 1995:139). It is simply undeniable that certain individuals manage to manipulate the macro-system of choreophobia through micro-interactions and avoid its negative consequences. In fact, these individuals are sometimes admired for successfully circumventing and flouting societal rules. One may think of Ronald Reagan's "Teflon" nickname to imagine this quality. I shall term this characteristic the "Teflon factor" for purposes of this study.

Many years ago, during my student years at UCLA, I had two close Iranian friends, one male and one female, both of whom had Teflon characters. When Nilufar, a young, brilliant student with an enormous sense of humor, who came from a highly aristocratic background, rose to dance at a student party, I was considerably taken aback. Her performance was highly skilled and somewhat transgressive for the context, and even more surprising, everyone was delighted. When I asked a mutual friend about the performance, she shrugged and explained, "That's Nilufar," meaning that because it was Nilufar, her performance was perfectly acceptable. My other friend, Hossein, danced in the grotesque fashion of an infirm old man, which never failed to amuse everyone. He was constantly begged to perform. As a highly skilled athlete, he might, in the ordinary way, have risked his dignity and reputation, but because he was Hossein and everyone adored him, his performance was always acceptable, and, in fact, enhanced his reputation as "a great guy" (*bache-ye khubi-ye*) in the Iranian community.

While difficult and elusive to characterize, individual personality traits and character can not be discounted as important variables in how different individuals are judged by those around them. The individual who escapes censure is often considered extremely witty, entertaining, or perhaps naive, while another individual of the same sex, age, and social standing, in the same or a similar context, can arouse unfavorable reactions. Two women and a man I currently know push the borders of choreophobia, but somehow are never censured. All of them are older (forty-five to sixty-five years old), but nevertheless, when they throw caution to the wind and dance where others fear to, they are admired for their presumption and audacity. Mrs. "Elaheh," whom I described earlier, who was dressed in an obviously expensive evening gown, performed in a transgressive manner. Everyone admired and encouraged her for no discernible reason other than that she radiated enormous self-confidence, charm, and elegance. Unlike the unfortunate young dentist I described earlier, she wore a good deal of Teflon.

Part of this perception, as was the case with Mrs. "Elaheh" or Hossein, may lie within a particular individual's extraordinary ability to dance; their talent serves as a factor. Their extreme technical prowess over the dance movements to some degree symbolized their control— they could not therefore go "out-of-control." In my experience, most dancers have adequate rather than extraordinary ability. As I pointed out earlier, and underscoring the concept of choreophobia, with rare exception, when asked to talk about dance or invited to do so in a social context, every individual, no matter how proficient, denies his or her ability to dance in an elaborate display of *ta'arof*.

Normative, Transgressive, Out-of-Control

At this point in the discussion I would like to look at William O. Beeman's study of Iranian communicative processes to see how the categories I theorize—normative, transgressive, and out-of-control — can be conceptualized in Iranian dance events. I also look at Jane K. Cowan's important study of dance events in Northern Greece, which highlights issues similar to those raised in this study. These two works contain analogous concepts and have a direct impact on the way I attempt to theorize dance in a choreophobic context. The difference is that I am theorizing three states: normative, transgressive, and potentially out-of-control, while Cowan and Beeman seem to suggest only the existence of normative behavior and its contrasting state, which they discuss and characterize in different ways.

Beeman's Iranian Communication Model

In Chapter One I attempted to demonstrate how the performative act of dancing has an aesthetic component. It also contains an intensely social aspect. Beeman, a scholar of Iranian communicative phenomena, posits two poles of speech communication: "appropriateness" and "effectiveness."

> In contrasting appropriateness and effectiveness, then, the former can be seen as the ability to move toward predictable usage and the latter to vary from predictable usage in order to establish a revised framework for interpreting the elements of interaction. (1986: 9)

Beeman's terminology corresponds to mine in that "appropriateness" is what I term "normative," i.e., the dancer performs in an expected and predictable manner. His notion of "effectiveness" in speech communication corresponds to my concept of "transgressive" behavior in dance. In this case, as in Beeman's, the performer utilizes deliberate, perhaps provocative, movements to create an "effect." I would, however, add that communication in dance events can further break down, and therefore, in addition to the two categories that Beeman identifies in speech communication, I add a third, potentially "out-of-control," category. In speech this might be equated with a person who loses control and suddenly uses all of the words he or she was socialized never to use, thus causing a potential rupture in communication. In the convoluted traffic of Tehran, one may observe such breakdowns in speech communication on a daily basis. In Iranian dance events, a person who loses control is one who disrupts the event with the potential of causing a loss of reputation for his or her self and the family, or some other social sanction and possible censure and disapproval.

The reason that I place these terms on a continuum is that they are relative. That is to say, what one individual Iranian or Azerbaijani might consider as normative dance behavior or performance, another individual might look upon as transgressive, or even out-of-control. These considerations would depend not only on the background and experience of the observer, but also the individual who is dancing and the context for that performance. I wish to stress that I am attempting to ascertain the responses and reactions of Iranians, rather than my own personal opinions. In eliciting opinions, I interview and speak to groups and individuals watching dance performances to learn what ranges of reaction are expressed.

Let me again emphasize that the dancing in most participatory events is usually normative. As I explained, individuals may be found performing a solo, or small groups may participate at the same time. In this latter case, everyone is dancing individually in the dance space, although occasionally, a person will dance in reference to "a partner" or, more rarely, two or more "partners." The movements are still individual, spontaneous and improvised, not coordinated, although attempts at "mirroring," attempting to dance like one's "partner" or coordinate one's movement with that of the "partner," also occur. Shalinsky relates similar constellations of dancers among Afghan Uzbeks (Personal communication: July 20, 1995), and I witnessed a Tajik wedding in Dushanbe (November 6, 1986) which resembled those I had seen in Tehran ten years before and in Los Angeles on a monthly basis. Because of the possibility of multiple dancers, each dancing idiosyncratically, one might expect to witness a variety of styles and modes of performance, including transgressive and out-of-control, occurring simultaneously. However, if outrageous behavior occurs, most dancers make room for these dancers, quickly forming an audience and framing such behavior.

I wish to make a clear distinction between what I label as transgressive and potentially out-of-control behavior in this dance context. The major difference that I posit between the two categories is that transgressive behavior is always planned, even when the dance is improvised. This assumes, as Beeman suggests, that the performers have "knowledge of their social environment, control of their linguistic repertoire, and some knowledge of the probable effects of their use of one form as opposed to another" (ibid.). The transgressive dance performance may, in its movements and gestures, be considered far more outrageous by the viewer than out-of-control behavior, but it is expected, whereas out-of-control dancing is always potential and unexpected. I argue that out-of-control behavior is contextual; that is, such behavior is often less extreme or sensual than transgressive dancing movements, but the social status, and the sex of the individual and the location of the performance will be the determining factors, rather than the movements, for how Iranian individuals perceive this behavior. In Cowan's case study of Aphrodite, whereas Cowan saw nothing "extreme," the Greek participants in the event described her transgressive behavior as "the way in which Aphrodite performed," when in actual fact it was Aphrodite's social position as a single woman from another town that caused her to be ostracized. As we have seen, in Iranian contexts, gender, age, social class, and context, as well as the individual's personality traits, all have an impact on such judgments.

It is doubtful that the observer can always analyze or theorize the reasons why an individual might perform in an out-of-control fashion. Dance scholar P. Sterling Stuckey makes an attempt, however, which is partially applicable in the Iranian case. He states, "For in the dance, such is the speed with which the mind can work, and the body respond to it, that the time between thought and action all but disappears" (1993:55). I indicated in Chapter One that the rapidity with which an Iranian dancer improvises generally leaves little time for premeditated planning. This factor contributes to the uncertainty that an individual faces when rising to dance in any situation, especially when strangers are present. Other factors also contribute to the uncertainty: in most

social situations, the dancer does not know what music will be played at
a particular event. In Iranian contexts, each occurrence must be analyzed separately, for it is unique in terms of context, social status, age
and gender of the individual, the number of other people present, and
other highly specific contingencies.

In certain performance contexts, not to perform transgressively
would be the exception, which is why I wish to examine the whole participatory—performance continuum that Nahachewsky (1995) posits.
For example, in the *ru-howzi* or *siyah-bazi* theatre (detailed in the following chapter), the black-face servant figure tempts the *hajji* to dance:
he juts his buttocks suggestively toward the *hajji* as he dances. The *hajji*, seemingly mesmerized by the compelling rhythm, also begins to
dance, ultimately presenting his backside to the black-face clown. In
doing so he is feminized by the clown and, in Bakhtin's terms, the world
is turned upside-down. I will analyze the performances, and the questions of gender and ethnicity that they raise in these specific theatrical
contexts, in Chapter Six.

In these examples of transgressive behavior I wish to stress that the
performances are generally for fun and entertainment. Historically, this
was a fact often missed by many European travelers (1500 - 1940) who
witnessed and described many professional dance performances, and it
is still true today. These travelers almost universally condemned the
loose morals of the Persians. Transgressive dancing can present sensual
or sexually provocative aspects of movement, as these travel accounts
suggest. In this sense it is most often connected with commercial sex,
and it is the movements and gestures of this style of dancing which, in
my opinion, create the negative symbol which dance represents to many
people in this area.

There are certainly parallels between the way aspects of this dance
form and flamenco, tango, and jazz, for example, are regarded in their
respective societies. Flamenco scholar Timothy Mitchell observes that
"Spaniards concerned about the moral tenor of their society came to
look upon deep song (flamenco *canto jondo* or *hondo*) with deep con-
tempt. There is much to be learned from people who find certain musical styles transgressive and threatening" (1994: 45). The periodic attempts to ban this dance tradition in the Iranian culture sphere, including
those attempts made in present-day Iran, as well as the manner in which
many Iranians regard this genre, demonstrate the similarities with the
way turn-of-the-century moralists in the United States reacted to jazz.
"American jazz is best understood by studying the reaction of those who
were hostile toward it. Alarmed musicians, clergymen, journalists, and
even philosophers heard the new music as sensuous and indecent, suitable only for houses of prostitution; its primitive rhythms aroused animal passions; jazz embodied a spirit of lawlessness and a general revolt
against authority" (ibid).

For an excellent parallel example in an Iranian context, in his famous *Kashf ol-asrar* (Discovery of Secrets), Ayatollah Ruhollah Khomeini, later spiritual and temporal ruler of Iran, proclaimed that "Music which encourages the spirit of passion and love among the youth is forbidden in the shariat and should be taken out of school programs" (1971: 313-14).

Out-of-control behavior is always potential in a participatory event. It can occur if an individual who is dancing is perceived to have lost control of him- or herself, usually by performing in what is perceived by onlookers as a transgressive manner. Men occasionally transgress during dancing if they have had too much to drink. Jamal stated that, "it would be rare to have an event in which someone did not dance in a way that was considered transgressive or out-of-control" (Personal communication: March 20, 1996).

I have seen a woman from a good family get up on the top of a table to dance at a large party in a hotel, attended by over a thousand guests, considerably shocking some of those around her, while amusing others. Several people made negative comments, and the woman's reputation (and that of her family) suffered, at least to some degree (January 1990).

Those who are strict in their moral standards sometimes call out-of-control behavior in dance *fetneh* (disturbance). The terms *sabok* (light, unserious) or, worse, *jelf* (vulgar) are also popularly used as adjectives applying to people who dance transgressively or in a flamboyant or vulgar fashion. *Fetneh* is the most serious of these terms and, in an Islamic context, attaches to behavior that is conceived of as threatening to the social fabric, and, according to many scholars, constitutes the underlying reason for sexual segregation in Islamic societies (see Mernissi 1975 for a full discussion of this issue).

I argue that among other considerations, the context and the social standing of the individual are crucial. Such perceived out-of-control behavior can damage reputations, lower social status, and in the case of the unmarried, make the finding of a proper and desirable mate more difficult. The family of the transgressor is also held accountable for allowing a family member to exhibit such behavior in a public space. This establishes dance as a negative activity for many, especially outside of carefully regulated private venues. And yet, certain individuals, in spite of class, status, gender, or age, manage to defy all of the unspoken rules of proper behavior and perform in an almost identical fashion as one who has been condemned as wanton or out-of-control, without incurring criticism. As I pointed out earlier, some aspect of their specific personality, often advanced age, seems to enable them to break the rules with impunity.

I believe that the identification of transgressive and out-of-control behavior provides fresh insights into Iranian views of appropriate and inappropriate behavior that will also identify Iranian notions of social,

class, and gender roles, and the types of behavior which, in part, identify
them. These studies also enable the interested scholar to better understand how "choreophobic" attitudes are expressed individually and socially, as well as organizationally, that is, official governmental reactions.

Cowan's Study of Dance in Northern Greece

I primarily cite the differences between the 1993 study conducted by
Jane K. Cowan in Northern Greece and my study of solo improvised
dance in the Iranian culture sphere, since her study, more than any other
that I have found, in some ways parallels the observations which I present here. Cowan's study looks at the ways in which Greek society is
gendered, and dance events are her focus because they act as a major
arena where men and women gather together socially and act out what it
means to be male or female in that society. During such events an individual, particularly a female, may transgress and ruin her social status.

Although my study focuses on many of the same questions posed in
Cowan's, it also raises different questions. Like Cowan (although she
phrases it somewhat differently than I do), I am concerned with issues of
transgressive and out-of-control behavior, how they are viewed by individual members of Iranian society, and what their potential social reper-
cussions might be. There are, however, major differences between
Greek and Iranian societies, and these are reflected in the format that
Cowan chose for her study compared to the approach that I use. The
situation is also different in that in Iran, dancing as an activity is regarded with great ambiguity, while in Greece, the activity of dancing,
per se, generally constitutes a positive activity that is considered an important part of the communal social life that everyone participates in at
some point in his or her life.

In Cowan's study (and, indeed, from my own numerous personal
observations), in Greek dance events, the participants go to dance as
their primary activity. As in English, the Greeks may "go to a dance."
It is a positive activity that almost everyone seems to enjoy (although, as
in many societies, certain individuals or groups, such as elderly wid-
owed women, rarely attend specific types of events). In general, people
freely get up to dance within what I would call the framework of an unspoken, tacit etiquette, similar to that of the choreophobia I analyze for
this study. Unspoken rules for behavior exist, and most members of the
society follow them as they do the rules of grammar they internalized as
children. In a Greek context, this would include such questions as
where to place oneself in the line of dancers and, in certain events, if a
man pays the orchestra for a *zembekiko* (a solo dance), only he, or his
close friends, dance. (This custom is also common in Greek *tavernas*
[nightclubs] in the United States). As I detailed earlier, until an Iranian
event is in high gear, following the performance of several individuals

or perhaps a group of dancers, or numerous entreaties by a hostess, and perhaps not even then, individuals do not freely get up and dance, with the possible exception of large public events for which there is no host or hostess.

A second point of departure of my study from that of Cowan is that I place more emphasis on movement and its description. Concerning movement description, Cowan states:

> This study...is relatively unconcerned with delineating the structural or morphological features of particular dance forms or of dance more generally or with issues of classification...Though it is impossible to understand So-hoian dance-events without knowing something about the forms and the social and historical connotations of particular dances, the analytical level here is that of the ever...Detailed descriptions or analysis of steps, body movements, or the structural aspects of individual dances are, for the most part, not directly relevant to the basic questions explored here. (1990: 18)

In her analysis of how "Aphrodite" transgressed (1990: all of Chapter Eight), the reader is left with the question of whether the specific movements which Aphrodite performed caused her to be perceived as out-of-control, or whether it was the social context and her particular status. This chapter forms Cowan's longest and most detailed case study of the consequences of losing control, a danger that Cowan asserts all women in this society face if they veer from the slippery slide of normative behavior. As an investigator of dance, I wanted to know specifically, in terms of movement, what had distinguished Aphrodite's transgressive performance, one that had, in the words of some of Cowan's informants, "gone too far" (1990: 219) and was "sexually wanton, out of control" (1990:217), and set it apart from other "normative" performances of this dance. In other words, if the reader were able to account for differences in movement, he or she could then look at other behavioral and social factors—which I attempt to do in my study.

On the one hand, Cowan's informants say, "it is Aphrodite's performance of the *tsifte teli* that confirms this" and another claimed that, "what offended people was the 'way' Aphrodite performed it" (1990: 222). In only one sentence does Cowan contrast these findings with her own observation: "I myself would not have interpreted her gestures in such extreme terms" (ibid.).

One might draw parallels between Cowan's depiction of Aphrodite and my   analysis of "Jaleh" at the beginning of this chapter. These were two performances of a solo, improvised dance judged to be out-of-control by those who witnessed them. Although Cowan did not specifically analyze Aphrodite's movements, they may well have been less transgressive than Jaleh's, but the consequences for Aphrodite were more serious: almost total social ostracism and a reputation as a woman of low morals, while Jaleh suffered only a few momentarily raised eyebrows. The difference between the two situations and their results must be sought among other factors: Aphrodite was an outsider in a small town, Jaleh was an insider with high social standing. Aphrodite was single and young, presenting a real threat to married women, while Jaleh was middle-aged and married, with her husband in attendance; she was also among people who knew her well. The dance that Aphrodite appropriated, the *tsifte-teli*, was perceived as non-Greek, "other," and potentially threatening, whereas Jaleh danced the same dance as everyone else, only the details of her performance setting her dancing apart from that of Nazi. Unlike Aphrodite's small space, Jaleh sat at her husband's side with four other close friends at a table at some distance from the other guests. Aphrodite's context was a small intimate party of married couples, whereas Jaleh danced among a larger heterogeneous group, including non-Iranians, which may well have contributed to her boldness. Thus, in my opinion, the most crucial factors leading to Aphrodite's downfall lay in a myriad of details of age, social and class status, and context.

In contrast to the dancing of Greece, in the Iranian culture sphere, the solo improvised dance is often the only dance performed at an event where dance occurs. A few groups, such as the Kurds, Armenians, and Azerbaijanis, in the northwestern regions of the Iranian culture sphere, perform group dances and one may see these dances alongside the solo improvised dance at a wedding, for instance. However, patterned group dances are not part of many urban dance events in this region, and, instead, generally only the solo improvised dance is performed. The solo improvised dance is considered "native" and "Iranian."

Cowan's excellent study, which uses dance events to demonstrate how gender ideals and behavior actually operate in a small Greek town, provides a model of how a study of dance illuminates wider social issues such as gender, hierarchy and ethnicity in the society she examined. I also look at these issues, but in a departure from Cowan's study, I also utilize dance to make aesthetic connections with other forms and processes of expression.

Conclusions and Summary
In this chapter, I have presented examples and analyzed the elements of choreophobia: the ambiguous and negative attitudes toward solo improvised dance that can be found among many individuals in Iranian-American society in Southern California. Elements of gender, social class, age, religiosity, and context, along with individual personality traits, contribute to perceptions of an individual's dance performance as normative, transgressive or out-of-control behavior.

Utilizing the elements I have described, it is possible for an investigator to construct an analytic tool to lay out a graph with the elements I described: 1) gender—male or female, 2) age—child, young adult, adult, middle-aged adult, senior adult, 3) social status—married or unmarried, high, upper-middle, middle, or poor economic and/or social class, 4) religiosity—devout to non-believer or non-practicing, 5) context—a range which includes very private and intimate gatherings and to large public social events, and 6) individual personality characteristics, what I call the "Teflon factor," which creates a dynamic, random element that must be factored into any analysis of a specific performance and how it is perceived. Using such a hypothetical graph, one might draw lines from point to point to see how they interact, because the data I present in this study reveals the capacity to interpret empirical occurrences of solo improvised dance. Keeping in mind the elements I enumerated, I am able to lay out the relative salience represented by the elements I described on a hypothetical graph. I turn to analyze several of the examples I presented in this chapter in light of these six elements, their relationships to one another, and how they can be compared in each individual case.

The first example is the elderly woman of high social class I depicted in the Beverly Hills penthouse. She is 1) female, 2) very elderly, 3) of high social status, 4) not Moslem or particularly religious, 5) performing in the context of a large, non-intimate party, and 6) a personality with enormous dollops of Teflon. This Teflon factor might perhaps have resulted from her age, which confers authority, her social status, and an indefinable amount of personal charm. The context, a large non-intimate event, certainly mitigated against the perception of proper behavior, at least in the eyes of the hostess, but the lady's extreme age, impeccable social standing, her wit and humor, and her "Teflon factor" canceled the contextual element in the view of the other guests.

Jaleh, described at the beginning of the chapter, provides an example in which the intersecting points form a very different pattern: she was 1) female, 2) middle-aged, but still young enough to be perceived as sexually threatening, 3) of high social status, causing her to lose dignity in the eyes of several onlookers, 4) a non-practicing Moslem, 5) in a semi-safe context, and 6) without sufficient personal Teflon to save her from a largely negative reaction. Perhaps, had she added some wit and humor to her performance, she might have escaped the negative reactions she excited. Whatever her intent, the explicit movements she used, which were widely perceived as being directed at strange men and culturally negative for her gender, were taken seriously by the onlookers. In addition, she was young enough for her behavior to be perceived as wanton, improper, and out-of-control by the onlookers with whom I spoke. Thus, gender and age were highly salient elements in a context similar to the one described for the elderly lady in Beverly Hills, in a private party with friends and strangers. Jaleh's social class, at least as high as the elderly woman's, only added to the perception of a person dancing out-of-control.

How did such an evaluation by onlookers differ from the way in which Nazi, in the same context, was regarded? Nazi's points of intersection differed in several respects: Nazi was 1) female, 2) elderly, 3) of high social status, 4) a non-practicing Moslem, and 5) in the same context as Jaleh—semi-safe, that is, private but not intimate, with both friends and unknown people. Like the elderly lady in the penthouse, Nazi had 6) considerable charm contributing to her Teflon factor, and she danced with wit and humor. Her use of *"gheir"* was studied and deliberate, which drew laughter, as did her facial expressions. In addition, she, unlike Jaleh, was elderly. She did not direct her dancing toward any specific individual as Jaleh did. The result was that, while her husband was unhappy with her public display of what he regarded as undignified behavior, no one else present regarded her dancing negatively. In fact, most of the viewers found it delightful. Thus, her age and her "Teflon factor" saved her from negative reactions.

Earlier I described two individuals who did, in fact, regularly escape censure. Using the elements of the graph which I constructed, how did the elements intersect in such a way that this became possible? Nilufar, my UCLA classmate, was 1) female, 2) young, 3) aristocratic, 4) Moslem, but not strictly so, and 5) the context was invariably in small, intimate student gatherings. Her dancing skills, per se, though good, were not out of the ordinary, although she moved with a recognizable grace which many enjoyed watching. Thus, in my opinion, the determining factor was 6) her individual character. Like Jaleh, Nilufar often danced in a slightly transgressive manner by punctuating her movements with a deliberate *"gheir,"* but unlike Jaleh, she always performed with wit and humor. She never took herself or her dancing seriously. This was manifest in "mugging" with funny facial expressions, pseudo-flirtation with a hankie whipped out to serve as a veil, or dancing with a man's hat that was much too large. Yet the "Teflon factor" also existed, for Nilufar could also tell jokes, make slightly outrageous statements, and express unorthodox opinions, and in doing all of these things absolutely charmed everyone. Nilufar possessed a highly independent character and the kind of charm and personal social skills that led one of her friends to wryly observe: "Nilufar could wear a gunny sack and make it appear as if Yves St. Laurent had especially designed it for her." This independence of character, much admired, contributed, in my opinion, to the impression that Nilufar created: that she was an individual who was always in control.

The second example, Hossein, falls differently on the graph, creating a different configuration. He was 1) male, 2) young, 3) of merchant family background, 4) Moslem, but with unknown religious convictions, and 5) he danced in a variety of contexts, including public ones. Thus, he, like Nilufar, displayed 6) a Teflon factor consisting of personal characteristics that not only allowed him to dance, but also caused people to beg him to do so. He was popular among his age mates and widely viewed as a "good guy." In particularly popular demand was his performance of a dance in which he imitated a feeble old man. Hossein was an outstanding athlete (weight lifter) with a highly muscular body, which in a general way, coupled with his overall demeanor, put any questions of a threatening or effeminate sexuality out of consideration. In addition, his dancing was always humorous, using elements of the grotesque, to the point that people would laugh until it hurt. In his dance imitating an old man, he would push one bent knee straight, only to almost fall when the other collapsed as a result. Unlike Nilufar, whose dancing skills were only slightly above average, Hossein's dancing ability was remarkable in a highly masculine style.

I now address the question of how these elements might be compared, how they interact and which can be considered the most salient positions in a particular analysis. In short, the answer to this question is that the way in which the elements are configured varies; in each situation, the dominant element(s) will be different. For example, as I showed in Jaleh's situation, her gender, coupled with her age, were the most salient elements in people's evaluation. In the case of the elderly woman in Beverly Hills, in my estimation, her age and humor canceled the potentially negative elements of gender and context. In Nazi's case, in a manner similar to the elderly woman, her age canceled the potentially damaging element of gender. Even more important in her case were her personality traits, which in her dancing showed as a sense of humor. "I'm not being sexy, I'm having fun!" was the message choreographically sent and received.

Given that these elements must be differently weighed and sifted in each empirical instance, are any of them more or less important? In Southern California, where I conducted my principal research, I would without hesitation state that religiosity carries the least salience, whereas in Iran this would probably be a more important element in such a dance analysis. Investigators wishing to, perhaps, create a similar analytical tool for use in other Middle Eastern societies need to take such issues into account.

Among Iranians, context, after individual character traits, carries the most variability, since an individual can not change age or gender, or to a lesser degree, social position. Is there any place an individual can not dance? Under no circumstances could any of the individuals I described appear professionally in a nightclub, nor might I add, would any of them consider such a career. In such a case, as Jamal stated, "no one would take a professional dancer seriously. They never know when to stop—that is what characterizes a professional dancer. That is why the expression *raqas-bazi* (acting like a [professional] dancer) is a popular way of describing behavior that is low-class, untrustworthy or out-of-control" (interview: January 7, 1997). Dancers in the concert dance field, including myself, consider context more than any other element when deciding where and when to dance. Were I, or any of the professional concert dancers, to appear in the context of a nightclub or as a professional dancer in a wedding, loss of credibility and reputation would be irretrievable—and has been for some individuals. Several times in the text I alluded to the opinions of Iranians toward professional dancers. I remind the reader that these attitudes contribute powerfully to the perception of and reaction toward dance and dancers. These attitudes and reactions allowed the Islamic regime to ban dance as one of its first acts when it came to power. Whether Ms. Najafi, in fact, danced for "benefits" for her mother in Iran of the 1940s is open to interpretation, but her analysis of how professional dancers are perceived is right on the mark:

> Often when my mother had guests she would call me in to dance. In Persia one dances for a good cause—what you call in America a "benefit." It would not be appropriate for me to dance for money, to entertain strangers, to make a career. I know here in America entertainers are well thought of. Professional entertainers in my country are applauded but they do not belong to the upper classes. (Najafi 1953:28-29)

Notice that Najafi categorizes the idea of dancing in front of strangers as improper behavior. These reactions stem in part from the historical and current reactions toward professional dancers and their associations with commercial sex. Thus, context becomes one of the most important elements for the investigator to analyze. Is the dancer of this genre on the concert stage or in a nightclub? In a Western context such a difference might not appear important, but in an Iranian-American context in Southern California, it is crucial.

Slightly less important than context is the element of gender. As I am sure the reader has noted, the examples I furnish mostly feature women. Gender figures prominently in the evaluation of choreophobia, because transgressive, overtly sexual female dancing symbolizes an out-of-control individual—one who will dishonor her husband and family. Men who dance in a female manner are also scorned. "His dancing makes me afraid to get up and dance," Nader, a middle-aged man told me, speaking of the performances of a well-known professional male dancer (March 1, 1997). Women, in my experience, dance in public far more frequently than do men, increasing the potential that their behavior will be judged in a negative way. I suggest that dancing that is perceived as transgressive or out-of-control symbolizes women who are wanton, and such associations, emphasized in Iranian film portrayals, are made by the observer. The symbols of wanton behavior that characterized the film advertisements, as well as the portrayal of loose women found in Iran from 1950-1979, reinforce choreophobic attitudes. This style of solo improvised dance tradition figured in the majority of films from the 1950s to the revolution. "To satisfy the not-so-critical Iranian audiences of such films, who expected to be entertained, Persian singing and dancing and often a comedy character were almost always included in Iranian feature films" (Issari 1989:159). Iranian cinema historian M. Ali Issari's encyclopedic history of the Iranian cinema demonstrates that the majority of money-making films in any given year during this period fell in this music and dance category. Female dancing thus falls closer to the transgressive-out-of-control end of the continuum and constitutes a potentially ambivalent and negative category. This means that women are generally more vulnerable than men to being perceived as transgressive and out-of-control, as the films make vividly clear. Women's historical spatial restrictions to their own closed quarters precluded many physical recreations available to men. I suggest that for this reason, dancing as an entertainment figured more prominently in their lives. As I mentioned earlier, young girls used to get together after school and dance, something I never saw young boys, who often pursued other sports, do, although Jamal reported that when he was a soldier, dancing became an important pastime, particularly when they were physically confined to indoor quarters. For a man, dancing has the potential to cast doubt on his masculinity, whereas such an issue does not arise for women. For women, the danger lies in being perceived as wanton in sexually-mixed contexts, but not when transgressive behavior was historically allowed in the "safe" contexts of all- female gatherings.

It is important to stress that elements such as age, individual character traits, and context greatly mitigate the gender element. Women who are culturally aware know where the boundaries of perception are marked and do not trespass outside of safe contexts. Age forms another important, and connected, element to gender. The women that I described who received the least censure were generally, but not always, women who were old enough to no longer constitute a sexual threat; they were what Leslie Peirce described as "post-sexual." Coupled with age, there generally exists a high respect accorded in Iranian society to the elderly as people who are knowledgeable and who carry authority and thus, an older person is generally regarded as "in-control" and "aware of what he or she is doing." Another factor is that as women grow older, they are able to exercise more independence in their movements; this freedom comes earlier for men. I mentioned earlier that in many families, young boys, sometimes into their twenties, are as carefully supervised as girls, but when they attain their twenties, they generally have much more freedom to be out of the house. Iranian urban centers have many facilities, such as cafes and teahouses, *zurkhanehs*

and athletic centers, where men socialize. The public space of the cities
constitutes male space, whereas females generally socialize in the home.
Men tend to dance less as they grow older, but I have seen some elderly
men dance as well. In a party that I hosted at the Iranian Center in Orange County, in which both young and old participated, we played the
dance-game *mojasameh* (statue), in which the dancers must freeze in
their positions when the music ceases. The winners were a man and a
woman (unrelated) in their seventies, who were among the finest dancers I have ever seen (March 19, 1992). The audience was delighted by
their obvious enthusiasm and skill in dancing.

Censure and attitudes of choreophobia are by no means confined to
individuals. Censorship by the Iranian government currently forms an
extremely lively topic on Iranian talk programs, and the first example
exhibited is the reaction of the government to dance. Mr. Golshiri, a
frequently interviewed guest and a poet, discusses the Islamic government's choreophobic reaction to the very word "dance" (*raqs*) and the
extreme levels of censoring the word from printed poetic expression,
past and present. The poetic term *raqsan*, "dance-like," even when referring to flowers or leaves "dancing in the wind," attracts the red pencil
of the censor.

The elements of social position and social class, too, create distinctions. As Najafi correctly observed, entertainers do not belong to the
"upper classes." Highly popular vocalists, even when they are highly
capable dancers, carefully restrain their movements on stage, and significantly, and ironically, often hire non-Iranians to serve as dancers in
their live performances and video tapes to maintain their own reputations as "artists" (*honarmand*) rather than "entertainers" (*motreb*). *Dar
delesh miraqseh* (he or she dances in his/her heart) is a Persian expression used for people afraid of expressing themselves openly. No Michael Jacksons, Fred Astaires, or Gene Kellys, who both sing and dance,
figure, to date, among the biggest stars in the diaspora.

Social class figured in the exclamation that I cited earlier when a
woman reacted to the dancing of another woman, which the first woman
considered transgressive or out-of-control: "Why did she have to do
that? She's a dentist." Clearly, in this instance, for that observer, the
element of social class figured into her evaluation of the dancer's behavior.

Therefore, it is clear that familiarity with this cultural tradition and
the elements of choreophobia require Geertz's "period eye," that is, to
posses the ability to understand what is being observed in a specific time
and place, to analyze how these elements interact, to determine in which
situations the importance of one element cancels the potential salience
of another, and to identify which are the most salient in a given circum-
stance. For example, determining an individual's social class requires a
great deal of ethnographic and cultural knowledge, which is not readily

available without specific information such as family names and subtle sartorial clues. The configuration, I stress again, differs from one instance to another.

Were I to rank in order of importance which elements I consider the most salient for an analysis of a specific instance, I would, in the Iranian context rank them as follows:

1. individual personality characteristics
2. context
3. gender
4. age
5. social class
6. religiosity

In Iran, these elements would probably assume a slightly different configuration than in the diaspora, which constitutes a new environment for Iranians. In this new environment, various dancing activities occur in larger non-Iranian contexts which, to some degree, influences the thinking and attitudes of many younger Iranian-Americans. As I indicated in Chapter One, the Iranian-Americans, especially the numerous Moslems, form a population that is less religious than the population of Iran (and the formation of a theocratic state was one of the main reasons many of these individuals left Iran).

While the configuration of the relative importance of the elements forms a working tool for analysis, I stress that each case is individual. As we have seen, women of the same gender, religion and social class were perceived differently: Jaleh and Nilufar—one censured, the other praised—because their personality traits were different. Thus, religion, gender, and context were not the defining elements in this instance. In the situation with Jaleh and Nazi, the gender, social class, religion, and context were the same. The variables that tipped the scales of the perception of the two performances between transgressive and out-of-control were age and, more especially, personality traits. In the case of Nilufar and the elderly lady from Beverly Hills, both were encouraged to perform in their enjoyably transgressive fashion by those around them. Despite differences in age and religion, they came from the same social class and performed in a similar context. For these reasons I focused on their personality traits, the "Teflon factor," which I feel formed the most salient element of perception for both of their performances. Thus, we can see that in each case the relative importance of the elements varies, because I have identified gender, age, context, and personality traits in specific cases that I cited in this study. No doubt, in other circumstances, social class forms the salient element, as in the case when the pretender to the throne was reported dancing at the private wedding of a near relative. In other cases, religiosity might also form an important element. These latter two elements simply seemed less important in the cases that I personally observed.

   This chapter analyzed reactions in social, non-professional contexts using elements both quantifiable, such as age, social class, and gender, and non-quantifiable, such as the individual character traits I refer to as the "Teflon factor." In the four examples I analyzed above, I show how these elements can be weighed and evaluated in attempting to determine how a specific dance performance might be regarded as normative, transgressive, or out-of-control. These elements should be evaluated in tandem to produce a full picture of how choreophobia operates and how individuals successfully or unsuccessfully behave and perform, and how they are viewed within its parameters. In such evaluations, however, the configurations of the crucial defining element(s) may differ.

Chapter 6

Solo Improvised Dancing in Performance Contexts[1]

> Exoticism is a way of establishing order in an unknown
> world through fantasy; a daydream guided by pleasurable
> self-reassurance and expansionism. It is the seemingly
> harmless side of exploitation, cloaked as it is in playful-
> ness and delirium. Exoticism is a practice of representa-
> tion through which identities are frivolously allocated. It
> is also a will to power over the unknown, an act of indis-
> criminately combining fragments, crumbs of knowledge
> and fantasy, in disrespectful, sweeping gestures justified
> by harmless banality. (Savigliano 1995: 169)

*H*aving analyzed and described the principal topic of this
study—solo improvised dance in its social contexts, in Chapter Five, in this chapter, I wish to briefly describe and characterize this
dance tradition in its other manifestations—traditional and modern theatrical contexts, for purposes of contrasting its performance in social
contexts. I will first outline how dance formed part of the traditional
comic theatre and briefly describe those forms, and how Mikhail Bakhtin's notion of the "World Upside Down" provides an excellent lens for
their analysis. I will follow with a discussion of contemporary stagings
of solo improvised dance in the Iranian-American community and how
many of these productions contain romantic and exotic images which I
believe constitute orientalist and self-exotic portrayals of this dance tradition. Of particular interest in this discussion are what I call the politics
of representation. How are Iranians represented, not only in the dances
that are staged, but more particularly, how does the choreographer, in
program notes and interviews, articulate that representation? This discussion does not focus on issues of authenticity, such as whether a particular dance company utilizes exact replicas of steps or movements,
costumes, or music in their dance productions, but rather how the artistic

director of dance groups represents Iranians through the use of images, and even more importantly, words.

Traditional Contexts
Traditional Theatre in the Iranian Culture Sphere
(ru-howzi, siyah-bazi, bazi-ha-ye namayeshi)
Among the most important sources for the study of solo improvised dance are the various forms of traditional comic improvised theatre found in different areas of the Iranian culture sphere. As in many Asian societies, dance forms one of the most important movement elements within traditional comic Iranian theatre practices, and dance and theatre are sometimes conceptually difficult to separate. Indeed, Iranian theatre historian Bahram Beiza'i (1965:167-170) claims that comic theatre gradually grew out of professional dance performances during the late Safavid and Zand periods (seventeenth and eighteenth centuries), when certain itinerant dance troupes began to settle in major cities. Thus, dance forms a basic element of traditional comic improvisational theatre and any systematic study of solo improvised dancing in the Iranian culture sphere requires the investigator to become familiar with these theatrical forms and the role that dance plays in theatrical performance practices. Traditional Iranian comic improvisational theatrical forms also constitute an important source for information concerning such elements of Iranian life as gender and sexuality, social classes, religion, politics and power distribution, race and ethnicity, and humor. Theatre history and analysis, however, lay beyond the parameters of this study. For the interested reader, studies by Beiza'i (1965), Beeman (all), Chelkowski (all), 'Enjavi-Shirazi (1972), Farahnakianpour (1977), Gaffary (1980), Safa-Isfahani (1980), and Shay (1995b), provide information concerning traditional theatrical practices in Iran.

The three comic theatrical forms that I describe below, along with the newer concert-style performances, are all occasionally performed in Southern California. However, these traditional forms are increasingly confined largely to the older elements of this community, both as performers and as audience members. The younger people, by and large, possess neither the linguistic skills nor the grasp of the historical and social contexts that originated in a homeland they barely know to apprehend these theatrical presentations. These performances truly epitomize Geertz's concept of the "period eye": they require knowledge of a specific time and place for their full comprehension. Increasingly, they seem to serve as a kind of garnish to *No-ruz* (New Year) television program celebrations to fill in the gaps between the performances of currently popular vocalists.

In addition to European-style theatre, introduced to Iran in this century, there are three basic areas of traditional theatrical practice in the Iranian culture sphere: religious, patriotic, and secular-comic (which includes the women's domestic theatre, *bazi-ha-ye namayeshi*). It is in the latter that dancing forms a basic performative practice. Briefly, the other two theatrical forms are the *ta'ziyeh*, a type of religious theatrical production, depicting the martyrdom at Karbala (Iraq) of Hossein, the son of Ali, the fourth caliph,[2] and patriotic theatre, which consists largely of the dramatization of the *Shah-nameh*, the epic history of Iran.[3] Professional storytellers known as *naqqal* perform the *Shah-nameh*.[4] These two forms lay beyond the scope of this study.

A little-known form of comic improvisational theatre is the women's theatre, called by the foremost collector of its texts, 'Enjavi-Shirazi, *bazi-ha-ye namayeshi* (theatrical games).[5] Women's theatre is characterized by the same performative elements as other traditional comic theatrical forms, but these simple plays have been created, developed and performed by and for women. Unlike the men's theatrical performances, these are strictly amateur, domestic productions. The content deals with issues that are reflective of the lives and concerns of women. Because of their unique qualities and functions, they differ principally from the men's comic performances in that they use more patter verse and dancing and less spoken dialogue. For purposes of this study, women's theatre forms an intermediate space between contemporary social settings and professional theatre, because while it is performed largely in social settings, it utilizes elements and performing characteristics of professional theatre. The dancing I described in Chapter One furnishes the movement practices in conjunction with which the miming and patter verses are performed. The dancing and horseplay in this tradition can be highly transgressive, since the performance context, always among friends and family members, is "safe." Nevertheless, the hostess in these settings always begins the proceedings, even among close friends and family, by begging the guests to dance, thus providing a link to the current practices which I described in Chapter Five.

Dance forms an important element of the traditional comic theatre, and in this way represents a theatrical experience unique to the Middle East, and a major difference from the *commedia dell'arte* with which it has been compared.[6] All Iranian theatrical performances are characterized by improvisation, thin plots, and stock roles, all well-known to potential audiences. It is this quality, most closely related in form and content to the European *commedia dell'arte,* that gives the performers enormous scope for performance opportunities and makes each performance unique and fresh for the spectators.

Today, the principal urban professional forms of this theatre are *si-yah-bazi* (the black play), so-called because the main character is a clown played in black-face, and a closely-related type, *ru-howzi* (above the pond), so-called because, in the past, one of its most typical urban performance venues was a temporary stage created of planks constructed above the pool that is a fixture in most older Iranian homes.[7]

Both forms use the black-face clown and other stock cast members, improvisation, earthy, sometimes bawdy, language, double-entendre jokes and puns, and sight gags. According to Ardavan Mofid, a renowned player in this form, as well as some other informants, the two forms differ in emphasis in that the *siyah-bazi* is a political theatre utilizing biting satire to expose political folly, whereas the *ru-howzi* is a social theatre that satirizes domestic life, and thus uses more dance and music. *Ruhowzi* also refers to both dance and music styles that can be performed exclusively of any theatrical or dramatic performance.[8]

Bakhtin: Carnivalesque and Grotesque

Bakhtin's concept of carnival as a subversive, disruptive "World Upside Down" (WUD) event, in which the repressive views (and lies) and hypocrisy of the officially-run and dominated everyday world are unmasked, provides a powerful theoretical concept for any study of Iranian theatrical and related choreographic forms. In many ways, *siyah-bazi* and *ru-howzi* embody Bakhtin's notions of the grotesque and the carnivalesque. *Gholam-siyah*, the black faced clown, always wins over his master: the World Upside Down. *Gholam-siyah's* extravagant clothing, movements, speech and lower stratum language demonstrate Bakhtin's dictum that "the grotesque. . . can not be separated from folk humor and carnival spirit." *Gholam's* bright red costume and conical hat, for example, are probably the closest thing to carnival costume in the entire Middle East. William O. Beeman, the Iranian linguistics scholar, discusses the black-faced clown:

> His movements are also grotesque. The clown distorts
> normal physical movement by jumping, running, flailing
> his arms, and twisting his body into odd shapes...This is,
> of course, part of his repertoire for sight gags make up
> much of the comedy of traditional comic theatre. This
> grotesque twisting of the body is also part of the dancing
> that occurs in the comic theatre, especially by the male
> characters. (1981:515)

In brief, the clown figure, *Gholam-siyah*, is the clever servant, played in black-face, with a quick tongue and ready wit, who gets his master, the *hajji* (someone who has been on pilgrimage to Mecca and therefore a person of high status in an Islamic community), the other principal stock character, in and out of trouble. The *hajji* is a venal hypocrite on the order of Tartuffe. There is a constant stream of wit, verses, puns, and double-entendres from the *gholam-siyah*. In the world of the *siyah-bazi*, as in all of the Iranian comic improvisational theatrical forms, the underdog always wins. In other words, power relationships are turned upside down and choreographically visualized. I suggest that this is because in a hierarchical society such as that of Iran, everyone feels that he or she is an underdog in relation to someone else. Beeman (1981), Chelkowski (1991), 'Enjavi-Shirazi (1975), Safa-Isfahani (1980), and Shay (1995b) all stress that this portrayal of the World Upside Down provides the participants and observers with important psychological tools with which to cope with their social and psychological environment. I suggest that Iranian traditional theatre, in all of its forms, embodies Bakhtin's notions of carnivalesque and grotesque, and this framework provides the most useful theoretical approach for its understanding. It uses lower body stratum humor, depicts the World Upside Down in which the weak, at least temporarily, are on top, and satirizes the powerful. Improvisational comic theatre is a mirror of Iranian culture, but a mirror which reflects the opposite of the political and social reality of everyday life, and therefore might be said to operate as a safety valve for expression of political and social discontent and frustration. Traditional comic theatre also utilizes solo improvised dance in its performances, creating a unique Middle Eastern performing genre.

Dance in Theatrical Contexts
Throughout the Middle East, the Balkans, North Africa, and Central Asia, solo improvisational dance displays enormous potential for sensuousness, explicit sexuality, and grotesque movement and therefore, transgression. This is the dancing form that is often found in the context of the *bazi-ha-ye namayeshi*, *ru-howzi* and *siyah-bazi*. Mofid stated that this dancing marks both the opening and closing of *siyah-bazi* (March 4, 1994: interview). During my interviews with actors in the tradition, two of the seasoned performers with whom I spoke said in no uncertain terms that, "dance is the basis of the *siyah-bazi*" (Mofid, Ardavan and Bahman January 27, 1994: personal interview).

The movements of the performers in the improvised comic theatre can often be transgressive—exaggerated and grotesque versions of the solo improvised dance form that one encounters in any social event at which dance is seen—with comic and at the same time strangely sensuous and sometimes outrageously explicit sexual movements and gestures. The movements of the body can be disjointed, with both spasmodic and smooth isolation movements. The performers not only use distorted muscle contractions, but also carry the body in such a way that the rear end is hyper-extended and shaken and wiggled, along with every other part of the body. This is especially true of the black face clown, who then entices the *hajji* or some other staid character into mimicking him, and thus, losing all dignity. The *hajji's* daughter, the ingenue, on the other hand, invariably performs the dance in the normative fashion usually performed by any young woman at any party.

In spite of all attempts by the *hajji*, the clown is not successfully feminized, because of his cleverness and quick wit, although attempts are made to do so by putting him in his place. It is through the dance

that this is often depicted. This solo dance form, as I described in
Chapter Five, is considered to be extemely undignified for men of high
social status, so that when the clown induces the *hajji* or some other
figure of power to follow his suit and begin to dance, it is cause for mer-
riment—the World Upside Down. Visually, a comic theme is enacted
during the dancing sequences or elsewhere, in which one of the male
characters representing a power figure all too "unknowingly" presents
his buttocks to the *Gholam*, further emphasizing the clown as "on top,"
in power. In another typical instance, the *hajji* "teaches" the clown to
walk properly and as the clown follows him, he thus presents his backside to the clown, "unknowingly" feminizing himself.

I have described the dancing as it appears in theatrical contexts for
two reasons: 1) no other investigator of dance, except Rezvani, has discussed the way in which dance forms an important aspect of comic theatrical performances, and 2) it is in the theatrical context where solo
improvised dance can be found in its most carnivalesque and transgressive manifestations, embodying the World Upside Down. Thus, such a
description rounds out the portrayal of Iranian solo improvised dancing.

Modern Performance Contexts:
Orientalism and Self-Exoticism in Presentational Dance
in the Iranian Culture Sphere
For purposes of this discussion, orientalism is defined as any distortion,
exoticizing or romanticizing of the Orient by Western visual artists, choreographers and dancers. Auto-orientalism describes instances in which
individuals from the Iranian culture sphere and other parts of the Middle
East and North Africa incorporate romantic and/or Orientalist images
and staging strategies into their works. The results obtained are often
strikingly similar, but as I show below, the process of authenticating
research often distances the one group from the other. Some Iranians
choose to self-exoticize productions. A woman who called me recently
said: "We wish to educate Americans about Iran and so we are constructing a harem on the high school football field. We will use lots of
fresh flowers" (Jan. 9, 1997). This woman was from the Iranian Jewish
community and came to the United States as a child and, outside of a
Hollywood film, had most likely never seen a harem.

For the non-Iranian choreographer who uses orientalist images, choreographic and verbal representation sometimes signal that he or she is
an initiate into the "Mysteries of the East," and all of its attendant and
timeless spirituality. The choreographer will guide the audience members through the intricacies of Persian poetical metaphors, serving as
translator of Iranian culture, helping them to "transcend cultural boundaries" in order to grasp some of its simpler spiritual riches—a momentary
peep into a timeless and frozen universe of simpler, more profound values. It is he or she who has the power of representation and interpreta-

tion. "Kismet" is a fairy tale entertainment, designed with a tongue-in-cheek look at the Middle East, which one can, perhaps, accept in the spirit of fun intended. However, when choreographers describe themselves as serious artists and educators, they owe their audiences a different level of artistic and cultural experience, one that reflects the original milieu accurately. Whereas an adult can be expected to discern fact from fantasy, children of both Iranian and non-Iranian backgrounds, who often witness these performances, can not.

In the presentation of Iranian dance, orientalist and exoticizing elements might consist of several features: music purged of "ugly-sounding microtones" that the "American audiences can not understand"; costumes in matching colors, with hairdos, seams and hemlines altered to create more contemporary silhouettes, appealing to twentieth century, Western-based tastes; sets created to provide a Thousand-and-One-Nights atmosphere; dances devoid of any movements that might offend middle class sensibilities. Such alterations unfortunately obscure the actual movement practices of solo improvised dance, which constitutes a rich aesthetic source for performance. Since many of these groups claim that educating the public, particularly the young, about life in Iran is a major goal, the usefulness and appropriateness of such productions as educational tools becomes questionable.

I confine the observations about these performance groups to what they say about their work, either in program notes or interviews, and their actual stagings. I do not enter any discussion regarding the quality of performance or the actual aesthetic success or failure of the final result.

Orientalism

No serious discussion of dance in the Middle East, North Africa and Central Asia, of which the Iranian culture sphere forms a major portion, can afford to omit the topic of orientalism and self-exoticism in the performance and staging of dance. Certain aspects of Edward Said's (1978) discussion of orientalism are germane to the topic of solo improvised dance in the Iranian culture sphere. Orientalism and auto-exoticism appear in the investigation of this dance tradition in several aspects. First, the writings of European travelers, whose observations serve as crucial historical eyewitness accounts of dance, are rife with orientalist attitudes, in Said's terms. Also, orientalism informs topics such as the appearance of orientalist and self-exoticized elements used in public, staged performances of this dance genre, which forms a crucial aspect of this study.

Stagings of dance in concert events, both those by Iranian and non-Iranian choreographers, are filled with images informed by orientalism. Orientalist and self-exoticized images flood productions throughout the Iranian culture sphere. In Iranian, Uzbek, and other dance productions in Pahlavi Iran, the former Soviet Union, and in the Iranian diaspora, miniatures come to life, sultry beauties dance in scanty garments never seen or worn in these areas, kings dance with chorus girls, poets dream in paradisiacal gardens, whirling dervishes whirl. Orientalism and exoticism flow from a number of causes and reasons, rather than one simple factor. It is a multi-layered and complex phenomenon.

While these images may originate in Western productions of operas, music, paintings, and musical comedies, what is unique in the Iranian culture sphere is that auto-orientalist, romantic images are often produced that are based on native sources, such as historical miniatures or Persian poetry. Thus, the choreographic depiction of Iran that is often presented on the stage embodies the Orient as a place which Said characterizes as a site of "imaginative geography" or, as Kiernan called it, "Europe's collective daydream of the East" (quoted in Said 1978: 52 [Kiernan 1969: 130]). Said claims that this imaginative geography results in certain aspects of the lives of the people, such as spirituality, becoming overvalued, while other aspects, such as native arts, are undervalued.

Said describes his subject as: "...in short, Orientalism is a Western style for dominating, restructuring, and having authority over the Orient" (1978: 3). He adds: "To speak of Orientalism therefore is to speak mainly, although not exclusively, of a British and French cultural enterprise" (1978: 4). I wish to contest this latter point, as Bryan Turner (1994) does, but on a different level.

Bryan Turner (1994) adds a highly important observation to Said's: in addition to Said's focus on the English and French, there are other national orientalisms, such as German. I would add to both Turner and Said that there are several other kinds of orientalisms, if by this term we mean "a distortion of the Orient," in Said's words. There are not only national orientalisms (German, French, English, as Turner points out, and I would strongly add Russian and American), but I argue that orientalism is also manifest across genre lines—orientalist images and viewpoints are expressed in dance, films, music, theatre, literature, politics, and anthropology, to name a few areas. (For an excellent discussion of this topic see MacKenzie 1995, in which he addresses orientalism in music, art, design, theatre and architecture—but not dance, and, more importantly, he challenges Said's notion that orientalism is totally pernicious.) These are in turn highly colored by time and place. For example, scholars have largely ignored the considerable outpouring of orientalist ballets, music, operas and literature produced by various Russians, both Tsarist and communist, primarily characterizing their own colonized Moslem populations in Transcaucasia and Central Asia—an orientalist project fully as egregious as that of the British and French. I emphasize this last point because the Russians' vision of the Orient has had, first through Diaghileff's productions of orientalist ballets such as

"Scheherezade," with costumes and sets designed by Leon Bakst, and subsequently through the Moiseyev and other dance companies, a major and vital impact on dance production and its accompanying capacity to create images throughout the world. "Scheherezade" set styles for Hollywood and Broadway, and Moiseyev, since World War II, has influenced the depiction of Moslem peoples both within the former Soviet Union as well as in Egypt, Iran, and other Moslem countries.

> The sumptuous costumes and settings designed by Leon Bakst for this ballet [Scheherezade] helped to create the special twentieth century stereotype which was perpetuated not only in revivals of this production, but which, in a less elevated style, has been embalmed in the often preposterous incongruities for which cinematic productions with Biblical or Arabesque themes are notorious. (Wood and Shay 1976: 29, note 17)

One of the major critiques leveled at Said (see Winder 1982, Al-'Azm 1984, Turner 1994, MacKenzie 1995) is that Said, himself, treats the orient as one large, frozen and timeless place. In addition, it is a passive place and the West casts orientalist images upon it. I challenge these notions because in the Iranian culture sphere, what I call auto-orientalism occurs in addition to orientalism, and I detail instances of it in this chapter. For example, in the production of images in the visual arts, such as modern versions of the miniature, and in dance productions, auto-orientalist images, based on older historical miniatures, paintings, and pre-Islamic monumental art, are produced on a large scale. Western-produced images are appropriated as well, creating a different phenomenon than that described by Said, in whose work romanticized native productions are largely ignored.

Thus, while Said's seminal work provides a useful starting place for the discussion of orientalism, I question several of his assertions. Unlike Said, who looked primarily at Europeans as active agents and Asians as passive recipients, I look at both orientalist images and thinking produced in the West and the auto-orientalism produced by Iranians in the diaspora.

The former national company, the Mahalli Dancers, provided a model for many productions found in the Iranian-American community of California. Therefore, it is useful to give a brief description of that company and its staging strategies and the stated philosophies that animated them, as expressed by its former director, Robert De Warren. Many contemporary stagings of Iranian solo improvised dance, as well as regional folk dances created for the stage, rely principally on western ballet and Moiseyev-inspired choreographies as sources for their creative impulses.

In Chapter Two, I showed the impossibility of reconstructing dance from historical periods due to the paucity of extant historical sources. Contemporary presentations, even the best of them, in no way constitute "authentic" historical reconstructions of how Iranian solo improvised dancing was performed 2000, or even 200 years ago.[9] Because adequate research materials for historical documentation do not exist, the choreographer who wishes to portray how he or she thinks dancing might have appeared has no recourse except to his or her own imagination. As an example, Robert De Warren claims for his piece "Haftpaykar," the Seven Portraits, a work based on a poem by Nezami-Ganjavi, that: "Each step and gesture is a reproduction of the real traditional painting, choreographed after almost two years of research" (Mahalli Dancers program 1976:n.p.). The result becomes an example of romantic orientalism, because, except for adjectives such as "lascivious," travelers' journals do not provide enough description of movement, nor do the many paintings of the period depict more than static poses, both of which are insufficient for historical reconstruction. There is no intrinsic artistic objection to creating dance pieces that can honestly be described as "this is possibly how dancing might have appeared." However, to claim that a work can accurately constitute a replica of the dancing performed 400 years ago and be reconstructed by "laying twenty or so miniatures side by side" (1973: 29), as De Warren claimed, is providing misleading information. One of the hallmarks of many orientalist portrayals of Iranian dancing is the often copious program notes justifying the choreographer's research.

Issues of Representation
In Said's formulation, orientalism is a desire by the West to dominate and speak for the East. Certainly, although individual intentions might not be so considered by those involved in stagings of dance, in fact, the individual choreographer is placing him or herself in the position of representing the Other. This establishes a potential power relationship that is not necessarily pernicious, but is often, in Marta Savigliano's terms, "disrespectful" and "banal" (1995). In fact, the intention often originates from the intense love an Iranian or non-Iranian choreographer has for these dance traditions, and a sincere desire to prove to those unbelievers in the Iranian-American community that dance truly constitutes an art form and not merely lightweight, low class entertainment. They "speak" for the silent Orient by providing "cultural understanding" of the misunderstood.

A pertinent example of representing and speaking for the silent Orient comes from the program notes of a San Francisco Bay area-based group, Ballet Afsaneh:

> Ballet Afsaneh is dedicated to presenting the traditional
> dance and music of the Silk Road...to promote apprecia-
> tion and understanding of these enduring cultures...Along

with political conflicts, social and religious misunder-
standings have masked the beauty and humanity of these
cultures for much of the American public. The need for
cultural understanding has never been greater—Ballet Afsaneh offers these rare and exciting art forms to build a
bridge of world peace and understanding. (Ballet Afsaneh 1994: cover)

I do not subscribe to the notion that the result of staging Iranian dance is
always a romanticization of the Orient.[10]   While research and concern
for authenticity is stated by most non-Iranian choreographers who involve themselves in creating stagings of traditional dance forms, in fact,
the production or reproduction of Orientalist and self-exotic images often infuses the creation of choreographies that infer and create a kind of
"Thousand-and-One-Nights" never-never land.

Most of the self-exotic and orientalist images found in productions
of solo improvised dance in California originate in Iranian visual arts
and poetry, and therefore, the investigator of dance needs to be familiar
with them. *I remember from my early days in college, over forty years
ago, that certain individuals from the Iranian culture sphere, such as
Leila and Shahla (pseudonyms), were not loathe to dance on stage in
what I call "Kismet" style costumes in order to appear glamorous and
exotic in the Hollywood environment where they might just possibly be
"discovered."   Shahla danced in the student union wearing a turquoise
blue bra and harem trousers with a matching skirt, and gloves worn to
the elbow, all covered in rhinestones and sequins.   The Iranian students
were aghast at her appearance in a costume taken from a Hollywood
fantasy of Arabic dancing.   The costume was not specifically Arabic
either, but rather a concoction worn by Hollywood stars such as Hedy
Lamar or Debra Paget.   Amazingly, the dance itself was extremely
authentic, because it was all that Shahla knew.*

Although not plagued with romanticism and fantasy to the same degree as depictions of Egyptian belly dancing, some Iranian individuals
are not immune to picturing dance in imaginative and fictitious ways to
please or amaze gullible foreigners, as Shahla's costume and Ms. Najafi's description at the opening of Chapter Two amply demonstrate.

One of the most commonly asked questions that non-Iranians ask,
after seeing a performance of the solo improvised dance, is: "Do the
hand gestures mean anything?" They are, of course, responding to the
well-known fact that in certain types of classical dances from the Indian
sub-continent, the hands, and other parts of the body, in fact do have
codified meaning (see Ohtani 1988: 9-13, Massey and Massey, 1989:1-
16, Singa and Massey 1967), as do some dances of certain Polynesian
areas (Kaeppler 1972). Certainly, among the finest dancers of the Iranian culture sphere, both professional and amateur, highly elaborate,
graceful, and intricate movements are articulated with the hands, arms,

and fingers that might suggest the possibility of such a similarity, which Najafi (and a few of her compatriots) suggests to make her mendacious account more appealing. But, as Al Faruqi asserts in a more forthright fashion, "there is little or no evidence of an attempt to coordinate steps, formations, movements or gestures with a story or with the description of events or things. . .It is an 'abstract' rather than a descriptive or delineative art" (1987: 7).

A newspaper reporter in Redlands attended a recent workshop that I conducted for a large crowd of children and some adults. Seeing a few Iranians present, she inquired of them how authentic the presentation had been. Amongst the effusive comments that accompanied this question, one of the women gushed enthusiastically, "and every step and movement of the hands has meaning." Overhearing this, Jamal hurried over to the reporter and her enthusiastic informant and asked the Iranian woman, "what meaning?" He then demonstrated a basic movement of the dance. "Exactly what does this movement mean? I certainly never knew it had meaning." The woman looked embarrassed and quit the lists. Jamal then turned to the journalist and said, "These are just movements, there is no meaning in the sense that Indian classical dances have meaning. The woman was trying to make your story 'interesting'" (July 27, 1996).

In other words, there is no codified movement vocabulary with meaning that people learn in a systematic fashion. This is not to say that mime is totally absent from the Iranian culture sphere; certain miming gestures exist in the women's domestic theatre games and plays, and in rural folk dances depicting agricultural movements, but they are individual and not codified. They suggest, for example, the washing of clothes or the winnowing of rice. They are not the elaborate stories told in *Bharata natyam*, for example.

Najafi's subtle suggestion of the low status of dancers is accurate and clear, although she does not go so far as to state that many connect it with prostitution. In contrast to Najafi's mother pushing her daughter to dance in public, several of my female informants relate how their horrified mothers warned them against dancing in public "as the first step to prostitution" (Shahla Haeri, personal communication: Nov. 20,1994; Parvaneh Azad, personal communication, September 7, 1995). Considering the venal nature of the historical dancers described in European travelers' accounts, it is difficult to imagine the "dancer with the heart of gold" that Najafi depicts who gave up a prince in exchange for a broken heart.

I do not wish to suggest that in what I have described as traditional performances, dancers had no imagination, nor that the manner of performance remained frozen and timeless. On the contrary, Beiza'i, in his history of Iranian theatre, states that comic improvised theatre derived from professional dancing and that its movement vocabulary is still the basis for traditional theatre. He recounts how a troupe of dancers in sixteenth-century Isfahan had themselves carried into the performance area in trunks, like gigantic versions of the dolls or puppets that itinerant performers (*lo'bat-baz*) carry around and make dance. Each dancer was dressed in a different color. They also performed "*ghahr va ashti*" (quarrel and make up)" (1965: 169). Beiza'i suggests that the professional dancers were always in search of imaginative ways in which to present themselves in order to keep audiences returning. One method was to perform skits between the dance acts when the dancers needed to change costumes. These skits expanded until they supplanted dance as the main attraction, thus creating traditional comic theatre. Dance, however, continued to constitute an important aspect of theatre. It is clear from the descriptions, and particularly the paintings in the nineteenth century, that professional dancers consciously developed techniques and "specialty acts" featuring elaborate displays of gymnastic feats in order to create a unique niche and attract patronage. One must keep in mind, however, that these were not Western strategies of staging.

The Iranian National Dance Company, The Mahalli Dancers
For those familiar with the history of state dance companies, worthy of a study in itself, the Ballet Folklorico de Bellas Artes from Mexico City, under the direction of its founder, Amalia Hernandez, launched a movement in which, throughout Mexico and the Mexican-American community in the United States, scores of companies were founded in emulation. At first, many directors of these companies copied Hernandez's work, but eventually, several of them developed unique styles and visions. In the same way, some Iranian and Western choreographers have adopted the choreographies created by Robert De Warren. Others have utilized choreographies by Mukharam Turganbaieva, the founding director of Bahor, the national company of Uzbekistan, or have followed the choreographies of the Azerbaijan, Georgian and Armenian State companies. Some directors of local companies performing dances from the Iranian culture sphere are choreographically parting company with the models created by Turganbaieva and De Warren, striking out in new, creative directions.

I viewed a concert featuring a copy of De Warren's work at the University of California, Santa Barbara (March 9, 1996), in which the musical director of the program properly announced that the Iranian choreography presented that evening had been copied from a film of the Mahalli dancers. Indeed, the non-Iranian dancers gamely attempted to recreate the movements seen on the film. This performance was recorded and broadcast the following week by *Sima-ye Ashena*, one of the national television programs originating in the Iranian community of Los Angeles. The costumes of the dancers resembled Islamic *hejab* clothing and elicited howls of protest from the call-in viewers of the broadcast.

The stagings of the national company have had a strong impact on the manner in which Iranian dances are staged in Southern California, since video cassettes of this company have been generally available for the past two decades. Several individuals have copied or borrowed copiously from De Warren's works, perpetuating his images for audiences in the United States. A brief look at De Warren's choreographic strategies is instructive, for some of them are redolent of orientalism.[11] De Warren was the artistic director of the company, which became the Iranian State Folk Ensemble, known also as the Mahalli Dancers, from 1967-1978. He had served as the head of a classical ballet company in Tehran, and according to him, in 1967, the Minister of Culture asked him to be the head of a new company (De Warren 1973: 28). In addition to the depiction of various ethnic groups performing regional folk dances, itself worthy of a full study, De Warren produced several works purporting to originate from historic Iran.[12]

Like many non-Iranian choreographers of staged versions of traditional dance forms, De Warren (1973) took great pains to explain his research strategies in order to justify the authenticity of his choreographies. For example, in addition to his use of historical miniatures, he states that he saw the solo improvised dance form at parties and that his stage versions of dances set in historical periods contained movements garnered from his observations at these social events. He states that women perform this dance primarily for their husbands or for other women, a standard line from belly dance enthusiasts, who utilize this approach to justify and mute the frankly sensual content and perception of their dances. As Deaver (1978) has shown for Saudi Arabia, and Safa-Isfahani (1980), Bolukbashi (1964), and 'Enjavi-Shirazi (1973), among others, have demonstrated for Iran, until recently, this dance was performed in domestic female space. Women performed for and entertained other women. All of those whom I interviewed rejected the notion of a woman dancing privately for her husband as an Orientalist fantasy, not the widespread practice suggested by De Warren and some belly dance devotees. The notion of performing in sexually mixed social occasions is a very recent, largely middle class, occurrence.

Native Iranians now resident in California have utilized De Warren's images, including depictions of Sufis and shahs dancing with harem girls. Not only does De Warren claim to utilize miniatures for research sources, he places them on the stage, the dancers posed like the famous tableaux vivants of the Follies Bergeres in the 1930s. One of the well-known wall murals from the *chehel sotun* pavilion in Isfahan from the Safavid (1501-1722) period, depicting dancers entertaining the shah and a Mughal ruler of India, who is on a state visit, served as the visual setting for one of his choreographies. In De Warren's depiction and similar scenes set by local choreographers, the shah rises and dances with the dancing girls. Such a possibility did not exist. The hue and cry surrounding the rumor that the current pretender to the throne was seen dancing at a private wedding event provides ample evidence of what historical attitudes must have been. (See Footnote 7, Chapter Five).

De Warren claims that members of the Safavid dynasty, in the manner of the French court, welcomed artists and dancers to the court to perform, and while they did not exactly develop an official Academy of Dance, or even a system of dance, the implication he makes is that the practices at the Safavid and Qajar courts paralleled those of the Capets. In point of fact, as travelers such as Chardin and Olearius indicate, the professional dancers did not live at court but were rounded up by a female charged with this duty, and taken there. The characters and performances of these professional dancers deeply shocked many Europeans. By hinting at royal patronage, De Warren sidesteps the problematic marginal social position of the professional dancer, who was so stigmatized as immoral that Schimmel (1990), in her article on dance in the *Encyclopaedia of Islam,* indicated that they, like their European counterparts, were not allowed to testify in court. Beiza'i (1973) points out that zealous Shi'i clergy attempted to drive professional actors and dancers out of certain parts of town. Thus, the portrayal of a shah rising to dance with public women becomes a romantic, orientalist fantasy.

In true orientalist style, spirituality is also emphasized. De Warren staged a "scene" from the ritual of the whirling dervishes. This order of sufis (only one among scores of mystic groups), founded by Jallal al-din Rumi (1207-73) in the thirteenth century in Anatolia, never spread to Iran to my knowledge, although De Warren claims that it "was founded in Persia in the 12th century" (1973: 29). In any event, the ritual he depicts is the one associated with the Mevlevi dervishes of Konya, Turkey. In his choreography we are given a scene of spirituality in the orientalist tradition. The actual dervish order in Konya turns for hours to classical Turkish music, during which time some of them attain ecstatic states. De Warren's dancers all enter trances after five to seven minutes and, all at once, fall on the floor in a picturesque geometric pattern. Theatrical necessity may require shortening of production time, but De Warren's choreography is a misrepresentation of the actual practices that could have at least merited explanations in the program notes.

Local Companies in California
The current presentations of this dance tradition in the Iranian diaspora, since the Revolution of 1979, have also taken on new symbols of patriotism and nostalgia in addition to adapting choreographies from the Iranian state company. Certainly, the circumstances of presentation are different than those in the Iranian culture sphere. There is, for example, no state support. The movement tradition, however, remains largely the same as that which I have seen both here and in Iran, Azerbaijan, Uzbekistan, and other parts of the Iranian culture sphere over the past

forty years.

At the time of this writing there were at least eight dance companies operating in California devoted to the performance of dance from the Iranian culture sphere.[13] Maintaining a dance company requires arduous effort, and unfamiliarity with important aspects of management, administration, finances, and fund-raising has caused more than one company to fold. It might be stretching a point to call some of these agglomerations "companies ". Several are temporary or close down within a short time. For the most part, they do not rehearse in any regular fashion; some have only one or two dancers, while others hire a group of dancers and hold two or three rehearsals prior to a performance. State companies from the Iranian culture sphere have influenced many, but not all of these companies. In addition to the local companies I described above, other performances of a one-time nature are prepared for public performance, such as the one I viewed in Santa Barbara (March 9, 1996).

Perhaps because of the presence of so many companies and an inevitable limit of possible engagements, a certain rivalry occurs between some of them, which is occasionally manifest in an insider-outsider discourse. The question of "authenticity" rears its head in such a discourse. For example, one young Iranian woman was informed by a panel judging auditions for a performance in San Francisco that her dancing was not as "authentic" as that of an American woman who often performs dances from the Iranian culture sphere, and the young Iranian was very affronted. In such a discourse, the differences between orientalism and self-exoticism form an interesting topic. Visually the results may appear the same—a depiction of a miniature coming to life, for example. One difference resides in the program notes of companies directed by non-Iranian artists, including De Warren, which often include extensive and defensive "proofs of authenticity" that attempt to underscore extensive research. Iranian choreographers, on the other hand, generally present no documentation or explanation for the images which they choose to produce, except, perhaps, the invocation of a great poet such as Hafez. They often offer an essentialist position that as an Iranian, one needs no explanation for the choices one makes. As one Iranian dancer, defending the authenticity of her movements, phrased it, "It's in my blood" (September 1991).

I asked another Iranian woman what inspired the atypical dance movements she used in a work accompanied by Persian music and poetry. These movements consisted of profile posing with arms bent at the elbows, positioned like figures from ancient Egyptian tomb paintings. No articulation of the wrists and hands, typical of contemporary Iranian solo improvised dance, was utilized. "It's inside," she replied (January 21, 1997).

For purposes of brevity I will use three examples among the local companies in order to represent trends of performance and how orientalist and self-exotic images in the Iranian diaspora of California inform them. The first company example is a performance by Saba. This company, according to several of its dancers, rehearses one or two weeks before full-scale concerts. The core group consists of four or five dancers who work with the director at weddings and video recordings. The corps, some thirty dancers, was hired for specific concerts. I saw this company twice at UCLA's Royce Hall, the last time in 1992. These performances were elaborately mounted with sets, a hired orchestra, and many lighting effects. The large company has not performed since this time. The Saba repertoire was largely derivative of the Mahalli dancers and others. For example, in his suite from Bojnurd, almost a step-by-step copy of De Warren's piece, Saba went to great expense to hire a donkey for a wedding scene, as shown in the video of the Mahalli Dancers. Saba also has a miniature scene depicting a Safavid shah viewing a court entertainment, based on De Warren's earlier work, in which a painting comes to life, and the director, in the role of the shah, rises and dances with the professional entertainers. The orientalist image of a painting coming to life, and the shah and his harem dancing, forms one of the most durable and popular exotic choreographic themes.

In contrast, another Iranian choreographer directs Ballet Pars, which performed largely as a modern ballet company in Iran for twenty years prior to the 1979 Revolution, and according to the souvenir program, boasted a large, wide-ranging repertoire. In Los Angeles, where he began working in the mid-1980s, the director's works appear to be more heavily informed by Iranian themes. His company, the three times I saw it in Los Angeles, appears to have seven or eight female dancers who form a corps to support the solo turns of the artistic director. The company appears publicly four or five times a year, and each performance features a single story ballet. The artistic director attempts to create works with a unique and sometimes avant-garde vision, such as a production that used the life of the famous poetess, Forough Farokhzad, as its organizing theme. His work differs from that of De Warren, because he primarily uses a ballet movement vocabulary, whereas De Warren attempted to use "authentic" Iranian movements, although De Warren's use of western ballet movements is clear in his choreographies. Nevertheless, the director of Ballet Pars, like De Warren, uses self-exotic images, including dancing shahs. Depictions of a poet in a dream-world of exotic beauties clad in harem clothes with eye-catching bras covered in large gold coins, appropriated from Hollywood, not Persian miniatures, appear in his works as well (viewed at UCLA, Mar. 1996). The piece opened with a dramatic reading of Hafez's poetry and the women, apparently *houris*, carried candles on to the stage and disappeared. The choreographer, dancing the role of the famous poet, is also dressed in Hollywood Middle Eastern clothes. He appears to be searching for something, perhaps poetic inspiration, and then performs an arabesque.

Somewhat later, the women run about the stage carrying a large, blan-
ket-sized, chiffon scarf and finally envelope him in it.

A non-Iranian woman based in the San Francisco area directs another California company, Ballet Afsaneh. This group has been in existence since at least the 1980s. The company, like several other local
companies, varies in the number of dancers who perform in different
concerts. They often perform with a live Persian orchestra. In budget,
scope and number of performances, Ballet Afsaneh seems to be the most
stable of all of the companies I surveyed. This company recently portrayed the Iranian world in a performance of dances. This performance,
and the program notes accompanying it, embody another aspect of orientalism, which Said characterized as overvaluing the spiritual. In this
portrayal, the choreographer had chosen to depict Persians as poets and
mystic Sufis contemplating God and the Universe in a timeless and
beautiful Orient. The themes of poetry and spirituality are invoked in
the program a number of times. In a number called *Barg-e Behesht* (The
Gardens of Paradise), the notes read: "According to Persian poets, paradise is a garden filled with the bounty of the earth yet free from all
worldly cares. Like a Persian classical painting come to life, dancers
swirl in a dream of perfect harmony." But, in point of fact, in Persian
classical paintings, as I took pains to demonstrate, the dancers do not
"swirl in a dream of perfect harmony," but rather are depicted in highly
static and stylized poses, indicative and symbolic of dancing rather than
portraying actual movements.

In the next selection, a group of dances listed in the program under
"Samarkand" start with the premise that Samarqand had "opulent
courts...[which] were the meeting place for travelers along the Silk
Road. The most respected women were educated in art and literature as
well as the sciences and at times wielded great influence in the affairs of
state. In this suite, women from many regions have gathered together..." (Ballet Afsaneh 1994: 4). These women come from Mongo-
lia, where a dancer personifies a "carefree Mongolian girl on the grassy
steppes," the Mughal court of India, and several locales in Central Asia.
This suite brings together several geographic, social, and historical in-
congruities. The suggestion that any woman, excluding a few exceptional royal ones, was educated in literature and the sciences, strikes an
anachronistic note. A few of the highest royal women did carry some
political influence, but the notion that any group of women from these
diverse geographical regions would have "gathered together to enjoy
each others' company and entertain one another with music and dance"
at some informal salon is highly unlikely. Women simply did not have
the freedom or means in the medieval Islamic period to travel the hundreds, even thousands, of rugged miles suggested in the program notes.
What common language would they have spoken? Even as late as the
early twentieth century, one could securely assert that "Women in Qajar

harems lived their lives in seclusion. They traveled rarely and, if at all, in total seclusion" (Paidar 1995:38). In fact, women in Iran have never been able to travel without the permission of their husbands or some other male guardian. In the 1970s, this caused protests from feminists, in response to which the Iranian government in 1978 (the beginning of the Islamic Revolution) announced "that a woman would not be required to obtain her husband's permission for each trip abroad and once permission was granted it would be sufficient for multiple trips" (1995:158).[14] Thus, the suggestion that a class of learned women existed who traveled widely and entertained, in the manner of geishas and hetaeras, is simply not borne out by historical, or even contemporary, facts.

The last suite in the Afsaneh program is a combination of both orientalism and self-exoticism, for its creation is credited to an American and two Iranians. In this suite, the company depicts the love of Jallal aldin Rumi and a "ragged dervish, Shams-e Tabrizi, 'the sun of Tabriz'. In that face Rumi sees the image of the timeless Beloved and till the end of his life he turns bewildered with love,—shattered, humble, magnificent, angelic. When Shams vanished, Rumi created the turning dance of the Mevlevi dervishes to express the longing for the lost Beloved." Here in this interpretive dance we have the conflation of love and faith, religion and sensuality.

In their program, Ballet Afsaneh states, "these dances while shaped by modern influences and artistic interpretation, aspire to express the sacred mysteries of their roots and that which transcends boundaries of time, place, and culture" (1994: cover). Thus, whatever Orientalist images are created and projected must be acceptable because of the lofty stated ideals of "world peace" and "building bridges of understanding." The program speaks eloquently for itself and brings to life Savigliano's concept of the "seemingly harmless side of exploitation," which allows the "legitimate practice of discrimination, where otherwise secretive fantasies can be shared aloud" (1995: 169).

Conclusions
In this section I have attempted to show that Orientalism and self-exoticism are a multi-layered process involving representation and who has the right to it. It involves the question of who possesses power in speaking for and marginalizing the other, whether practiced in the banal presentation of a dance by a seemingly well-meaning local dance company, or the conveying of serious political messages by a state dance company. Representation constitutes a form of power, and any artist who appears in public contexts, whether or not one conceives of his or her position in terms of providing representation, exercises that power through words and choreographic images. In my opinion, the power of representation bears a heavy responsibility. A modern dancer, for ex-

ample, represents her or himself, but a choreographer who stages dances from specific cultural traditions is, in fact, representing not only his or her personal view of how that dancing should appear, but by implication, the choreographer also represents the people who created the tradition.

It is not only the creative artist who shapes the exotic and romantic excesses that I have described. The audiences also come with their expectations. As Naficy demonstrated earlier, the exilic discourse often centers on the fetishizing of a romanticized past (1993). The processes that I depict have created stereotypes that Iranian audiences often buy into and internalize as their own. This can be seen in these performances when the audience bursts into applause as a dancer garbed in orientalist shah-clothing and his harem finish dancing and resume their frozen positions in a picture frame. As Graham-Brown points out about orientalist paintings: "There is an increasing interest in 19th century Orientalist painting among Arabs themselves, particularly those who can afford to purchase art. Like old photographs, these paintings are seen, sometimes quite uncritically, as a representation of life in the Arab world: as it used to be...Thus what was appropriated by Europe can be reappropriated and is in danger of becoming part of national memory and heritage" (1984: 59). Jamal agrees: "the truly ugly aspect of Orientalism, is that it creates expectations within us Iranians that this is how we ought to look and act. We lose our authentic arts to cheap imitations. Bad artists hide behind poetry as an excuse for their inadequate productions" (personal interview: September 1, 1995). The consequence of such orientalist images projected upon audiences of young people who have never been to Iran is to deny them access to their authentic heritage. "We are here tonight to present this program to preserve our heritage and promote Iranian culture," the young co-ed gushed in introducing the ballet of Hafez danced by Ballet Pars, in which Hollywood/Arab clothing replaced the historical clothing that would have been worn during Hafez's period. The musical accompaniment was played by a symphony orchestra. Young Iranians brought here as infants or born here rarely have an accurate picture of the aspects of movement, costume, or music required for an authentic production. This is not to say that every dance artist is required to produce authentic Iranian dancing. Rather, she or he is ethically responsible to state that the work in question is from his or her imagination and must be evaluated on its own terms, not as a representation of Iranian history or traditional styles of dancing. This latter aspect is particularly crucial when one remembers that due to the ban on dance activity in the Islamic Republic, California has become the chief site of its public performance. Knowledgeable Iranians often turn away from dance because the projected images I described are insulting to their intelligence, which removes the potential support that they might provide for this aspect of their cultural heritage.

Chapter 7

Summary and Conclusions

"Dancing is the loftiest, the most moving, the most beautiful of the arts, because it is no mere translation or abstraction from life; it is life itself."
Havelock Ellis, The Dance of Life (1923)

*I*n the formulation of this study, two individuals existed side-by-side, the scholar and the artist. As hard as I tried to excise the artist in this scholarly pursuit, I finally realized that the two were inseparable, and that without my artist's persona I could not truly construct this study.

While traversing a great deal of scholarly ground in the process of addressing the ways in which Iranians and Iranian-Americans perform and regard solo improvised dance, I posed questions and attempted to provide some possible answers in three major areas of inquiry. The most important is: 1) the study of a population for whom their own unique dance tradition constitutes a largely negative or ambivalent activity, and the suggestion of the existence of an amorphous, but perceptible set or "system" of reactions and attitudes within this population, for which I have coined the term "choreophobia." I also identified two other themes that relate to and accompany this main topic: 2) how the links between dance and other forms of aesthetic visual and performative expression constitute an important element in its aesthetic and social construction. The seemingly formless, improvisatory character of this dance genre sets it apart from the generally, clearly-patterned aspect of regional folk dancing. I suggest that this seemingly formless quality sometimes establishes a feeling of unease in the viewer who never knows what is going to happen next. For many years I had felt these connections, and this study provided me with the opportunity to articulate and demonstrate these linkages. 3) The use of a conceptually larger geographical, historical and cultural area of investigation, which I call the Iranian culture sphere, serves as the historic and cultural background for the Iranian population that I studied and continue to study. I main-

171

tain that this background has, to a large degree, shaped the thinking and attitudes of these people. Thus, the geographic and historical boundaries that I have adopted for this study stand in contrast to the narrower political borders of the current nation state of Iran that are commonly adopted for dance and music (but not literature or visual art) studies for this cultural area. I feel that these three topics constitute new areas of investigation in Iranian dance, and to some degree have wider implications for the study of dance and other aesthetic practices in the larger area of the Middle East, Central Asia and North Africa as well. To address some of the conclusions I reached in this ongoing study, I briefly recapitulate and reconfigure some of the contents of the chapters.

This study has proven to be a pioneer work on several levels: it is the first attempt to systematically describe and analyze the movement practices and combine this aspect of solo improvised dance with its social and historical contexts in one study. In addition, it connects this dance tradition with other Iranian visual and performance genres of expression and demonstrates the aesthetic bases of its performance. I suggest that currently, dance does not largely constitute a form of art among the peoples of the Iranian culture sphere, including the Iranian-American community of Southern California. Rather, for a considerable majority, dance constitutes a pleasurable social activity or a "lightweight" entertainment. By emphasizing that the movement practices of dance proceed from the same aesthetic principles, namely geometry and improvisation, as highly esteemed art forms such as calligraphy and architectural ornamentation, I identify and reconfigure dance as an important cultural practice with the potential to be considered an art form by its creators.

Choreophobia
In this study I characterize the phenomenon that I call "choreophobia," which I suggest is an amorphous set or "system" of reactions and attitudes that largely ranges between ambivalent and negative and that characterizes the reactions of many, if not most, Iranians, both in the Iranian culture sphere and in the Iranian diaspora. I assert that the term choreophobia is a useful concept to characterize these attitudes. Because of its amorphous character, choreophobia remains unarticulated by many individuals, although, as I showed in Chapter Three, some religious figures, speaking officially and unofficially for both the Islamic Republic of Iran and Afghanistan, have pronounced its performance an anathema, causing it to be banned. This ban underscores the significance of this dance tradition: one never bans an unimportant activity. Even among academics, dance remains a topic to be avoided by many individuals who are made uncomfortable by it or who regard dance as not a serious or valuable topic.

In Chapter Five, I established a model for analyzing how dance in social contexts might be regarded and apprehended as normative, transgressive, or out-of-control by culturally competent observers. I described and analyzed several dance performances that I witnessed by contrasting and comparing the six elements that I identified to create this model: 1) gender, 2) age, 3) social status, 4) religiosity, 5) context, and 6) specific character traits. The development of such a model may aid other observers in using this method to determine how culturally competent observers might socially and culturally evaluate a particular dance performance. Future studies might further refine and develop this system, perhaps identifying several other elements. For example, Katherine St. John, in her study of women's dances in Herat, Afghanistan, suggested that "payment for services" constitutes a possible element of negative reactions to dance. While in her thesis she proposes that payment for services constitutes the primary reason for disdain of public dance performances in Afghanistan (1993:24), by contrast, I suggest that payment for professional dancing could serve, after careful investigation, as a subtext under the categories of "context" or "social status." I further emphasize this as but one of several possible components of the complex and ambiguous reactions to solo improvised dancing. Unlike the case for the Afghan society that St. John studied, it might equally be determined that "payment for services" does not form a viable element in the Iranian community, or other similar communities such as Arab-Americans, for while certain public entertainers in Southern California excite negative reactions, others do not. My findings indicate that the context in which the performances occur, the manner of their performances, including movements employed and costumes in which the performers possibly expose parts of their bodies, and personal, individual behavior and reputations create the reactions, positive or negative, rather than professional or amateur status. For example, two of the Iranian dancers in my company refuse payment, perhaps in order to avoid the possible stigma of being a professional public dancer, although their stated reason for not accepting payment is to support the company by contributing their honoraria back to the company account for costumes and other expenses. Meanwhile, other Iranian-American members accept their honoraria gladly. Nevertheless, paid or unpaid, these dancers all appear in the same professional contexts, and the audience cannot know who does and who does not receive honoraria. This model may provide researchers in the Arab world, Turkey, North Africa, and Central Asia a starting place for understanding how dance, with its physical presence and immediacy, invokes such powerful reactions and attitudes. Fear of such immediacy and embodiedness, often symbolizing gendered sexuality, provide powerful insights into cultural values and attitudes toward sexuality and religion.

These reactions also emphasize the manner in which the Iranian-American community constitutes a dynamic part of the Iranian culture sphere, reflecting historical attitudes from the Iranian culture sphere, and changes in attitude as expressed by these individuals. For example, in response to my question regarding what they want to learn in my class on Iranian dance, many students of Iranian-American background state that they come to my classes as a means of expressing and learning more about their Iranian heritage, which constitutes a major departure from practices in Iran or Afghanistan, where the dance is banned. This also demonstrates changing views about dance among the young, who see other ethnic groups, such as Mexican or Indian students, effectively promoting the richness of their respective cultures by giving programs of dance to celebrate their heritage. Such changing attitudes suggest a rich topic suitable for long-term documentation and research.

Such attitudes, I maintain, are widely understood, if unarticulated, by those individuals whom I term as "culturally competent." Even if an individual does not agree with these attitudes and reactions, he or she recognizes their existence and the consequences that may ensue when they are ignored.

On a recent tour of AVAZ in the San Francisco area, the local Iranian community hosted the members of the company. During the reception, which included all ages, male and female, a great deal of improvised solo dancing occurred. Several company members and I were driven to our hotel by Maryam (pseudonym), a woman who wears a *rusari* (Islamic head covering) and one of the generous helpers of the sponsoring organization. She explained to us that just because she was religious (*mazhabi*) did not mean that she was fanatic (*ta'sob*). Since several young girls in their teens and early twenties were going to dance in the AVAZ performance, Maryam explained that she had nothing against dancing—in the right context. She and her husband had decided to let their teenage daughter, Nahid, sing in the young people's chorus, but not dance—a compromise. "You know how Iranian men think about dancing in public," she explained, unconsciously underscoring my finding of the general cultural knowledge and acceptance of choreophobia in the Iranian-American community.

The next day, at the performance, which her family attended, Maryam said, "Dr. Shay, my husband was upset when I told him that I had said to you that he would not like Nahid to dance. He said Nahid may dance as long as she is respectably dressed, so she may dance with you." As it turned out, however, Nahid herself was too embarrassed to perform. (March 1-2, 1997).

The above passage underscores some of the concepts I have presented and sums up several of the findings of this study:

1) Maryam assumed a choreophobic attitude on her husband's part, one that she characterized as, "you know how Iranian men think about dancing in public." By her statement she also suggested that all of us who were listening were culturally competent, aware of and accepting

this cultural generality as well. Her assumption of the existence of cho-reophobia was later and separately echoed by a man at the reception who also pointed out, "how wonderful it was to have your group as our guests—you know how we Iranians are about dance" (M. Niknia [pseudonym] personal interview March 1, 1997). The cultural general-ity of the existence of choreophobia among the Iranian-American popu-lation was thereby underscored by these observations.

Kathleen Fraser (1993: 58-66), in a brief, preliminary presentation of her research on belly dancing ("oriental dance" in her terms), and using informants in the Egyptian-Canadian community of Toronto, presaged the findings I have made in this study. "Egyptian Canadians truly love this dance but could not bring themselves to say they give it high esteem as an art" (1993:59) or that "they think dancing is a first step to prosti-tution" (ibid: 60). Her findings parallel attitudes that were expressed many times throughout my study of Iranian-Americans. Thus, such a study as this one about solo improvised dance in the Iranian-American community, and the Iranian culture sphere generally, has implications beyond the attitudes and reactions of the Iranian community alone.

2) While in most cases I did not find that religiosity forms a major element in choreophobic reactions in California, Maryam's reaction suggested that the element of religiosity still has some degree of salience among some individuals, and must not be discounted by the knowledge-able observer. As Jamal observed, such an association with and support for a dance performance and "chauffeuring a group of dancers by a re-spectable Moslem woman would likely not have occurred in Iran, which suggests a mellowing of attitudes among Iranians in the United States because of AVAZ's excellent reputation" (March 7, 1997). This sug-gests that cultural change is occurring, initiated by the presence of a company like AVAZ, which stresses the positive aspects of this dance tradition, even among the most socially conservative elements of Ira-nian-American society.

3) AVAZ, because of its growing reputation as a respectable and professional company, one which represents Iran "properly" and "authentically," in the words of many Iranian informants, perhaps serves as a catalyst for many individuals to change their attitude toward dance and its propriety. One young man e-mailed the sponsors of a concert held March 2, 1997, saying that AVAZ's professionalism and use of Iranian, rather than western movements and staging strategies, made him proud of his heritage (March 3, 1997). Such reactions suggest that the phenomenon of performing dance companies and the images they project within ethnic communities offer a rich field of research. This also affirms the possibility that AVAZ and other companies are cur-rently in the process of creating a new, highly visible space for dance to be considered as a serious form of art by the Iranian community throughout the diaspora. This has been underscored by recent AVAZ

performances in Washington, D.C. and New York City before sold-out houses sponsored by one of the most important media, Radio Seda-ye Iran (October-November 1998). Following a command performance in New York, Empress Farah Pahlavi of Iran, patroness of the former Iranian national dance company, mounted the stage, shook the hand of each performer, and stated, "I am proud to see the art of Iranian dance performed by such a talented group of artists of different ethnicities" (November 22, 1998).

Positive representations of Iran through AVAZ's dance performances, and its accompanying pleasurable elements of nostalgia, plus the lack of choreophobic attitudes in the United States, are all possible elements that permit such a change of attitudes. I argue that this study documents the beginning of a development of a shift of attitudes. Dance, the most embodied of art forms, produces social and cultural meanings contingent on context in the Iranian-American community.

As I pull together the pieces of this large picture puzzle, in order to make sense of the elements I have identified, I realize that my dance company has provided me with the means to attach these fragments into a meaningful whole. AVAZ serves as a powerful tool for measuring the changing reactions and attitudes within the Iranian-American community. Reactions and attitudes of audience members, board members, performers, and the media, often very immediate and honest, appear in response to performances, rehearsals, and other activities. In the beginning of the company's existence, several well-known individuals often came to and left AVAZ performances in the dark, to avoid being visually connected to a dance performance. For many years, obtaining Iranian board members was difficult, but now such participation is increasingly considered highly desirable and sought after. Multiple reasons for the company's current popularity are expressed by the various performers, board members, and supporters: nostalgia, pride in the representation of cultural heritage, having a good time, and sheer love for the movements, music and costumes, among others.

Choreophobia has historically determined, and to a large degree still determines, the reactions of Iranians and Iranian-Americans to solo improvised dance. This dance form, considered by most individuals as a formless collection of movements, which, through the use of improvisation, symbolizes unpredictable, potentially out-of-control behavior, sometimes provokes negative reactions among certain individuals. Phobias derive from the fear of unknown or unpredictable elements, but companies like AVAZ and studies like the present one shed light on this dance genre, demonstrating a coherent system of aesthetics and movements. Currently, a constellation of elements, including a new environment in which dance is considered a positive and valuable activity, and the formation of local companies like AVAZ, which present dance in a positive light, constitute a dynamic new intersection of changing values and attitudes in Southern California.

Solo Improvised Dance as an Art Form

This study contributes an original element to the study of Iranian solo improvised dance: it articulates the manner in which the performance of this dance tradition does not derive from a formless, meaningless collection of movements, but rather forms a coherent movement system. I demonstrated in Chapter One the concept of logic of choice, the mechanism by which the dancer proceeds from one movement or gesture to another, particularly through the use of intricate, geometrically-based movements of the hands and arms. This shows that, like Persian classical music, dance is capable of being systematized, a prerequisite for the creation of an aesthetic system. The logic of choice utilized by dancers illuminates an improvisatory practice that follows the type of performative logic utilized by the storyteller or the musician, who operate within specific stylistic constraints and who select specific motifs during the course of a performance.

This study calls into question what constitutes "art" within different societies. Fortunately, my long association with Iranians, as I demonstrated in the opening of Chapter One, revealed to me attitudes that were at sharp variance with those I had internalized living in American urban society. Therefore, at the beginning of this project, I was not intellectually seduced into the assumptions with which I was raised, that is, that dance is universally an art form. However beautiful as a movement practice I, as well as some Iranians of my acquaintance, may find this dance tradition, it remains, at least currently among the Iranians of California, "the least of the arts," if an art form at all. For the majority of Iranians, dance functions instead as a social activity in which they themselves often participate, or as a professional entertainment, whose professional exponents often excite disdain. However, these attitudes are changing, especially in the relatively new milieu of the United States, with increased exposure to a wider cultural world and its accompanying values. Increasingly, I meet young Iranian-Americans planning to enter dance as a profession, generally much to the sorrow, opposition, and reluctance of their parents and families. These parental reactions and resistance stem from the traditional view of professional dancers as out-of-control, as I showed in Chapter Five, and which were reflected and reinforced in the pre-Revolutionary Iranian cinema, which was flooded with a multitude of such scenes. In addition, dance concerts of this dance tradition are attracting increasingly larger Iranian audiences, albeit still much smaller than those who attend music performances of popular singers, whose audiences can run into the thousands. This may change, since Yaffa Soleimani, director of a major television program in New York City, stated that "the AVAZ concert broke previous records for attendance" (November 22, 1998).

"I would like to speak to Mr. Shay," one of a group of three women, all of whom were crying, told Jamal after a recent concert. Seeing that I was busy, Jamal said that I could talk to her in a moment; however, she said, "Please, don't disturb him. Just tell him that I have been here for thirty years and I came for a good time." Jamal, noting the tears running down her cheeks said, "I hope that you did not have a bad time." "Oh no," she said, "but instead of merely a good time he took me back to Iran— and I am most grateful" (March 2, 1997).

These women's initial reactions demonstrate the traditional view and expectation of dance as an entertainment. However, their positive reactions, brought about by an experience of dance treated as an art form, and the transformation of these women's attitudes and reactions to dance as art rather than entertainment, demonstrates the dynamic element of change occurring in the Iranian-American community. Because of the attitudes of many Iranians and Iranian-Americans that dance constitutes a form of entertainment rather than an art form, this dance tradition has not yet reached its potential capacity as an aesthetic and performance practice. Such changes as those experienced by the three women I describe above probably occur for a number of reasons. First, AVAZ performances project a specific image of this dance genre as a rich, varied, and serious movement practice, without orientalist accouterments and choreographic strategies. In staging several pieces in the repertoire, the dancers are often encouraged to improvise rather than following a set choreography. Story plots of orientalist imagination are avoided, and the stagings rely on the abstract elements of the rich movement and musical traditions, and additional aesthetic effects are largely produced through effective costuming and lighting. AVAZ performs regional folk dances as well as solo improvised dancing. Many Iranians regard regional folk dances differently and far more benignly than solo improvised dance, and several individuals, who ignored or disdained such regional dances as "peasant" dances in Iran, avidly seek to have their children perform them as a legitimate form of patriotic expression in their new environment. Regional folk dances, with their patterned movements, reassure with their predictability and the respectability represented by their all-enveloping costumes.

Second, the Iranian-American community largely realizes that it is now here to stay. In spite of the rhetoric one hears and reads in the electronic and print media of a return to the homeland, increasingly, many individuals in the community are conceptually shifting from exile status to an immigrant community, realizing that their children can not return. As people remain longer, most of the upcoming generations demonstrate increasingly weaker linguistic competency in Persian, an issue often discussed in the media. Thus, the linguistically-based forms of performances of literature, theatre, and cinema become increasingly closed to many Iranian-American youth. Concerned parents, in search of paths for inculcating the succeeding generations with a sense of Ira-nian-ness and pride in their ethnic origins, increasingly find themselves considering dance. Along with music, dance constitutes one of the ma-jor forms of cultural expression for which language is not needed as a means for maintaining a cultural continuity.

Although the term "*sonnati*" (classical) is sometimes applied to fine performances of solo improvised dance, this word in such usage is im-precise. In spite of claims that this is a classical dance form, this genre lacks a specific technical vocabulary (although in Soviet Uzbekistan and Tajikistan, one has been created and developed for pedagogical pur-poses in the choreographic institutes and dance manuals [see Karimova 1973, 1975, 1977, 1979]), and an academy such as the ones found in Azerbaijan, Uzbekistan and Tajikistan. Such a method and vocabulary remain unknown to Iranians because the political conditions in Central Asia after the Soviet era formed a political and cultural *terra incognita* for Iranians of Iran. These qualities—a codified, standardized movement vocabulary and academy with standardized pedagogical practices, con-stitute the hallmark and *sine qua non* of a "classical" tradition. While these elements of specialized vocabulary, presence of an academy, and standardized pedagogical methods existed in Iran for the learning and performance of Persian classical music, no such standards existed in the field of dance. One of the projects that resulted from this study is the future development of both a technical vocabulary, for which the dance manuals from the former Soviet Union (see Karimova, Tkachenko, for examples) provide a useful guide, and a teaching method to accompany it, and AVAZ's plan to form an academy.

Thus, the articulation of solo improvised dance as a systematic, co-herent movement practice and aesthetic system provides an important first step in establishing this dance genre as a potential art form. This study demonstrates that, like music, this improvisational movement system proceeds logically, within specific stylistic parameters. The per-formances of this genre by a skilled dancer can constitute a teachable artistic practice possessed of an internal logic, rather than a formless, inchoate, meaningless series of gestures and movements.

The attempt to develop positive attitudes toward dance as an art form did not begin among Iranians in the diaspora. The Pahlavi dynasty, es-pecially through the support of the Empress Farah, promoted the staging of native dance traditions in artistic performances through the estab-lishment of the Mahalli Dancers. The Iranian State company bore a re-semblance to Bahor, Lalah and the other state-sponsored companies of Uzbekistan, Azerbaijan, and Tajikistan, which had in turn been modeled after the Moiseeyev Company of the former Soviet Union. In Iran, folk and traditional dances were usually choreographed and staged in a fashion that departed from traditional professional contexts, often rely-ing on classical ballet productions as a model. This garnered a great deal of support from both the Iranian government and some members of the public. These stagings departed from previous practices, for example, by the replacement of improvisation as the primary aesthetic element, with set choreographies, often danced in unison by large groups of dancers trained in specific routines to specific musical selections. I demonstrated in Chapter Six how such a departure from traditional, improvisational practices impacts the resulting movements used in the new stagings. In Iran, the traditional, and highly negative, words for dancer, *raqas* (male) or *raqaseh* (female), were replaced by the more neutral term *raqsandeh*, a word that applies to either sex, for dance performers of the legitimate stage.

These stagings in Iran, the former Soviet Union, and the Iranian diaspora often resulted in a spate of productions informed by orientalist and romantic self-exotic images. Rather than relying on the vast possibilities of the movement and aesthetic practices of this genre, many choreographers and dancers have turned instead to spurious historical and poetic inspiration as frameworks for their productions.

Analysis of the contents of both the performances and the written descriptions of them provided by the government in printed programs provides fascinating information for political analysis as well as the social and aesthetic impact both in Iran and among the exile and immigrant Iranian communities. Such analysis forms a potentially important topic, reflecting elements of nationalism and ethnicity and their choreographic representation. The revulsion of the mass of the Iranian population against the overarching Westernization sponsored by the Pahlavi regime claimed dance as one of its first victims. With the arrival of the Islamic Revolution of 1979, all dance activity was banned—a ban that still extends to the public performance of solo improvised dance, although regional dances seem to be permitted socially in the countryside, if not the cities.

Such companies, their repertoires and the ways in which they are characterized in movement and in print, raise important issues of representation on a wide variety of levels—political, historical, ethnic, economic, gender, and aesthetic—among others. Performances of these companies over the past five decades raise questions of who is represented, and perhaps, even move importantly, who is not represented, in the repertoires of these state-sponsored companies. In addition, how are different ethnicities represented? For example, within the now-defunct Iranian State Ensemble, known in the West as the Mahalli Dancers, the Persian dances are "graceful" in contrast to those of the Turkoman (sic) dances, which are "simple, but strong" (Mahalli Dancers Program 1976: n.p.). Since Iran is a multi-ethnic nation, with the Persian-speakers numbering about one half of the population, and because the Mahalli Dancers constituted an official representation by this dominant political and ethnic segment, such characterizations take on multiple meanings.

To date, no scholarly inquiry has been conducted concerning the establishment, maintenance, and representations of these large-scale dance companies. With the collapse of the former USSR, some of these companies, which are extremely expensive to maintain, are beginning to wane, and with the historical perspective of the past fifty years, now is the time to assess the impact of these companies and the various messages they conveyed, and still convey. In the post cold war world, what will be the role of such surviving ensembles? Has their representation changed?

Many of these state companies also spawned a number of look-alike companies in the West, including several in the California diaspora. These were founded both by individuals within ethnic communities, and individuals like myself, whose origins are not Iranian. "Authenticity" became a central issue with layered meanings and may be regarded in a number of ways: 1) Ethnographic: How close were the stage representations to dances and music found in the field and performed natively? 2) Politically and ethnically: Did these ensembles "represent" the ethnic groups properly? Such questions of "authenticity" and "representation" form an important focus for future studies.

Another important question of such inquiries concerns the role of these dance companies in transforming dance into an art form. Linked to the study of the state ensembles is the notion of dance as art, because these ensembles operate on the assumption that they are art ensembles, as stated in all of their promotional materials. I attempted to demonstrate in Chapter Six that if one can not presently term solo improvised dance as "art," one can perhaps more comfortably characterize it as a form of expression, sometimes an aesthetic one. However, an important preliminary finding of this study is the indication of a major shift in the attitudes of many Iranian-Americans regarding the cultural role occupied by dance, an unanticipated result of my research. Thus, following Geertz (1983), I maintain that what constitutes "art" can be seen to be a social and historical judgment and set of attitudes and reactions of a particular group, or generation, at a particular time and place. Like all other forms of cultural expression, dance, and the way in which it is regarded, is a dynamic phenomenon, subject to change. Future, more detailed, studies of the movement practices, and especially, the mechanics and aesthetics of improvisation, may reveal exciting aspects of aesthetic behavior and more formal links with musical practices, for example. Establishing such linkages forms an original aspect of this study, in which I have moved this dance tradition from its position as a socially and historically marginalized activity, to a foregrounded position worthy of serious investigation and analysis.

Such changing attitudes impact the behavior of people in Iran and Afghanistan as well, because the communication between the immigrant communities and the homelands form a dynamic interaction. Thousands of Iranian-Americans travel to Iran. Videos and musical tapes, magazines and newspapers, e-mail and telephone calls, and radio and television broadcasts from both communities constantly circulate between these two environments.

Change occurs and the sensitive investigator must be ready to see, accept, and document it. Such change is illustrated by the many young Iranians who frequent discotheques, such as Club X and the Rendezvous, specifically established for their use and the social performance of this dance tradition. A pop music industry based in Southern California pumps out music for this dance genre that is featured in homes, concerts of popular vocalists, and discotheques.[1] The Islamic Republic immediately closed down such establishments, which briefly flourished in Tehran in the 1960-70s, in 1979. It is an established mode of dating among some young Iranian-Americans, thus ensuring the continuity and development of this dance tradition amid social change.

Through vignettes and thumbnail sketches I have shown how I have been the recipient of the various shades of choreophobia through the workings of my dance company, AVAZ: the fiery reaction of a westernized woman rejecting the earthy production of the women's theatre games, the gray disdain of the talk-show host who considers his show too serious to discuss dance, the bland beige tones of the second talk show host, who wishes to treat dance as low entertainment and me as amusing and naive for participating in dance, the warm glow of the religious woman trying to cross a bridge and gain new appreciation for dance as a permissible activity in spite of the choreophobic attitudes that surround her, the dark brown rejection of the musician who considers all dancers as "motrebs," the golden glow of a community reception of men, women and children, the blue coloring of the pointedly unreturned calls of a UCLA professor, the hot retort of the graduate student for whom the topic of dance is "all prostitution," and warm tones created by the man with tears in his eyes who told me that I took him to Iran for the duration of an evening. As I unroll this unstretched canvas, upon which I and others—performers, supporters, critics, and audience members—have been adding brush strokes of different hues and colors, it has become AVAZ, through which I have created a portrait of this dance tradition in its many contrasting colors. Fortunately, most of the brush strokes have been bright and added with passion by those whose love for this dance has matched my own. For me, and increasing numbers of others, this is an art, the one I have chosen for my own expression.

As the Persians say, "mah posht-e abr hamisheh penhan namimanad" (the moon does not remain hidden behind the cloud forever).

Introduction

[1] For purposes of this presentation, the Iranian culture sphere stretches in a wide arc from Western China through Central Asia to the Caucasus to Iraq and the Persian Gulf, as well as the Iranian diaspora. The Southern Californian counties of Santa Barbara, Ventura, Los Angeles, San Bernardino, Orange, and San Diego, which are home to between one and two million Iranian-Americans, constitutes the largest diaspora settlement. In addition, areas with populations numbering 5,000 or more each also exist in several cities in Germany, in Paris, London, Rome, Madrid, Qatar, Abu-Dabai, Istanbul, Tokyo, New York, Seattle, Houston, Dallas, Austin, Atlanta, Toronto, Quebec, Vancouver, San Francisco, Salt Lake City, and Chicago.

[2] After the 1979 Revolution, the Islamic Republic banned all dancing. Later the ban on group dances seen in tribal and rural areas seems to have been partially lifted (see Mortensen 1993: 373 for example). Solo, improvised dancing remains interdicted. In 1993, two well-known male television personalities were dismissed from their jobs for performing this dancing at a private wedding party. (Parviz Kardan, TV news item, November 1993). Regional group dances are currently permitted, and men from tribal areas are periodically seen dancing in television programs, even though many people think that a total ban on dancing exists (personal observation of *Aftab* program, recorded in Iran, December, 1993).

As examples of resistance to the ban on dancing in the Islamic Republic, several travelers to Iran, both Iranian and American (Anthropologist Gene Garthwaite, Iranian social sciences scholar Houchang Chehabi, and dancer Cynthia Word), have confirmed that dance is widespread in secret, and this places the participants at risk. Chehabi indicated in an interview (November 15,1995) that people dance at weddings, even in processions on Shah Reza Blvd, where there is a risk of arrest or beating. He attended a wedding in Tehran, summer 1995, with live music, dancing, and alcohol allowed in exchange for heavy bribes. Such bribery can only be afforded by the rich. Garthwaite attended a similar wedding in Shiraz where guards were bribed to allow dancing (personal interview: July 6, 1995). As another example, at the Women's World Conference held in Beijing, September 1995, *Radio Seda-ye Iran* (Voice of Iran Radio) reported that a delegation of Iranian women, diaspora dissidents of the Islamic Republic, donned both Western and national costumes and danced to taunt and anger the Islamic regime and its delegation of *hejabi* (a term for proper, or legal, Islamic dress, i.e. head covered, loose coat or tunic, but not necessarily veiled face) women, using the dancing as a highly visual and emotional manifestation of resistance. The representatives of the Islamic Republic vigorously protested (newscast September 5, 1995).

[3] Seen and photographed by a friend and informant, Pary Azad, in 1992, who gave me a photograph that she took in a bus in 1993 that shows people dancing. They had closed the curtains and one of the passengers placed himself on watch to be on the lookout for the highway police. She stated later (July 3, 1996) that some buses are known to carry cassette players and one or two lively university students are given free passage to encourage the passengers to dance and create a festive atmosphere, and that people attempt to find rides on such buses.

[4] In a recent radio broadcast (KPFK April 3, 1996) to which I invited a Moslem and a Jewish guest to discuss choreophobia, both acknowledged the power of ambiguity toward dance throughout all elements of Iranian society.

[5] The individuals I interview in many ways embody what Sally Ness termed, "the ideal culture bearer, that extraordinary character renowned in her community as a

'keeper of tradition.' She was the one who could remember details, the one who would venture to discriminate between true and false, the one who could enjoy my esoteric interests in her world" (1992: 163-164). Alter (1992), Lewis (1992), Ness (1992), and Cowan (1990), during their participant-observation research, all conducted in-depth interviews with individuals who were widely perceived by the community as possessing special information or embodying the tradition.

As an example of "the ideal culture bearer," Jamal (Khosrow Jamali) is a visual artist who loves Iranian dance and sees its potential as an art form. He is my partner in the direction of AVAZ. His professional association with me and AVAZ dates back to 1990. He creates, or co-creates with me, choreographies, sets, and costumes, as well as performing. His memories of dancing that he has seen and experienced in Iran form clear visual images because of his training as a visual artist. From childhood, in a large extended family in an old neighborhood in Tehran, he witnessed many dance events by women of his family, and later, among his friends and during his years of basic training in the army, dancing formed a frequent entertainment. His sister-in-law, an outstanding dancer, provided a model for many of the movement practices he learned. Thus, he is that "culture bearer" with the intense interest in this study. Because I see him on a daily basis, and because of our partnership in the company, he furnishes the most frequent information of all of my contacts.

Jamal suggests that the well-known negative reactions of Iranian society against dancing in public allow the parents to exercise further control over the children whose marriage and career plans are of great concern. "It is not merely dancing, but any art form they dislike. Children should be doctors and lawyers and make lots of money" (Feb. 16, 1996).

[6] One need only remember that the Empress Theodora was a public actress and dancer as a young woman. She was vilified by Procopius, the Byzantine historian who was her contemporary, in his *Secret History*, and her public excesses were exposed [some say exaggerated] by him. Meanwhile, the considerable propaganda machine of Justinian's government were employed to make her respectable. See for example A. A. Vasiliev 1964: 132, 180.

[7] During this period I was also conducting research in other dance traditions. I made several trips to the Balkans and Turkey throughout the 1960s and 1970s. I created over one hundred works for the ensembles I directed, the Village Dancers and AMAN (1960-77). In 1976 I made an extensive tour of Iran, Afghanistan, and the Central Asian republics of Uzbekistan and Tajikistan. I had also conducted extensive correspondence with the republics of Uzbekistan, Tajikistan, Armenia, Azerbaijan, and Georgia, as well as Bulgaria and Yugoslavia since 1961. This resulted in the acquisition of a major collection of books, recordings, films, photographs and other research materials on dance, music, costume, ethnography, history and language of these areas. It also greatly facilitated my research plans when I arrived in the USSR in 1976.

[8] Children who are acting wildly or behaving badly are sometimes told: *raqas-bazi dar naiavari* (don't act like a dancer).

Chapter 1

[1] Asad Torfeh has remained a friend and informant since the 1950s.

[2] So important is the symmetrical and "beautiful" (in Iranian terms) alignment of the body in the performance of this dance that in one version, a playful, game-like dance called *"mojassameh"* (statue) or *"raqs-e mat"* (death dance, i. e. "freeze motionlessly") in Iran, and *Logari* (place name) in Afghanistan, the dancer stops and as-

sumes a pose when the music stops. The mark of good dancer is one who can assume a "beautiful" pose with all of the limbs and torso attractively arranged like a dancer in a miniature painting.

Several years ago (Persian New Year, March 21, 1993), I served as a host at a New Year celebration for about 200 Iranian guests. I had the musicians play a piece for this dance and almost everybody in the room participated. If a performer moves after the music stops, he or she must retire from the dance space until a single dancer is left.

[3] As an example of this point, Cynthia Word, a modern dance choreographer and instructor who is married to an Iranian citizen, has taught dance in Iran, although she was required to call it "theatrical movement," and was unable to recognize solo improvised dance as a coherent aesthetic and movement system even after observing it for several years. She also informed me that this dance tradition is still widely performed behind carefully closed doors (personal communication: November 3, 1995).

[4] Iranian students in my classes, many of whom were born here or were very young children when brought to the United States, sometimes exhibit some embarrassment or surprise when viewing some of these performances on film, which often contain transgressively sensual and/or grotesque movements. Some of them claimed never to have seen such dance styles, while others laughed in delighted recognition. The women's harem games, *bazi-ha-ye namayeshi* (see Shay 1995b), are often characterized by highly transgressive movement practices. An Iranian student in one of my classes stated that they are still performed in her family circle (Feb. 16, 1998).

[5] While I find Levi-Strauss' notion of bricolage a useful model, in no way am I interested in his notions of what constitutes "primitive" or "savage" since such terms can not be useful in discussions of the Iranian culture sphere.

[6] In contemporary Iran, as with other areas with which I am familiar, it is difficult to assign terms like "traditional" and "modern," since highly educated scholars at the University of Tehran, physicians and lawyers, artists, intellectuals, and many other individuals are distinctly "modern," at least in most aspects of their lives. On the other hand, many rural dwellers and uneducated urban Iranians practice what I would term "traditional" life styles. As in the United States, a so-called "modern" nation, where many individuals conduct their lives utilizing a mixture of traditional and modern elements, so, too, in Iran, a nation which has existed historically along major trade and invasion routes, many individuals live their lives exhibiting both elements of the so-called "modern" and the so-called "traditional." Thus, I use these terms, for purposes of this study, as a convenient means for explaining conceptual approaches to aesthetic expression. For example, children in all societies and of all classes learn games and children's verses traditionally, that is, through mimesis and by rote through copying other children and, sometimes, adults. That is how Americans learn to sing "Happy birthday to you," a song which has not changed an iota in the sixty years I have heard and sung it.

[7] It is beyond the scope of this study to delve deeply into the niceties of what constitutes "modern dance." For purposes of this discussion, my use of the term "modern dance" also includes the genre of post-modern dance, which I, perhaps in contrast to many dance scholars, consider a continuation of modern dance. I believe that most culturally competent individuals in the United States who are not experts in dance, would do so as well. While some scholars might object to categorizing modern dance, I follow dance scholars Roger Copeland and Marshall Cohen's idea that "most critics and historians of the dance remain firmly committed to the practice of categorization. Indeed, throughout most of the century, they have routinely divided Western, theatrical dancing into two sometimes antagonistic genres, ballet

and modern dance. More recently, during the last fifteen or twenty years, a third major designation, that of post-modern dance, has been added." (1983:225). I fully understand their caveat that no one "pretends that every individual example of theatrical dance can be easily and unambiguously assigned to one of these three genres" (ibid). While "the designation 'modern dance' is usually and more properly reserved for choreographers such as Mary Wigman, Martha Graham, and Doris Humphrey who emerged during the period between the two wars" (1983:231), dance based on the techniques created by these individuals was still being widely taught throughout academia in the United States in the 1960's and 1970's, and I suspect, currently. In fact, so strongly did the devotees of modern dance become entrenched in academia, that the hostility toward classical ballet debarred its teaching in many of the same university and college dance programs for many years. The transition to "cutting edge" and "post-modern" is often more apparent than real, and, for most individuals, non-existent. In looking for "new solutions" for choreography, as Copeland and Cohen wryly observe, "post-modern dance—at least in its early minimalist manifestations—ran the risk of purifying itself right out of existence" (1983: 235).

[8] Since the banning of this dance in Iran, Farzaneh Kaboli, former soloist with the national dance company, holds semi-secret classes, for women only, which are in great demand, and even the daughter of President Rafsanjani attends. Currently, classes almost exclusively attended by women are more popular in Southern California because many of the traditional venues for learning no longer exist due to the social and geographic fragmentation of the Iranian community in Southern California. The *Iranian Yellow Pages* and Iranian television interviews and advertisements (December 1995) disclose at least four instructors holding classes for those who would like to shine in social events or for parents who would like their children to acquire this skill. I am personally approached after each public appearance to hold classes for adults and children.

[9] For the interested reader, there are numerous excellent articles and books about various aspects of calligraphy because it is such an important art form. I recommend the Yusofi article in *Encyclopaedia Iranica* (1994) as both succinct and well-researched. A longer study with many illustrations is the work by Khatibi and Sijelmassi (1976). The work by Maheronnaqsh (1991) demonstrates through copious illustrations the connection between calligraphy and tile work and the geometric forms upon which they are based.

Chapter 2

[1] A review of medieval miniatures from the various cities throughout this region from the fourteenth to the sixteenth century, and even later, show dance scenes that have an enormous uniformity of visual representation. These miniatures were produced in cities such as Herat, Samarqand, Bukhara, Tabriz, Isfahan, and Shiraz, as well as Moghul India.

[2] The one exception is Ettinghausen's 1984 study of carnivalesque dances performed in animal masks—a highly specialized topic. In addition, there are several miniatures showing dervishes in attitudes of movement. As depicted, the artists sometimes wryly depict them as sots, while in others they are in various states of ecstasy. I argue that this is not dance in the Western sense (Shay 1995). Clearly, in these depictions the dervishes are not practicing coordinated movements but, rather, appear to be "out-of-control."

[3] Chardin stated that "Prostitutes in Persia were more recognized than in other countries, although they were clothed and veiled like other women. Apart from their

veil being shorter and looser, their posture gave them away at first glance."
1996:118.6

[4] Authors Lloyd Miller and Katherine St. John have self-published a book, which is called *Radif-e Raqs:Collection of Dance Sequences of the Persian Tradition* (1987), to accompany video tapes of dancing by St. John and two other dancers, and it is provided as an aid to learn what the authors term "miniature" dancing (1987:iii). They claim these:

> ...dances have been formulated from the texts of poetry which accompanies the various *gusheh* (melodic sequences) which have been chosen to represent the various *dastgah* (modes). The dances and costumes have also been formulated from the system of colors and elements assigned to the *dastgah* by master Safvat and the emotion and mood set by each according to Safvat's system (1987:ii).

In order to learn this dance tradition properly, according to Miller and St. John:

> The first step to success in understanding and eventually performing these dance sequences is to forget the ego, the audience, any fame and fortune and to perform only for the pure beauty and the possibility of a feeling of unity with the divine source" (1987:ii).

The authors further claim that:

> ...the dance descriptions can serve to remind dancers of the movements which are appropriate for the emotion or symbolism to be interpreted. The study of music, symbolism and movements to poetry are instrumental in elevating a dancer to the role of interpreter of inner meaning and metaphysical wisdom. A prime ingredient for a traditional art is a spiritual path or some path of self improvement which is totally void of ego and of materialism. Some claim to know and even dare to teach Persian dance without abandoning the ego and without understanding the importance of a path. Modern Persian dance in night clubs is not Persian dance but only an incorrect representation as if viewed in a smudged mirror without the living essence which needs to be transmitted by a spiritual master. (1987:iii)

Several qualities are claimed for this dance form by Miller and St. John: 1). "Persian miniature dance depicts the qualities of perfection which are described in Persian poetry and miniature paintings of past eras" (1987: 8). Although eminent scholars of Persian literature such as Michael Hillmann (1990:76-78) stress that the idealized beloved is most often a generic young male, Miller and St. John claim that the idealized beloved is the "ideal perfect woman" (1987:8). 2). They also claim that dance is some type of mystic practice:

> Thus, although Persian miniature dance is not purposely intended to be a dance of devotion to God as are certain dance forms of India, the dancer portrays the qualities of perfection described in poetry and depicted in paintings which awaken the

viewer to a higher consciousness beyond the material plane"
(1987:9).

3). Like Rezvani and De Warren, Miller and St. John also claim a historical period
when dance was venerated. While acknowledging that "Historical data on Persian
dance is rather scarce" (1987:9), they nevertheless claim that "Ancient Persian dance
must have shared the same purpose and respect in which dance of ancient India or
China was held" (1987:9), without citing how such a conclusion was reached. Following Rezvani and De Warren, they also state that "When Islam came to Persia,
dancing was relegated to a low social category" (1987:10).

They go on to describe how miniature dancing came about:

> Persian miniature dances have been developed from drawing on
> Persian miniatures, from dance styles of neighboring areas
> which have been formed by influence and interchange with Per-
> sian culture and from the traditional poetry used in the vocal
> music.... (1987:10)

The authors present a description of dance movements with a vocabulary which they
developed (1987:23-29) and toward the end of the tape, Miller and St. John demonstrate how to interpret a poem with Miller reciting a translated line and St. John
producing the movements that "interpret" the meaning.

The authors are not forthcoming in clearly indicating that "miniature dancing" is
an invention of their own making. Throughout the text they give the impression that
this is a venerable and practiced tradition such as that described by Rezvani. In the
tapes, for instance, when the three dancers, including St. John, dance, they largely
perform to non-rhythmic classical Persian music, a practice not found in the Iranian
world where a rhythmic musical form known as *reng*, in 6/8 tempo, is generally
utilized for dance, although other rhythms might be employed. The use of specific
colors and times of day for each selection is also not a feature of traditional dance
and music. Equally significant, the implication of an Iranian dance tradition which
utilizes specific, standardized movements, such as mudras, to interpret poetry is
misleading. Solo, improvised dance in the Iranian culture sphere is an abstract form
of expression. Its professional practitioners have never been noted for mystic wisdom, and this work seems to be another noble, orientalist attempt to lend dignity to a
form of expression which clearly excites negative and ambiguous reactions from a
large portion of the Iranian population. Another problematic aspect is St. John's
portrayal of emotion in the dancing. As Hillmann points out:

> ...a significant feature in the Persian aesthetic: (is) its enduring
> classicism, exhibited through the adherence to convention in
> terms of subject and manner of treatment and through the em-
> phasis on generalized, typical, almost impersonal experiences as
> opposed to romantic or modernist lyrical statements that empha-
> size individuality, reality, subjectivity, and uniqueness.
> (1990:72)

In other words, the aesthetic described by Hillmann is the exact opposite of the
emotional displays suggested by the performances and their descriptions found in
Miller and St. John's book and tapes.

[5] The Topkapi Scroll is a 15th-16th century series of discrete patterns which Necipoglu utilizes to advance several important and revolutionary arguments regarding

aspects of Iranian aesthetic expression that I am advancing in this study. The timely appearance of this work allows me to deepen my observations regarding such topics as improvisation, geometry as a basis of Iranian expression, the role of geometry in art, and the notion of many Islams, among others.

The Topkapi scroll is a series of work patterns on the *girih* (*gereh* or knot), which "refers to the nodal points or vertices of the web like geometric grid systems or construction lines used in generating variegated patterns for architectural plans and decorative revetments in two and three dimensions" (1995: 9). This is much the pattern I describe in the way I envision this dance form in my own mind at the opening of Chapter One. The scroll is very rare and was found after several centuries in the Topkapi Museum Library. It is rare because it is a workbook of basic design formulae (*tumar* [scroll]—the same word used by storytellers for their cue books), which were carefully guarded trade secrets by families of guild members.

[6] Jamal, a professional painter, suggests that there are several reasons why the miniature, which was primarily used for manuscript illustrations of famous poetry, particularly the *Shahnameh* (the epic history of Persia), has such a grasp on the Iranian imagination. It has been the major form of representational art in Iran for nearly 1000 years, and perhaps longer, and even though few eyes saw these works initially, they embody Iranian aesthetic elements. As Pope has suggested, representational and figural painting is not an important art form in Iran, even though there have been important painters in Iranian history. Thus, painting has not progressed technically, beyond the aesthetic canons established during the Timurid period, and elaborated only slightly through later history. Since almost all painters were employed by the courts, there was no alternative vehicle for this mode of artistic expression.

Western art has never replaced miniature painting and this is, in part, due to the lack of understanding of Western aesthetics among Iranian painters. Those few Iranians who have made this departure are severely criticized for abandoning their traditional forms. (personal communication: May 9, 1994)

[7] Personal observation also demonstrates that sometimes older dancers and singers were in great demand because of their skill in the entertainment business. In 1986, in Tashkent, Uzbekistan, my tour party and I were honored by a visit to my hotel by Tamara Khanom, a legendary performer then in her eighties, and the hotel staff all applauded and bowed. Jamileh, perhaps the best known local professional dancer, is in her sixties.

[8] I am grateful to Dr. Houchang Chehabi, UCLA, for the suggestion that with the emigration of the aristocracy and upper classes, Iran is more than ever a middle-class nation and society and the aristocratic disdain for public dancing has disappeared, and more people are willing to dance than previously. (personal interview: November 15, 1995)

Chapter 3

[1] For a full discussion of patterned, non-dance movement practices see Shay (1995a).

[2] Java, for example, is an Islamic region that values dance and music. Therefore, the negative attitudes in the Middle East, Central Asia, and North Africa are not universally found in all Islamic areas.

[3] The terms *pai kubidan* (verb) or *pai-kubi* (noun), meaning dance, also exist, but they are mostly confined to literary use.

[4] During the regime of the late shah, professional ballet and folk dance companies

were established, as they had been in the Soviet-dominated adjacent areas in previous decades. Perhaps as a result of this, the term *raqsandeh,* meaning a dancer of
either sex, came into use. It does not seem to carry negative connotations and seems
to be a locution of recent provenance (over the last thirty years as evidenced by a
search through several Persian language dictionaries) to give respectability to professional dancers such as those in state companies.

[5] While carrying negative connotations in terms of street performers, the term *luti*
also refers to a kind of positive male behavior that is considered chivalrous and generous. An English equivalent might be someone who would "take the shirt off his
back" for one. I am indebted to Dr. Peter Chelkowski for his clarification of this
issue.

[6] It should be mentioned that several references to dancing at funerals in Luristan
have been cited. Morentsen observes that, "A testimony of dancing at funerals is
found on funeral stelae in the nomadic cemeteries in Luristan depicting women with
arms linked as if dancing (cf. e.g. Figs. 6,67 and 70, and Mortensen, I.D. 1983; Figs.
6 and 10). Modern Iranians look horrified when asked about dancing at funerals."
1993:373) Jamal also observed such "dance" or movement activities when traveling
in Luristan with his relatives prior to the 1978/79 Revolution. (personal interview:
February 8, 1999.)

Chapter 4

[1] A sampling of opinion is possible to some degree since one of the chief ways in
which Iranians in the United States keep in touch is through call-in programs on
both radio and television where I often appear as a guest and hold a dialogue with
both the host(s) and members of the listening public. These broadcasts are national
in scope and thousands of people listen and participate. For example, I was recently
the guest on an Iranian talk show (October 1, 1995), in which the hostess, Mojgan
Moghadam (whose family frequently invites me to social and ritual events) interviewed me for two hours about the subject of ambiguity regarding dance. As a result I received dozens of calls and invitations. For the purposes of gathering data
concerning the practices of Iranian solo improvised dance my particular venues form
the foci for my study.

[2] The term "Persian" derives from the Greek, which designated the Achaemenians
who originated in the province of Fars or Pars (thus Persis). In 1935, the Iranian
government formally requested all nations to refer to the nation-state as Iran, the
self-designated term in Persian. The use of "Persia" to designate the current nation-
state of Iran is anachronistic.

[3] It should be noted that many works in Middle Persian were penned after the Arab
conquest and express the ethnic and religious concerns of a beleaguered Zoroastrian
community.

[4] The importance of this Islamic cultural identity must be underscored because to a
large extent, it determines how the physical world of the Iranian/Islamic city, the
primary site of solo improvised dance, is ordered and organized. I look at sites such
as the women's quarters or the public coffee house, both popular sites of this dance
tradition. There is a perception that the sacred and non-sacred aspects of life can not
be separated in an Islamic context because Islam is an all-encompassing life style.
Historian Gene Garthwaite points out that "it is a truism that in Islam there is no
distinction between the sacred and profane" (1991:25), but I contest this position
because dance in an Islamic context cannot be performed in a sacred context or
space, and therefore a discussion of space in an Islamic context becomes crucial for
the study of dance, a distinctly non-sacred activity, in such a society.

The mosque, in anthropologist Sherry Ortner's (1973) term, is a "key symbol" of Islam. It is the decoration of these mosques and other sacred structures, with their elaborate calligraphic and abstract geometric designs, that gives the first and most basic clues of the aesthetic parameters of the Muslim physical and aesthetic environment. I discussed in Chapter One how these aesthetic visual patterns become translated into movement in the performance of the solo improvised dance.

After the advent of Islam, in contrast to London or Paris, the capital city of historical Iran (and sometimes there were multiple, sub- and competing cities) has changed many times: Samarqand, Ghazneh, Bukhara, Herat, Shiraz, Marv, Isfahan, Tabriz, and Tehran, among others, have served as centers of both politics and culture. This change of cities often occurred with changes of dynasty and we can see how this change of cities created a certain uniformity in the way space was employed in cities throughout this region. Thus we have an Iranian culture sphere with a shifting center. As ethnomusicologist Johanna Spector notes:

> While the geographical location of a culture center shifted from place to place as musicians followed the court, the culture traits and culture complexes of the music remained essentially the same or altered little, since the same musicians and the schools they established continued to practice the art and to set the standards regardless of geography. (1994: 36)

Like music, dance, too, maintained its stylistic integrity and uniform characteristics, informed by geometric forms and improvisation.

Another key symbol in Iranian society is the arabesque, a highly popular visual design element in both sacred and secular contexts. It is found everywhere in the decorative arts and it is so ubiquitous that scholars describing non-visual expressions such as poetry, including Iranian literature scholar Michael Hillmann (1990: 75), unhesitatingly use the arabesque as a basis of comparison. I use this key symbol to demonstrate how it is created in the performance of dance. Gulru Necipoglu's magisterial study, *The Topkapi Scroll-Geometry and Ornament in Islamic Architecture* (1995), supports Ortner's theory. Necipoglu's contention is that historians of Islamic art have developed an "Orientalist discourse on the so-called arabesque, singled out as a unifying essence of Islamic visual art," thus essentializing the entire art tradition as decoration without meaning beyond its intrinsic beauty, a timeless, immutable search for purity in design. However, Necipoglu successfully demonstrates that each of the various dynasties—Timurid, Safavid, Ottoman, Mughal, and others appropriated a different visual aspect, and thus, these geometrically informed design aspects have semiotic meaning.

Ortner uses the example of an American flag as a popular and positive key symbol. In contrast, I look at dance, a secular activity in Islamic society, as an ambiguous, sometimes negative, symbol. Unlike Ortner, I suggest that multiple and conflicting meanings may attach to such symbols (which is why some wish to burn the flag and others die for it); that dance creates both the positive symbol in the Iranian culture sphere, represented in poetic metaphor as freedom of movement and grace, and the negative symbol of loose morals, and transgressive, and potentially "out-of-control" behavior. I argue that because dance forms such a powerful and ambiguous symbol, the Islamic regime banned its performance, and because of this, individuals put themselves at risk to perform it, thus creating a new symbol: dance as an act of resistance to the Islamic regime. Dance, like most other human activities, does not occur in a vacuum. People perform it and people watch and react to it, and because people react to it, particularly in specific Iranian contexts, it is capable of forming symbols.

[5] For representative, in-depth studies see Fathi 1991, Asgari 1991, Bozorgmehr and Sabagh 1991, 1993, Kelley 1991, 1993, Srebreny-Mohammadi and Mohammadi 1991, Naficy 1991, 1993b. Some of those scholars have themselves emerged from that milieu, which may account for the fact that the pre-1978 population merits only the sketchiest coverage. Another reason that the pre-1978 population has not been studied in-depth is that population figures are sketchy and misleading. It was largely a student community, and was therefore, impermanent. For this reason, my personal observations of the pre-1978 community are, perhaps, most useful for the earliest period, the 1950s and 1960s.

[6] Parvaneh Azad, a resident of Los Angeles for over 40 years, states that the "old-timers" have little in common with the more recent exiles. This stems in large part because the new immigrants often "have their minds in Iran, while we pursue pastimes and activities that we have come to enjoy in America" (personal communication: March 30, 1996).

[7] Patoq on Alvarado, across from MacArthur Park, and Dinah's (Fried Chicken) on Western near Sunset Boulevard. Later, there was the Iran Shish Kebab House on Hollywood Boulevard. In addition there was a night club-restaurant, Delila, (from around 1975-1980), owned and hosted by a musician, Manuchehr Sadeghi, who played, in addition to Persian dance music, such popular Middle Eastern and Israeli hits as *Hava Nagila*, in order to attract a wider patronage. He also featured an Iranian dancer known as "The Persian Kitten" (personal observation and Joe Carson, musician who played *tonbak* [Iranian goblet drum] with Sadeghi, personal interview: June 24, 1996).

[8] Studies of the Iranian Revolution are many and varied. I highly recommend Ervand Abrahimian's works (1982, 1989, 1993), Keddie (1981), Lincoln (1989), Moaddel (1993), and Ramazani (editor 1990) as good sources about the revolution. Also of interest is Ehteshami's (1995) book about the current state of affairs in post-revolutionary Iran.

[9] I have film footage and I witnessed such performances in 1976. The performers were males, since females were not allowed in public spaces, with the exception of such large cities as Kabul and Herat. I also personally saw such a performance by a male dancer in Tehran (October, 1976), who was in his late sixties and had been a boy dancer during the late Qajar period.

[10] At a recent concert by an Azerbaijani singer (Zoroufchi, October 18, 1995), which included dancers and musicians from the former Soviet Republic of Azerbaijan, two audience members rose from their seats and danced with enormous energy and verve.

Chapter 5

[1] In the generic "anatomy of an Iranian dance event," I show that the hostess generally begins the dance, usually in a sketchy fashion, to entice the guests onto the floor. Since this host had no wife, he fulfilled this function.

Shalinsky states that recently, among some Afghan refugees in the United States, the solo improvised dance is being performed in mixed sex settings such as weddings, but a woman does not dance with anyone who is not a close relative such as a husband, brother or father. This is a new phenomenon because this same group of people, which Shalinsky studied in Kunduz, Afghanistan in the 1970s, danced in separate male and female locations. (Personal communication: July 7, 1995.) This practice of dancing in mixed gatherings began earlier in Iran. It was still fairly rare in the 1950s but spread through the 1970s and probably was one of the reasons this

dance form was banned in the Islamic Republic of Iran after the Revolution of 1979.
7. It has been reported that, on the occasion of Isma'il Mirza's wedding, Tahmasb (one of the Safavid shahs) was so delighted that he actually danced" (Gholsorkhi 1996:149) about which, Iranian history scholar Gholsorkhi comments in footnote that the spectacle of a shah dancing was certainly 30 (ibid): "an unregal public gesture by Tahmasb." Such reactions make fatuous the stage depictions of shahs and sultans who dance with dancing girls.

Such attitudes seem common throughout the Middle East. Metin And, the Turkish dance historian, reports that "A Moslem who visited a Paris ballroom [in 1905], asked 'when he is so rich, this gentleman gives himself the trouble to dance? Why doesn't he hire some one to do it for him?'" (1959:9, n. 3).

[2] A male Iranian friend of over twenty years' duration, but whom I had not seen for some time, was persuaded by his non-Iranian wife to dance. He moved with great ease and ability, but had the grace to give me a sheepish grin, since he had told me for years that not only did he not know how to dance but that he had never known how.

[3] The word *gheir*, and the concept of moving in a coquettish style, especially with the provocative movements of the torso which it implies, is the hallmark of many urban *motrebi* (professional entertainment) and *ru-howzi* songs, as well as the women's theatrical games. As an example:

amu sabzi forush (uncle vegetable seller?)	*baleh* (yes)
inja Tehrun-e? (Is this Tehran?)	*baleh* (yes)
gheir faravun-e? (Is there a lot of gheir?)	*baleh* (yes)

[4] I receive dozens of telephone calls from Iranians seeking to hire my company for their private events, and especially popular is the AVAZ version of *shateri* created by Khosrow Jamali. Friends who serve as freelance dancers for these events report dancing at as many as six events on a single weekend. In activities such as weddings, I only participate as a guest/participant; AVAZ performs only at formal, public events. Were I or AVAZ to perform in this informal context, I would lose all credibility as a serious researcher and artist.

[5] For Moslems, the *dowreh* can also include somber religious events, such as *sofreh-andakhtan* (religious feast). The guest list for such a religiously-oriented event would be more restricted, and non-Moslems would generally not be invited.

[6] In my opinion, the scrutiny of females in public contexts occurs because historically, public space (until 1935 in Iran) was considered male space. In practice, and what seems little known, is that in most Iranian families the behavior and whereabouts of male children is as closely scrutinized as that of female children.

[7] It has been reported that, on the occasion of Isma'il Mirza's wedding, Tahmasb (one of the Safavid shahs) was so delighted that he actually danced" (Gholsorkhi 1996:149) about which, Iranian history scholar Gholsorkhi comments in footnote that the spectacle of a shah dancing was certainly 30 (ibid): "an unregal public gesture by Tahmasb." Such reactions make fatuous the stage depictions of shahs and sultans who dance with dancing girls.

Such attitudes seem common throughout the Middle East. Metin And, the Turkish dance historian, reports that "A Moslem who visited a Paris ballroom [in 1905], asked 'when he is so rich, this gentleman gives himself the trouble to dance? Why doesn't he hire some one to do it for him?'" (1959:9, n. 3).

Chapter 6

[1] It is important to note that while the movement vocabulary of solo improvised dance is utilized for contemporary productions, unlike traditional contexts, the cho-

reographies are set rather than improvised. The choreographies originated as improvised practice by the original choreographer, but for group performances, the movements are frozen.

Much of the information for this section was gleaned from practicing actors of this traditional theatre form, and I am especially grateful to Ardavan Mofid, a gifted *naqqal* and *gholam-siyah* portrayer, for his patient and fruitful responses to my many questions. I first met Ardavan Mofid in joint performances given by AVAZ and his *siyah-bazi* group in the late 1970s and he has remained a friend and supporter ever since.

[2] As an artist, I make deliberate, conscious decisions and create choreographic strategies to achieve the effects I wish to produce. I clearly recognize that what I put on the stage is not a duplicate of what occurs in a specific village or historical period, but rather an evocation of such dancing. The most positive, and welcome, response I receive comes from the person who says, "that's just how it was when I was in Iran" or *"Tonight you took me back home for an evening I never again hoped to experience* (unknown audience member, August 3, 1996). The success of my work lies in its ability to create the feeling that an individual is experiencing a memory of an event in his or her life. *Like Alter, in an analogous position of participant-observer in another cultural context and genre, that is, the study of traditional wrestling in Northern India, confessed, "I hope that I have now exorcised from this picture the most malevolent orientalist demons"* (1992: 3). The methods I use for creating a new work include fieldwork, learning from individuals who possess specific knowledge about particular dance traditions, and research into scholarly and historical sources. This is a deliberate choice to avoid the stereotyped "harem" scene familiar to viewers of Hollywood movies and appropriated by several choreographers of Middle Eastern dance.

[3] For a full exposition of religious theatre practices, particularly the *ta'ziyeh*, see the works by Chelkowski (1979) (which includes a collection of essays by leading scholars of this form), Riggio (1988), and Beeman (1992).

[4] An excellent account of this practice is Mary Ellen Page's "Professional Storytelling In Iran: Transmission and Practice." *Iranian Studies*. Vol. xii, Summer-Autumn 1979. 195-216.

[5] According to Ardavan Mofid, my principal informant, if the rendering of these tales exactly follows the original work by Ferdowsi, it is called *shahnameh-khani*, whereas looser renditions are known as *naqqali*. Mofid, in addition to his ability in playing the black-face role of *gholam siyah*, is an outstanding *naqqal*.

[6] I first personally became aware of these plays when I was in Iran in the late 1950s and watched performances by Mahvash, a popular singer-entertainer who performed a few of these as part of her repertoire. Friends then informed me that such plays were commonplace among women. During my research on the *bazi-ha*, which began a decade ago, many wonderful Iranian women provided me with information. I am particularly grateful to Mrs. Azadeh and Mrs. Pary Azad for first-hand information.

In addition, Jamal, an individual who is the stage designer for AVAZ, has an acute memory of the performances of these plays in his own family, where they formed a regular part of the women's social activities.

I ultimately staged this genre for my dance company. A full description may be found in 'Enjavi-Shirazi, 1972, Safa-Isfahani, 1980, and Shay 1995b.

[7] A few women joined urban *ru-howzi* troupes, but this is a twentieth-century development, which obviously came to an end with the Islamic Regime that banned performances of *ru-howzi* and *siyah-bazi*.

[8] Mohammadi asserts that in the Qajar period, "the practice of putting boards over the garden pool became common." (1973:22). Azad stated that, "the practice of putting wooden pieces over the pool is an old one that was designed to protect the tiles from cracking during winter freezes, and then the planks were used during the rest of the year for any performances such as weddings or circumcisions held in the courtyard" (personal communication, February 28, 1994). *Siyah-bazi* was only one of the performing arts performed in this manner, and it was more commonly performed in coffee houses, public streets and squares, and later, in theatres and night clubs.

[9] Parvaneh Azad stated that in her childhood (during the 1930s), "*ru-howzi* was performed in homes, but *siyah-bazi*, with its more political character, was more common in coffee houses and other public areas which were commonly frequented by exclusively male audiences, who were more interested in political matters" (Personal communication: February 4, 1994). The most important and insightful comment on the difference came from Ardavan Mofid (January 27, 1994).

[10] In Tehran, in 1976, I did witness several times the performance of a man in his late sixties or early seventies who had been a professional dancer as young boy. He was recreating this dance tradition, so that to some degree, I have an idea of what dances looked like a century ago, during the Qajar period.

[11] As another example: "The dances you will see are echoes from a distant time and place...[and they] aspire to express the sacred mysteries of their roots and that which transcends boundaries of time, place and culture" (Ballet Afsaneh 1994: program cover).

[12] Among all of the well-known state dance companies of the world, I can think of no other example of such a sensitive position, that of portraying a nation state through dance, being handed to a foreigner for interpretation. Why a native Iranian was not selected raises many speculative possibilities, but in the final analysis, I feel it is one more point to support the entire concept of choreophobia.

[13] Having shown the orientalist methods and assumptions used by De Warren in exoticizing Iran, there are other aspects of the performances that are also of interest. The topic of representation by an official state dance company of a multi-ethnic state like Iran is a crucial one: who is represented and in what manner? I stress that one of Said's points is that political domination is one of orientalism's goals. Such a topic is beyond the scope of this study and merits a full-scale study of its own, but nonetheless, I wish to mention it in passing as an important issue. Dance is certainly not a means of direct domination, but rather, its performances by an official state dance company may serve as a reflection of social and political realities. I am extending Said's meaning to show, as Anna L. Tsing (1993) has demonstrated, that marginalization can contain many layers, as can colonialism. Messages of representation are embedded in the performances and program notes of the former Iranian State Folk Dance Company, the Mahalli Dancers. These representations deal with power and politics in the Iranian nation state disguised in quaint choreographic garb. In the program notes of the Mahalli Ensemble, the difference between Persian dances and those of other groups such as the Kurds, Baluchis, and Turkmen are briefly contrasted: those of the Persians are "refined and delicate" those of the other groups are rough, primitive, and vigorous (Mahalli Dancers program 1976: Introduction). Thus, Tsing's concept of layers of marginalization is vividly represented in such a dance performance. The Persians, peripheral and marginal to the West, are now the core; while the Iranian others, the Kurds, Baluchis, and Turkmen, are the periphery. They must be spoken for and interpreted to the world by the Persians through the vehicle of the Iranian National Dance Company and the Persian lan-

guage. Thus, in the nationalism of the Iranian state, the Persians are the center and
the other Iranians are presented as colorful natives. Significantly, the Azerbaijanis,
a Turkic group which constitutes a quarter of Iran's population, were not represented
in any of the performances I saw, either in Tehran or the United States.

[14] They are Shahrzad Dance Ensemble, Ballet Afsaneh, Kavkaz, Ballet Pars, Nama,
Ney Nava, Saba, and AVAZ. There are also dance companies in other areas of
North America, including a branch of Ballet Pars in Vancouver, Canada.

[15] One of my informants, Parvaneh Azad, a United States citizen for more than
thirty years, claimed that she was considerably taken aback when, upon attempting
to leave Iran in this period, the authorities demanded proof of her husband's permission for her to leave the country (June 19, 1994).It is important to note that while the
movement vocabulary of solo improvised dance is utilized for contemporary productions, unlike traditional contexts, the choreographies are set rather than improvised. The choreographies originated as improvised practice by the original choreographer, but for group performances, the movements are frozen.

 Much of the information for this section was gleaned from practicing actors of this
traditional theatre form, and I am especially grateful to Ardavan Mofid, a gifted
naqqal and *gholam-siyah* portrayer, for his patient and fruitful responses to my
many questions. I first met Ardavan Mofid in joint performances given by AVAZ
and his *siyah-bazi* group in the late 1970s and he has remained a friend and supporter ever since.

Chapter 7

[1] All informants who have visited Iran recently report that there is an intense demand for and availability of popular music, largely recorded in Southern California,
because it has become a "forbidden fruit." They also report that because of the banning of many entertainments, and boring television programming, the quality of
dancing and traditional music has greatly improved, because families must largely
provide their own entertainment in private, and dancing and music are among the
favorite activities for many. Mr. and Mrs. Abbas Chamanara, the owners of the
major Iranian music store, the Music Box, verify my personal observation in their
store, when they report that a sizable portion of their sales among the young is music
for dancing. Customer after customer asked for *raqs-e shad* (happy dancing) or
muzik-e shad bara-ye raqs (happy music for dancing). (Nov. 30, 1996)

Figure 1. Persian alphabet showing how letters are formed and proportions of lines and dots. Courtesy of Masoud Valipour.

Figure 2. Top: A line from the poet Nima Yushij. Bottom: The word *'eshq* (love), calligraphy by Masoud Valipour.

be ب

he (jimi) ح

Figure 3. Illustration showing how dancer creates similar movements to those used by calligraphers in the creation of letters *be* and *he (jimi)*.

(Illustration by Jamal.)

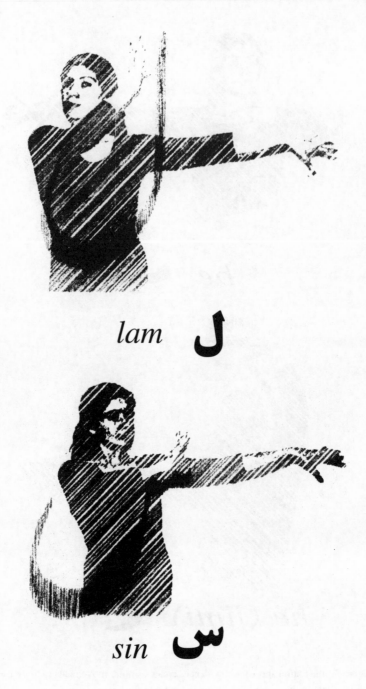

lam ل

sin س

Figure 4. Illustration showing how dancer creates similar movements to those used by calligraphers in the creation of letters *sin* and *lam*.

Figure5. A stone carving showing solo dancers in front of two "big men." (circa Third millennium from Zoka, part 2, 1978).

Figure 6a. Male group dance on dish, Fars 4th century B.C.

Figure 6b. Female dance group on potsherd, Fourth millennium, B.C.
(From Zoka, part 1 , 1978)

Figure 7. Dancing figure from Sasanian vase, possibly depicting the goddess, Anahtia.

Figure 8. Three fragments of Safavid period miniatures showing dancers in stylized positions indicating that dancing is occurring. Dancing indicated that a happy occasion such as an enthronement, wedding, or party was occurring. (from Soudavar)

Figure 9. Qajar period (circa 1850) professional dancer. (from *majmu'eh-i az naqashi-ha-ye irani*. n.d.)

Figure 10. Three aspects of solo improvised dance in social context photographed at the engagement celebration of Mojgan Moghaddam-Rahbar and Farzin Rahbar. (Courtesy of Afsaneh and Mojgan Moghaddam Rahbar.

Figure 11. Large hotel party showing solo improvised dance in social context. Courtesy of Afsar Moghaddam.

Figure 12. Siyah bazi group of Ardavan Mofid.   Left to right: Ardavan Mofid, Firuz, the black face clown, Rafi Khachatourian, first *hajji*, Behrouz Hashemi, second *hajji,* Ali Pourtash, Mehri, the *zan push* (transvestite hajji's daughter). Courtesy of Ardavan Mofid. (Photo by D. Young)

Figure 13. Film advertisement from 1950s showing images of "out-of-control," solo improvised dance. Video cover.

Figure 14. *Shateri*, performed by AVAZ International Dance Theatre.

Figure 15. Court dance from Samarqand performed by AVAZ International Dance Theatre.
(Photo by D. Young)

Figure 16. Solo improvised dance in performance context. Lynnette
Houston, AVAZ International Dance Theatre.

(Photo by D. Young)

BIBLIOGRAPHY

Abrahamian, Ervand. *Iran Between Two Revolutions*. Princeton, NJ: Princeton University Press, 1982.

_____. *Iranian Mojahedin*. New Haven, Conn.: Yale University Press, 1989.

_____. *Khomenism: Essays on the Islamic Republic of Iran*. Berkeley: University of California Press, 1993.

Al-'Azm, Sadiq. "Orientalism and Orientalism in Reverse." in *Khamsin, an Anthology*. n.p.: Al Saqi Books, 1984.

Al Faruqi, Lois Ibsen. "Dance as an Expression of Islamic Culture." in *Dance Resource Journal*. 10 (2). 1987: 6-17.

Alter, Joseph S. *Wrestler's Body: Identity and Ideology in North India*. Berkeley: University of California Press, 1992.

And, Metin. *Dances of Anatolian Turkey*. New York: Dance Perspectives. #3, 1959.

_____. *Pictorial History of Turkish Dancing*. Ankara: Dost Yayinlari, 1976.

Anderson, Benedict, *Imagined Communities*. London, NY, Verso, revised edition, 1991.

Anderson, Richard L. and Karen L. Field, editors. *Art in Small-Scale Societies: Contemporary Readings*. Englewood Cliffs, NJ: Prentice Hall, 1993.

Arberry, A. J. *Classical Persian Literature*. London: George Allen and Unwin, 1958.

Azizova, Aziza. *Raqs bo gulho* (dance with roses). Leninabad, Tajikistan: Oblastnoi Dom Narodnogo Tvorchestva, 1960.

_____. *Raqs bo kuza* (dance with jug). Leninabad, Tajikistan: Khanai viloiati khalq, 1960.

Baker, Roger. *Drag: A History of Female Impersonation in the Performing Arts*. NY: New York University Press, 1994.

Bakhtin, Mikhail. *Rabelais and His World*. Bloomington: Indiana University Press, 1984 (1965 in Russian). Translated by Helen Iswolsky.

BARDA (slave) (by various authors). *Encyclopaedia Iranica*. 1989:762-779.

Barthes, Roland. *Mythologies*. NY: Noonday Press, 1957 (translation 1972).

Beck, Lois. *Qashqa'i People of Southern Iran*. UCLA Museum of Cultural History, Pamphlet series #14. Los Angeles, 1978.

Beeman, William O. "What is (IRANIAN) National Character?: A Social-inguistic Approach." *Iranian Studies*, 9 (1976): 22-48.

_____. "Why Do They Laugh?" *Journal of American Folklore*, vol. 94, no. 374. 1981:506-526.

_____."Images of the Great Satan: Representations of the United States in the Iranian Revolution." in Keddie, Nikki, editor. *Religion and Politics in Iran.* New Haven, Conn.: Yale University Press, 1983.

_____. *Language, Status, and Power in Iran.* Bloomington: Indiana University Press, 1986.

_____. "Mimesis and Travesty in Iranian Traditional Theatre." in *Gender in Performance,* edited by Laurence Senelick. Hanover and London: University Press of New England, 1992:14-25.

_____. *Iranian Nationality and the Persian Language* (book review). Iranian Studies. volume 28, numbers 1-2 (Winter/Spring 1995): 86-88.

Behnam, M. Reza. *Cultural Foundations of Iranian Politics.* Salt Lake City, University of Utah Press, 1986.

Beiza'i, Bahram. *Namayesh dar iran* (Theatre in Iran, in Persian). Tehran: Kaivan Press, 1965.

Beliaev, Viktor. *Central Asian Music: Essays in the History of the Music of the Peoples of the USSR.* Edited and Annotated by Mark Slobin, Translated from the Russian by Mark and Greta Slobin. Middletown, Conn.: Wesleyen UP, 1975.

Berger, Bennett M. *Essay on Culture: Symbolic Structure and Social Structure.* Berkeley, CA: University of California, 1995.

Berger, Morroe. *Curious and Wonderful Gymnastic.* "Arab Danse Du Ventre." NY: Dance Perspectives, #10, 1961: 4-42.

Bier, Carol, editor. *Woven from the Soul, Spun from the Heart: Textile Arts of Safavid and Qajar Iran, 16th-19th Centuries.* Washington, D.C.: Textile Museum, 1987.

Blacking, John. "Movement, Dance, Music and the Venda Girl's Initiation." in Spenser, Paul, ed. *Society and the Dance.* Cambridge UP, 1985. pp. 64-91.

Blunt, Wilbur. *Isfahan: Pearl of Iran.* New York: Stein and Day, 1966.

Boroujerdi, Mehrzad. *Iranian Intellectuals and the West: The Tormented Triumph of Nativism.* Syracuse: Syracuse University Press, 1996.

Bosworth, Clifford Edmund. "Political and Dynastic History of the Iranian World (A.D.1000-1217)." *Cambridge History of Iran* (in eight volumes). Cambridge: Cambridge University Press, Volume 5, 1968: 1-202).

_____. *Mediaeval Islamic Underworld: The Banu Sasan in Arabic Society and Literature.* Leiden: E. J. Brill, 1976.

Bourguignon, Erika. *Trance Dance.* New York: Dance Perspectives, #35, Autumn, 1968.

Bozorgmehr, Mehdi and Georges Sabagh. "High Status Immigrants: A Statistical Profile of Iranians in the United States." *Iranian Studies.* Volume XXI, Numbers 1-3, 1988: 5-36.

_____. "Survey Research among Middle Eastern Immigrant Groups in the United States: Iranians in Los Angeles." *Middle Eastern Studies Association. Bulletin* 23. 1989:23-34.

_____. "Iranian Exiles and Immigrants in Los Angeles." Fathi, Asgar, editor. *Iranian Refugees and Exiles Since Khomeini.* Costa Mesa, CA.: Mazda Publishers, 1991: 121-144.

Bozorgmehr, Mehdi, Georges Sabagh, and Claudia Der-Martirosian. "Beyond Nationality: Religio-Ethnic Diversity." Kelley, Ron, editor.

Irangeles. Berkeley: University of California Press, 1993: 59 - 79.

Brend, Barbara. *Islamic Art*. Cambridge, MA: Harvard University Press, 1991.

Browne, Edward G. *Literary History of Persia*. In four volumes. Cambridge University Press, 1902 (reprinted in 1964).

_____. *A Year Among the Persians: 1887-1888*. New York: Hippocrene, 1984 (reprint of 1893 edition).

Bulliet, Richard. *Islam: the View from the Edge*. NY: Columbia Univ. Press, 1994.

Buonaventura, Wendy. *Serpent of the Nile: Women and Dance in the Arab World*. NY: Interlink, 1990.

Caiger-Smith, Alan. *Lustre Pottery: Technique, Tradition and Innovation in Islam and the Western World*. London, New Amsterdam, 1985.

Cefkin, Melissa. *Choreographing Culture: Dance, Folklore, and the Politics of Identity in Turkey*. Ph.D. dissertation, Rice University: 1995.

Chardin, Sir John. *Travels in Persia: 1673-1677*. NY: Dover, 1988.

Chehabi, H. E. "Staging the Emperor's New Clothes: Dress Codes and Nation-Building under Reza Shah." *Iranian Studies*. Volume 26, Numbers 3-4, Summer/Fall, 1993: 209-229.

___. "Sport and Politics in Iran: The Legend of Gholamreza Takhti." *International Journal of the History of Sport*. Vol. 12, No. 3 (Dec. 1995):48-60.

Chelkowski, Peter, editor. *Taziyeh: Ritual and Drama in Iran*. New York University Press, 1979.

___. "Popular Entertainment, Media and Social Change in Twentieth-Century Iran." in *Cambridge History of Iran*, Vol. VII, chapter 21:765-814. Cambridge University Press, 1991. Edited by Peter Avery et al.

___. "Ta'ziyeh, Indigenous Avant-Garde Theatre of Iran." *Interculturalism and Performance*. NY: PAJ Publications, 1991:226-236.

Chomsky, Noam. "Logical Basis of Linguistic Theory." In *Proceedings of the 9th International Congress of Linguistics*. The Hague: Mouton, 1964: 914-978.

___. *Aspects of a Theory of Syntax*. Cambridge: MIT Press, 1965.

Choudhury, M. L. Roy. "Music in Islam." *Journal of Asiatic Society* 23, No. 2 (1957).

Cohen, Selma Jeanne, editor, with a new section by Katy Matheson. *Dance as a Theatre Art: Source Readings in Dance History from 1581 to the Present*. Second Editon. Princeton, NJ: Dance Horizons, 1992.

Cole, Juan R. I. "Marking Boundaries, Marking Time: the Iranian Past and the Construction of the Self by Qajar Thinkers." *Iranian Studies*. Vol. 29, #1-2, Winter/Spring, 1996:35-56.

Comaroff, John and Jean. *Ethnography and the Historical Imagination*. Boulder, Colorado: Westview, 1992.

Confucius. *Wisdom of Confucius*. Edited and Translated with notes by Yu Tang. NY: Illustrated Modern Library, 1938:13.

Copeland, Roger and Marshall Cohen. "Genre and Style." in Copeland and Cohen, editors. *What is Dance?* Oxford: Oxford University Press, 1983: 225 - 237.

Cowan, Jane K. *Dance and the Body Politic in Northern Greece.* Princeton, NJ: Princeton University, 1990.

Curtis, John. *Ancient Persia.* Cambridge, MA: Harvard University Press, 1989.

Daryaee, Touraj. "National History or Keyanid History?: The Nature of Sasanid Zoroastrian Historiography." *Iranian Studies*, Volume 28, Numbers 3-4, Summer/Fall 1995 :129-141.

De Planhol, X. "Geography of Settlement." in W. B. Fisher, editor. *Cambridge History of Iran.* Cambridge: At the University Press, 1968: 409-467.

De Warren, Robert and Peter Williams. "Discovery in Persia." *Dance and Dancers.* January 1973: 28-32.

Du Ry, Carel J. *Art of Islam.* NY: Henry N. Abrams, 1970.

During, Jean. "Musique D'Extase et de Guerison du Baloutchistan." (record notes of disc, Iran, Vol. 5 and 6). Paris, Ocora, 1981.

___. "Emotion in Trance: Musical Exorcism in Baluchistan." in Caton, Margaret and Neil Siegel, eds. *Cultural Parameters of Iranian Musical Expression.* Redondo Beach, CA: Institute of Persian Performing Arts, 1986:36-46.

___. *Art of Persian Music.* Washington, D. C.: Mage, 1991.

Dzhavrishvili, D. *Gruzinskie Narodnye Tantsy.* (Georgian Folk Dances, in Russian). Tbilisi: State Publishing House, "Sabchota Sakartvelo," 1958.

Eagleton, Terry. *Literary Theory: An Introduction.* Minneapolis: University of Minnesota Press, 1983.

Eastman, Carol M. *Aspects of Language and Culture.* 2nd edition. Novato, CA: Chandler & Sharp, Inc., 1990.

Ehlers, Eckart and Willem Floor. "Urban Change in Iran, 1920-1941." *Iranian Studies.* Volume 26, Numbers 3-4, 1993: 251-276.

Eickelman, Dale F. "Re-Imagination of the Middle East: Political and Academic Frontiers." (1991 Presidential Address). *Middle East Studies Association. Bulletin.* Vol. 26, #1 (July 1992): 3-12.

'Enjavi–Shirazi, M. A. *Bazi–ha–ye namayeshi* (Theatrical Plays). (In Persian). Tehran, Amir Kabir, 1972.

Esposito, John L. "Ethnicity." *Encyclopedia of the Modern Islamic World*, Vol. 1. NY: Oxford University Press, 1995: 447-452.

Ettinghausen, Richard. "Dance with Zoomorphic Masks and Other Forms of Entertainment Seen in Islamic Art." in Ettinghausen, Richard. *Islamic Art and Archeology: Collected Papers.* Berlin: Gebr. Mann Verlag, 1984.

Farahnakianpour, Mehrangiz Hatami. "Survey of Dramatic Activity in Iran from 1850 to 1950." Ph.D. Dissertation, Brigham Young University, 1977.

Farhat, Hormoz. "Dastgah Concept in Persian Music." Ph.D. Dissertation. UCLA, 1965.

Farman Farmaian, Sattareh. *Daughter of Persia.* NY: Doubleday, 1992.

Farmer, Henry George. "Outline History of Music and Musical Theory." in Pope, Arthur Upham. *Survey of Persian Art.* 1964: Vol VI: 2783-

2804).

Fathi, Asgar, editor. *Iranian Refugees and Exiles Since Khomeini.* Costa Mesa, CA: Mazda Publishers, 1991.

Fermor, Sharon. "On the Question of Pictorial 'Evidence' for Fifteenth-Century Dance Technique." *Dance Research Journal.* Autumn 1967. Vol. 2: 18-32.

Firth, Raymond. "Art and Anthropology." in Coote, Jeremy and Anthony Shelton, editors. *Anthropology, Art, and Aesthetics.* Oxford: Clarendon Press, 1992: 15-39.

Fish, Stanley. *Is There a Text in This Class? The Authority of Interpretive Communities.* Cambridge: Harvard University Press, 1980.

Foster, Susan Leigh. *Reading Dancing: Bodies and Subjects in Contemporary American Dance.* Berkeley: University of California Press, 1986.

___. "Dancing Culture." *American Ethnologist.* Vol. 19, May 1992:362-366.

___. "Dancing Bodies." in Crary, Jonathan and Sanford Kwinter, editors. *Incorporations.* (Zone 6). NY: Zone, 1992:480-495).

Fraser, Kathleen. "Aesthetic Explorations of the Egyptian Oriental Dance Among Egyptian Canadians." *UCLA Journal of Dance Ethnology.* Volume 17, 1993:58-66.

Friedlander, Ira. *Whirling Dervishes.* New York: MacMillan, 1975. (reprinted in 1992).

Friend, Robyn C. and Neil Siegal. "Contemporary Contexts for Iranian Professional Musical Performance." in Caton, Margaret and Neil Siegel, editors. *Cultural Parameters of Iranian Musical Expression.* Redondo Beach, CA: Institute of Persian Performing Arts, 1986:10-17.

___. "Modern Persian Dance." *Encyclopaedia Iranica.* Costa Mesa, CA: Mazda, 1994. Vol. VI: 641-645.

___. *"chub–bazi"* (Stick Fighting). *Encyclopedia Iranica.* Costa Mesa, CA, Mazda, 1993. Vol. VI: 448–449.

Frishman, Martin and Hassan-Uddin Khan, editors. *Mosque.* London: Thames and Hudson, 1994.

Fry, Roger. "Some Aspects of Persian Art." in *Persian Art: An Illustrated Souvenir of the Exhibition of Persian Art at Burlington House London 1931.* Second Edition. London: Hudson & Kearns Ltd., 1931: xvii-xix.

Frye, Richard N. "Pre-Islamic and Early Islamic Cultures in Central Asia." in Canfield, Robert L., editor. *Turko-Persia in Historical Perspective.* Cambridge University Press, 1991: 35-52.

___. "Preface." *Cambridge History of Iran*, Vol. 4. Cambridge University Press, 1974: xi - xiii.

___. *Heritage of Persia.* Costa Mesa, CA: Mazda Publishers, 1993.

Fujii, Tomoaki, ed. *JVC Video Anthology of World Music and Dance.* In 30 video cassettes and 9 books. Tokyo: Victor Company of Japan, Ltd., 1988.

Gaffary, Farrokh. "Evolution of Rituals and Theater in Iran." *Iranian Studies.* 1984, Autumn: 361-390.

Garthwaite, Gene R. "Reimagined Internal Frontiers: Tribes and Nationalism—Bakhtiyaris and Kurds." in Eickelman, Dale F., editor. *Russia's*

Muslim Frontiers. Bloomington, IN: Indiana University Press, 1993.

___. "Popular Islamic Perceptions of Paradise Gained." in Blair, Sheila, S. and Jonathan M. Bloom, editors. *Images of Paradise in Islamic Art.* Hanover, N. H.: Hood Museum of Art, Dartmouth College, 1991: 25 - 31.

Gaube, Heinz. *Iranian Cities.* NY: New York University Press, 1979.

Geertz, Clifford. *Local Knowledge.* NY: Basic Books, 1983.

Gell, Alfred. "Technology of Enchantment and the Enchantment of Technology." in Coote, Jeremy and Anthony Shelton, editors. *Anthropology, Art, and Aesthetics.* Oxford: Clarendon Press, 1992: 40-63.

Gellens, Sam I. "Search for Knowledge in Medieval Muslim Societies: A Comparative Approach." in Eickleman, Dale F. and James Piscatori. *Muslim Travelers: Pilgrimage, Migration and the Religious Imagination.* Berkeley: University of California Press, 1990: 50 - 65.

Georges, Robert A. "Toward an Understanding of Storytelling Events." *Journal of American Folklore,* Volume 82, #326 (October-December, 1969): 313-328.

Ghaffarian, Shireen. "Acculturation of Iranians in the United States." *Journal of Social Psychology.* Volume 127, Number 6, 1987: 561-571.

Ghirshman, Roman. *Persia: From the Origins to Alexander the Great.* London: Thames and Hudson, 1954.

___. *Iran: Parthians and Sassanians.* London: Thames and Hudson, 1962.

Gholsorkhi, Shohreh. "Pari Khan Khanum: A Masterful Safavid Princess." *Iranian Studies,* Volume 28, numbers 3-4: 143-156.

Goldhizer, Ignaz. "'Arab and 'Ajam." in Stern, S. M., editor. *Muslim Studies,* Vol. I. NY: NY University Press, 1960: 101-136.

___. "Shuubiya." in Stern, S. M., editor. *Muslim Studies.* Vol. I. NY: NY University Press, 1960: 137 - 163.

Grabar, Oleg. *Formation of Islamic Art.* New Haven: Princeton University Press, 1987.

___. *Mediation of Ornament.* Princeton, NJ: Princeton University Press, 1992.

Graham-Brown, Sarah. "Orientalism in Color." *Merip Reports.* July-September, 1984:56-59.

Gray, Basil. *Treasures of Asia: Persian Painting.* Cleveland, OH: Albert Skira, 1961.

Grube, E. and Eleanor Sims. "Painting." in R. W. Ferrier. *Arts of Persia.* New Haven: Yale University Press, 1989: 200-224.

Haeri, Shahla. *Law of Desire: Temporary Marriage in Shi'i Iran.* Syracuse, NY: Syracuse University Press, 1989.

Hafez, Shams Ad-din Mohammad. *Hafez be s'ai-ye Sayeh.* Tehran, Tus: 1994-95. In Persian.

Hale, John. *Civilization of Europe in the Renaissance.* NY: Atheneum, 1994.

Halpern, Joel M. *Serbian Village.* NY: Harper & Row, 1967.

Hamada, Geoffrey Mark. "Dance and Islam, the Bojnurdi Kurds of Northeastern Iran." Unpublished M.A. Thesis, UCLA, 1978.

Hanna, Judith Lynn. *Dance, Sex, and Gender.* Chicago: University Press, 1988.

Harper, Prudence O. *Silver Vessels of the Sasanian Period. Volume One: Royal Imagery.* NY: Metropolitan Museum of Art, New York, 1981.

Hasanov, Kamal. *Azerbaijan Gedim Folklor Ragslari.* (Old Azerbaijani Folk Dances, in Azeri). Baku: Isig, 1988.

Hermann, G. "Art of the Sasanians." in R. W. Ferrier, editor. *Arts of Persia.* New Haven: Yale University Press, 1989: 61-80.

Hezar o yek shab (Thousand and One Nights, in Persian). (In six volumes). Edited by Mohammad Ramazani. Tehran: Aftab, 1937.

Hicks, Jim. *Persians.* NY: Time-Life, 1975.

Hill, Derek and Oleg Grabar. *Islamic Architecture and Its Decoration.* Chicago: University of Chicago Press, 1964.

Hillman, Michael C. *Iranian Culture: A Persianist View.* Lanham, Maryland: University Press of America, 1990.

Hirschkop, Ken. "Introduction: Bakhtin and Cultural Theory." Hirschkop, Ken and David Shepherd, editors. *Bakhtin and Cultural Theory.* Manchester, England: Manchester University Press, 1989: 1-38.

Hodgson. Marshall G. S. *Venture of Islam.* Chicago: University of Chicago Press, 1974. In three volumes.

Holub, Robert C. *Reception Theory: A Critical Introduction.* London: Methuen, 1984.

Hourani, Albert. *History of the Arab Peoples.* Cambridge, Mass: Harvard UP, 1991.

Huot, Jean-Louis. *Persia I: From the Origins to the Achaemenids.* Cleveland: World Publishing Company, 1965.

Hutchinson, John and Anthony D. Smith, editors. *Ethnicity.* Oxford University Press, 1996: v-vi.

Iranian Yellow Pages. Van Nuys, CA: Ketab Corp, 1995.

Issari, M. Ali. *Cinema in Iran, 1900-1979.* Metuchen, NJ: Scarecrow Press, 1989.

Kaeppler, Adrienne L. "Structured Movement Systems in Tonga." in Spencer, Paul, ed. *Society and the Dance.* Cambridge UP, 1985: 92–118.

Karimova, R. *Bukharskii tanets.* (Bukharan Dance, in Russian). Tashkent: Literatura i Iskusstvo, 1977.

___. *Ferganskii tanets.* (Ferghana Dance, in Russian). Tashkent: Literatura i Iskusstvo, 1973.

___. *Khorezmiskii tanets.* (Khorazmian Dance, in Russian). Tashkent: Literatura i Iskusstvo, 1975.

___. *Tantsy Ansambl'a Bakhor.* (Dances of the Bakhor Ensemble, in Russian). Tashkent: Literatura i Iskusstvo, 1979.

Karomatov, F. and N. Nurdzhanov. *Muzikal'noe Iskusstvo Pamira.* (Musical Art of the Pamirs, in Russian and Tajik). Moscow: Vsesouiuznoe Izdatel'stvo Sovetskii Kompozitor, 1986.

Kazemeini, Kazem. *"Tarikh–e mokhtasar–e zur khaneh va varzesh–e bastani va movajjedin–e an pahlavanan va 'ayeran va shaterian."* (A brief history of the *zur khaneh* and its members: the champions, the creators, and the servants). *Honar va Mardom*, 1967. #55:28–34; #56:55–62. In Persian.

Kazemi, Farhad. "Ethnicity and the Iranian Peasantry." Esman, Milton J. and Itamar Rabinovich, editors. *Ethnicity, Pluralism, and the State in the Middle East.* Ithaca, NY: Cornell University Press, 1986:201-214.

Keal, E. "Art of the Parthians." in R. W. Ferrier, editor. *Arts of Persia.* New Haven: Yale University Press, 1989: 49-60.

Kealiinohomoku, Joann. "Ethnic Historical Study." in *Dance Historical Research: Perspectives from Related Arts and Disciplines.* Proceedings of the Second Conference on Research in Dance. July 4,5,6, 1969. NY, Conference on Research in Dance, 1969.

___. "An Anthropologist Looks at Ballet as a Form of Ethnic Dance." *Impulse.* 1970: 24-33.

Keddie, Nikki, editor. *Religion and Politics in Iran.* New Haven, Conn.: Yale University Press, 1983.

Kelley, Ron, editor. *Iranangeles: Iranians in Los Angeles.* Berkeley: University of California Press, 1993.

___. "Iranian Political Demonstrations in Los Angeles, USA: A Photographic Essay."

Keyes, Charles F. "Dialects of Ethnic Change." in Keyes, Charles F., editor. *Ethnic Change.* Seattle: Washington University Press, 1981: 4-30.

___. "Towards a New Formation of the Concept of Ethnic Group." *Ethnicity* 3 (1976): 202-213.

Khaleqi, Ruhallah. *Sar gozashteh musiqi iran.* (History of Music of Iran). (in Persian). Vol. I. Tehran: Safiali Shah, 1974. pp. 465-486.

Khanlari, Parviz N. *Tarikh-e zaban-e farsi.* (History of the Persian Language, three volumes in Persian). Fourth Printing. Tehran, Nashreh no: 1990.

Khatibi, Abdelkabir and Muhammad Sijelmassi. *Splendour of Islamic Calligraphy.* NY: Rizzoli, 1976.

Khayyam, Hakim Omar. *Robayyiat.* Tehran: H. A. N. Esfandiary, 3rd printing, 1974.

Kheirabadi, Masoud. *Iranian Cities: Formation and Development.* Austin: Texas University Press, 1991.

Khomeini, Ruhollah. *Kashf ol-asrar* (Discovery of Secrets). First published in Qom, Iran, 1971. (see Paidar, bibliography).

Kuhnel, Ernest. "History of Miniature Painting and Drawing." in Arthur Upham Pope, editor. *Survey of Persian Art.* London: Oxford University Press, 1964: 1829-1827.

Lambton, Ann K. S. *Continuity and Change in Medieval Persia: Aspects of Administrative, Economic and Social History, 11th - 14th Century.* NY: Bibliotheca Persica, 1988.

Lawler, Lillian. *Dance in Ancient Greece.* Middletown, CT: Wesleyan University Press, 1964.

La Meri (Russel Merriweather Hughes). "Learning the Danse Du Ventre." in *Curious and Wonderful Gymnastic.* Dance Perspectives, Number 10, Spring 1961: 43-47.

Lazard, G. "Rise of the New Persian Language." in Frye, Richard N., editor. *Cambridge History of Iran.* Vol 4., Cambridge University Press, 1974: 595-632.

Lentz, Thomas W. and Glenn D. Lowry. *Timur and the Princely Vision: Persian Art and Culture in the Fifteenth Century.* Los Angeles: Los Angeles County Museum of Art, 1989.

Levi-Strauss, Claude. *Savage Mind.* Chicago: University of Chicago Press, 1966.

Levin, Harry. "Introduction." in Lord, Albert. *Singer of Tales.* NY: Athenaeum, 1960:3-12.

Lewis, Bernard. *Middle East: A Brief History of the Last 2,000 Years.* NY: Scribner, 1995.

Lewis, J. Lowell. *Ring of Liberation: Deceptive Discourse in Brazilian Capoeira.* Chicago: University of Chicago Press, 1992.

Lincoln, Bruce. *Discourse and the Construction of Society: Comparative Studies of Myth, Ritual, and Classification.* NY: Oxford University Press, 1989.

Lisitsian, Srbui. *Starinnye Plyaski i Teatrlinye Predstvleniia Armianskogo Naroda.* (Ancient Dance and Theatre Performance of the Armenian Nation, in Russian). Yerevan, Academy of Sciences of Armenia, Volume I, 1958; Volume II, 1972.

Loeb, Laurence D. "Jewish Musicians and the Music of Fars." Asian Music. Volume IV-1, 1972:3-13.

Lord, Albert. *Singer of Tales.* NY: Athenaeum, 1970.

Mackenzie, John. M. *Orientalism: History, Theory and the Arts.* Manchester, England: Manchester University Press, 1995.

Mahdavi, Shireen. "Women, Ideas and Customs in Qajar Iran." in *Persian Studies in North America,* edited by Mehdi Marashi. Bethesda, Maryland: Iranbooks, 1994.

Maheronnaqsh, Mahmud. *Khatt-e Banna'i.* (Mason's Script, in Persian). Tehran: Sorush, 1991.

Majmu'eh-i az naqashi-ha-y irani dar sadeh-ye davazdahom or sizdahom hejri-ye qamari. (Collection of paintings from the 12th and 13th centuries [19th century]). Tehran: Publication of HIH, Empress Farah (covered), 1972. (Persian translation of Falk, Toby. *Qajar Painting.*)

Manning, Susan. "Modern Dance in the Third Reich: Six Positions and a Coda." Foster, Susan Leigh, editor. *Choreographing History.* Bloomington, Indiana: University of Indiana Press, 1995: 165-176.

Manz, Beatrice Forbes. "Development and Meaning of Chagatay Identity." in Gross, Joann, editor. *Muslims in Central Asia: Expressions of Identity and Change.* Durham, NC: Duke University Press, 1992: 27-45.

Martin, Randy. "Agency and History: The Demands of Dance Ethnography." in Foster, Susan Leigh, editor. *Choreographing History.* Bloomington: Indiana University Press, 1993: 105-115.

Massey, Reginald and Jamila. *Dances of India.* London: Tricolour Books, 1989.

Melikian-Chirvani, A. S. "Aesthetics of Islam." in Falk Toby, editor. *Treasures of Islam.* Secaucus, NJ: Wellfleet Press, 1985.

Menashri, David. "Khomeini's Policy toward Ethnic and Religious Minorities." Esman, Milton J. and Itamar Rabinovich, editors. *Ethnicity, Pluralism, and the State in the Middle East.* Ithaca, NY: Cornell University Press, 1986: 215-229.

Menges, Karl H. "People, Languages, and Migrations." in Allworth, Edward, editor. *Central Asia.* Third edition. Durham, NC: Duke University Press, 1995: 60-91.

Mernissi, Fatimah. *Beyond the Veil: Male-Female Dynamics in a Modern Muslim Society.* NY: John Wiley and Sons, 1975.

Meskoob, Shahrokh. *Iranian Nationality and the Persian Language.* Washington, D. C.: Mage, 1992.

Meyer, Leonard B. *Style and Music: Theory, History, and Ideology.* Philadelphia: University of Pennsylvania Press, 1989.

Miller, Lloyd and Katherine St. John. *Radif-e Raqs: Collection of Dance Sequences of the Persian Tradition.* Salt Lake City, Utah: Society for Preservation and Propagation of Eastern Arts, 1987. (Includes 3 audio and visual tapes).

Mitchell, Timothy. *Flamenco Deep Song.* New Haven and London: Yale University Press, 1994.

Moaddel, Mansoor. *Class Politics, and Ideology in the Iranian Revolution.* NY: Columbia University Press, 1993.

Mohammadi, Dr. Ahmad. *"Negahi be tarikh-e namayesh dar Iran."* (A Look at the History of Theatre in Iran). in *Honor o mardom.* (in Persian). 1973 129:19-25.

Mo'in, Mohammad. *Farhang-e Farsi* (Persian Dictionary). (In six volumes). Tehran: Amir Kabir, 1992.

Moran, A. Vahid. *Turkce - Inglizce Sozluk* (Turkish - English Dictionary). Istanbul: Kagit ve Basim Isleri, 1945.

Mortensen, Inge Demant. *Nomads of Luristan: History, Material Culture, and Pastoralism in Western Iran.* London, Thames and Hudson, 1993.

Mottahedeh, Roy P. "Shu'ubiyah Controversy and the Social History of Early Islamic Iran." *International Journal of Middle East Studies.* Vol 7 (1976): 161-182.

Naficy, Hamid. "Popular Culture of Iranian Exiles in Los Angeles." Kelley, Ron et al., editor. *Irangeles.* Berkeley: University of California Press, 1993a: 325-364.

___. *Making of Exile Cultures: Iranian Television in Los Angeles.* Minneapolis: University of Minnesota Press, 1993b.

___. "Cultural Dynamic of Exilic Music Videos." Paper presented at Middle East Studies Association of North America, Phoenix, Arizona, November 19-22, 1994.

Nahachewsky, Andriy. "Participatory and Presentational Dance as Ethnochoreological Categories." *Dance Research Journal,* 27/1 Spring 1995: 1-15.

Najafi, Najmeh. *Persia is My Heart.* NY: Harper, 1953.

Najmi, Naser. *Tehran dar yek sad sal-e pish.* (Tehran, one hundred years ago). Tehran: Arghavan, 1367 (1988).

Nasr, Sayyed Hossein. *Islam and the Plight of Modern Man.* London: Longman Group, 1975.

___. *Islamic Art and Spirituality.* Albany: State University of New York Press, 1987.

Nassehi-Behnam, Vida. "Change and the Iranian Family." *Cultural Anthropology.* December 1985, Vol. 26, No. 5: 557-562.

Necipoglu, Gulru. *The Topkapi Scroll—Geometry and Ornament in Islamic Architecture.* Santa Monica, CA: Getty Center for the History of Art and the Humanities, 1995.

Ness, Sally Ann. *Body, Movement, and Culture: Kinesthetic and Visual Symbolism in a Philippine Community.* Philadelphia: University of Pennsylvania Press, 1992.

Nochlin, Linda. "Imaginary Orient." *Art in America.* May 1983: 131-139;187-189.

Novack, Cynthia J. "Body's Endeavors as Cultural Practices." in Foster, Susan Leigh, editor. *Choreographing History.* Bloomington: Indiana University Press, 1995: 177-184.

Nurdzhanov, N. *"Razvlechnniia i narodni teatr tadzhikov kartegina i darvaza."* (Entertainments and Folk Theatres of the Tajiks of Kartegin and Darvaze, in Russian and Tajik). in *Iskusstvo Tadzhiksogo Naroda.* 3rd Bulletin. Dushanbe: Donish, 1965.

___. *Istoriia Tadzhikskogo Sovetskogo Teatra.* History of the Tajik Soviet Theatre (in Russian). Dushanbe: Donish, 1967.

___. *Tadzhikskii Teatr.* (in Russian) Moscow: Iskusstvo, 1968.

Ohtani, Kimiko. "Techniques in Indian Classical Dance." in Fujii, Tomoaki, editor. *JVC Video Anthology of World Music and Dance.* Tokyo: Victor Company of Japan, Ltd., 1988: 9-13.

Ortner, Sherry B. "On Key Symbols." *American Anthropologist.* 75 (1973): 1338-1345.

Paidar, Parvin. *Women and the Political Process in Twentieth-Century Iran.* Cambridge, England: Cambridge University Press, 1995.

Page, Mary Ellen. "Professional Storytelling in Iran: Transmission and Practices." *Iranian Studies,* Summer/Autumn, 1979: 195 - 215.

Papadopoulo, Alexandre. *Islam and Muslim Art.* NY: Harry N. Abrahms, 1979.

Pechey, Graham. "On the Borders of Bakhtin: Dialogisation, Decolonisation." Hirschkop, Ken and David Shepherd, editors. *Bakhtin and Cultural Theory.* Manchester, England: Manchester University Press, 1989: 39-67.

Peirce, Leslie Penn. *Imperial Harem: Women and Sovereignty in the Ottoman Empire.* NY: Oxford University Press, 1993.

Phelan, Peggy. *Unmarked, the Politics of Performance.* London & NY: Routledge, 1993.

Pope, Arthur Upham and the editors. "Calligraphy. A. An Outline History." *Survey of Persian Art.* In 14 volumes. 1964-1965: 1707-1742.

Ramazani, R. K., editor. *Iran's Revolution: A Search for Consensus.* Bloomington: Indiana University Press, 1990.

Rasmussen, Susan. "Zarraf, a Tuareg Women's Wedding Dance." *International Journal of Cultural and Social Anthropology.* Winter 1995, Volume 34, No. 1:1-16.

Rezvani, Medjid. *Le Theatre et La Danse en Iran.* (Theatre and Dance in Iran). Paris: G. P. Maisonneuve et Larose, 1962.

Riggio, Milla Cozart, editor. *Ta'ziyeh: Ritual and Popular Beliefs in Iran.* Hartford, Conn: Trinity College, 1988.

Roaf, M. "Art of the Achaemenians." in R. W. Ferrier, editor. *Arts of Persia.* New Haven: Yale University Press, 1989: 26-48.

Robinson, B. W. *Persian Drawings: From the 14th Through the 19th Century.* Boston: Little, Brown and Co., 1965.

Royce, Anya Peterson. *Anthropology of Dance.* Bloomington: University of Indiana Press, 1977.

Sabagh, Georges and Mehdi Bozorgmehr. "Are the Characteristics of Exiles Different from Immigrants? The Case of Iranians in Los Angeles." *Sociology and Social Research.* Volume 71, Number 2, January 1987: 77-84.

Sachs, Curt. *World History of the Dance.* NY: Norton, 1937.

Sadiq, Mostefa. *"God–e moqaddas: peidayesh–e zur khaneh."* (The sacred pit: the discovery of the *zur–khaneh*). *Honar va mardom,* 1975. #145: 55–62. in Persian.

___. *"Zur khaneh va varzesh–e bastani."* (The *zur–khaneh* and the ancient exercise). *Honar va mardom,* 1964. #25: 6–15. in Persian.

Safa–Isfahani, Kaveh. "Iranian Culture:Symbolic Representations of Sexuality in Dramatic Games." *Signs,* 1980. Vol. 6, No. 1:33–53.

Safadi, Yasin Hamid. *Islamic Calligraphy.* London: Thames and Hudson, 1987.

Said, Edward. *Orientalism.* NY: Vintage Books, 1978.

Saleh, Magda Ahmed Abdel Ghaffar. *Documentation of the Ethnic Dance Tradition of Egypt.* Unpublished Ph.D. Dissertation, New York University, 1979. (University Microfilms International, Ann Arbor, Michigan).

Sauvaget, Jean. *Introduction to the History of the Middle East.* Berkeley: University of California Press, 1965.

Savigliano, Marta E. *Tango and the Political Economy of Passion.* Boulder: Westview Press,1995.

Schimmel, Annemarie. *Calligraphy and Islamic Culture.* NY: New York University Press, 1984.

___. *"Raks"* (dance). Encyclopedia of Islam. (1990:425-426).

Schuyler, Eugene. *Turkistan: Notes of a Journey in Russian Turkistan, Kokand, Bukhara and Kuldja.* New York: Praeger, 1876. (1966 reprint).

Scott, Virginia. *Commedia Dell'Arte in Paris 1644-1697.* Charlottesville, VA: University of Virginia, 1990.

Shahbazi, A. Shapur. "Dance in Pre-Islamic Iran." *Encyclopaedia Iranica.* Vol.VI, 1994: 640-641.

___. *Ferdowsi: A Critical Biography.* Harvard University, Center for Middle Eastern Studies. Distributed by: Costa Mesa, CA: Mazda Publishers, 1991.

Shalinsky, Audrey C. *Long Years of Exile: Central Asian Refugees in Afghanistan and Pakistan.* Lanham, MD: University Press of America, 1994.

Shay, Anthony. "Dance and Non-Dance: Patterned Movement in Iran and

Islam." *Iranian Studies*, Volume 28, Numbers 1-2, Winter/Spring 1995a: 61-78.

___. *"Bazi-ha-ye namayeshi*: Iranian Women's Theatrical Plays." *Dance Research Journal.* 27/2 Fall 1995b: 16-24.

Shelton, Anthony. "Predicates of Aesthetic Judgement: Ontology and Value in Huichol Material Presentation." in Coote, Jeremy and Anthony Shelton, editors. Anthropology, Art, and Aesthetics. Oxford: Clarendon Press, 1992: 209-244.

Shepherd, David. "Bakhtin and the Reader." in Hirschkop, Ken and David Shepherd. *Bakhtin and Cultural Theory.* Manchester, England: Manchester University Press, 1989: 91-108.

Shiloah, Amnon. *Music in the World of Islam: A Socio-Cultural Study.* Detroit: Wayne University Press, 1995.

Shiva, Shahram T. *Rending the Veil: Literal and Poetic Translations of Rumi.* Prescott, AZ: Hohm Press, 1995.

Shoberl, Frederic. *Persia.* London: R. Ackermann, 1828. In 3 volumes.

Singa, Rina and Reginald Massey. *Indian Dances: Their History and Growth.* NY: Georgre Braziller, 1967.

Slobin, Mark. "Conversations in Tashkent." *Asian Music,* 1971: Vol. ii-2: 7-13.

Smith, Anthony D. *Ethnic Origin of Nations.* Oxford, Eng.: Blackwell, 1986.

Snow, Maxine Leeds. "Dances of the Middle East." Fleshman, Bob, editor. *Theatrical Movement: A Bibliographical Anthology.* Metuchen, N.J., Scaracrow Press, 1986:551-561.

Soudavar, Abolala. *Art of the Persian Courts.* NY: Rizzoli, 1992.

Spector, Johanna. "Musical Traditions and Innovation." in Allworth, Edward, editor. *Central Asia.* Third Edition. Durham, NC: Duke University Press, 1995: 434-484.

Spier, David L. "Influence of Warfare on the Recreational Activities of the Ancient Assyrians and Iranians." Unpublished M.A. thesis, University of Oregon, 1976.

Sreberny-Mohammadi, Annabelle and Ali Mohammadi. "Post-revolutionary Iranian exile: A Study in Impotence." *Third World Quarterly.* 9 (1) January 1987:108-129.

St. John, Katherine. "Afghan Atan." *Viltis.* Volume 47, No. 1, May 1988: 23-24.

___. "Afghan Dance." *Folk Dance Scene.* Volume 24, No. 2, April 1989: 8-18.

___. "Cultural and Historical Study of Selected Women's Dance from Herat, Afghanistan. 1970-1980". Unpublished MA Thesis, Brigham Young University, Dec. 1993.

Stallybrass, Peter and Allon White. *Politics and Poetics of Transgression.* Ithaca, New York: Cornell University Press, 1986.

Stam, Robert. *Subversive Pleasures: Bakhtin, Cultural Criticism, and Film.* Baltimore and London: John Hopkins University Press, 1989.

Strauss, Gloria B. "Aesthetics of Dominance." *Journal of Aesthetics and*

Art Criticism. xxxvii/I, Fall 1978: 73-79.

Strinati, Dominic. *Introduction to Theories of Popular Culture.* London and New York: Routledge, 1995.

Stuckey, P. Sterling. "Christian Conversion and the Challenge of Dance." in Foster, Susan Leigh, editor. *Choreographing History.* Bloomington: Indiana University Press, 1993: 54-66.

Surieu, Robert. *Sarv-e Naz.* Geneva: Nagel, 1967.

Taj Al-Saltana. *Crowning Anguish: Memoirs of a Persian Princess from the Harem to Modernity.* Edited with Introduction & Notes, Abbas Amanat; Translated by Anna Vanzan and Ali Neshati. Washington, D. C.: Mage, 1993.

Tavakoli-Targhi, Mohamad. "Iran as Imagined Nation." (Mostafa Vaziri). Book Review *IJMES.* Vol. 26, #2, May, 1994:316-318.

____. "Contested Memories: Narrative Structures and Allegorical Meanings from Iran's Pre-Islamic History." *Iranian Studies,* Vol. 29, Numbers 1-2, Winter/Spring 1996: 149-175.

Tkachenko, Tamara. *Narodny Tanets.* (Folk Dance, in Russian). Moscow: Iskusstvo, 1954.

Tsing, Anna L. *In the Realm of the Diamond Queen.* Princeton University Press, 1993.

Turner, Bryan S. *Orientalism, Postmodernism, and Globalism.* London: Routledge, 1994.

Van Nieuwkerk, Karin. *"A Trade Like Any Other": Female Singers and Dancers in Egypt.* Austin, TX: University of Texas, Austin, 1995.

Varzi, Morteza. "Performance-Audience Relationships in the *Bazm.*" Caton, Margaret & Neil Siegel, editors. *Cultural Parameters of Iranian Musical Expression.* Redondo Beach, CA: Institute of Persian Performing Arts, 1986/1988: 1-9.

Vasiliev, A. A. *History of the Byzantine Empire.* Madison: University of Wisconsin Press, 1964.

Watson, Oliver. *Persian Lustre Ware.* London: Faber and Faber, 1985.

Welch, Anthony. *Artists for the Shah: Late Sixteenth-Century Painting at the Imperial Court of Iran.* New Haven and London: Yale University Press, 1976.

Winder, Bayley. Orientalism. (book review). *Middle East Journal.* 1982:615-618.

Wood, Leona and Anthony Shay. "Danse du Ventre: A Fresh Appraisal." *Dance Research Journal.* 1976 Volume viii/2, Spring/Summer: 18-30.

Yarshater, Ehsan. "Introduction." in Yarshater, Ehsan, editor. *Cambridge History of Iran.* Vol. 3 (1): The Seleucid, Parthian and Sasanian Periods. Cambridge University Press, 1983:i-xxvl.

Yusofi, Gholam-Hosayn. "Calligraphy." *Encyclopeadia Iranica.* London: Routledge & Kegan, 1994: 680-718.

Zakani, Obeid. *Koliyyat-e Obeid-e Zakani* (Complete Works of Obeid Zakani). With Corrections and Introduction by Abbas Eghbal Ashtiani. Conoga Park, CA: Eghbal Printing and Publishing, Inc., 1985 (date not given in book but ascertained by telephone from publisher, March 28,

1996). in Persian.

Zarinkub, Abd-al Husain. "Arab Conquest and its Aftermath." in Frye, Richard N., ed. *Cambridge History of Iran.* Vol 4. Cambridge University Press, 1974: 1-56.

Zinder, Jac. "Eternal 6/8 Groove: In the San Fernando Valley, the Persian Hit Factory Lives On." *LA Weekly.* January 17-23, 1992: 32-37.

Zoka', Yahya. *"Tarikh-e raqs dar Iran."* (A history of dance in Iran, in Persian). *Honar va Mardom,* 1978. This article is in four parts, with somewhat confusing dates, since it appeared just before the revolution, when the year designations were changed for some months. All are in volume XVI: Part 1 #188: 2-12; part II #189: 2-7; part III #191: 38-41; and part IV #192: 22-28.

INFORMANTS

Azad, Parvaneh. Persian Language Interpreter. Born in Tehran. Interviewed 1990 - 1998.

Bousseloub, Boualem. Personal Interviews, October 12–13, 1993.

Changizian, Hayedeh. Professional ballerina, soloist in Rudaki Hall in the National Ballet of Iran. Personal Interview, June 18, 1996.

Jamal. (Khosrow Jamali, Painter, born 1952, Tehran.) Interviewed and consulted 1992-1999.

Kaboli, Farzaneh. Former soloist with Iranian National Folk Dance Company, Mahalli Dancers. Interview, Sept. 5, 1994.

Miller, Lloyd Clifton. Musician and composer. Personal communication, October 26, 1993.

Mofid, Ardavan. Professional actor. Born in Tehran. Plays role of *Gholam Siyah.* Formal interviews: January 27, and March 4, 1994.

Mofid, Bahman. Professional actor. Born in Tehran. Plays role of *Hajji.* Formal interviews: January 27, and March 4, 1994.

Nasiri, Afshin. Former co-proprietor of Tassveer Bookstore, Born in Tehran. Interviews 1992 - 1995.

Pourtash, Ali. Actor, including role of *Hajji's* daughter in the Siyah Bazi. January 1,1994.

Valipour, Masoud. Proprietor of Ketabsara Bookstore and calligrapher. Born in Ahvaz. Interviews 1992-1999.

Videocassettes and Films

Afghan Village. 1972. Out take footage of dance scene provided by Smithsonian Institute.

Efriteh-ye Ma-chin. Stars Morteza Aghili as *Gholam-e siyah.* Made in Tehran in 1975.

Mohallel. Stars Ardevan Mofid. Made in Los Angeles in 1982.

Murcheh Dareh. Made in Tehran in 1970.

INDEX

Achaemenids, 59, 69, 70, 71, 78, 190
aesthetics, 5, 16, 58, 176, 181
Afghanistan and Afghans, 1, 2, 18, 22, 27, 46, 74, 77, 85, 96, 97, 103, 112, 115, 137, 172, 173, 174, 181, 184, 192
Afsaneh, 160, 161, 168, 169, 195, 196
Al Faruqi, 162
Alexander the Great, 70
Alizadeh, 132
Alter, 57, 79
Alternation, 31, 32, 33
Aman Folk Ensemble (dance company), 184
Amanat, Abbas, 8
Amini, Ali, 12
And, Metin, 3, 74, 83, 84, 88, 89, 90, 193
Anderson, Benedict, 103
Arabs and Arab world, 52, 58, 63, 66, 71, 72, 80, 81, 84, 88, 90, 91, 98-100, 161, 164, 170, 173
Armenia and Armenians, 18, 19, 22, 108, 111, 112, 142, 163, 184
Art as a cultural system, 3, 4-6, 62
Assyrians, 19, 108, 112
Auto-exoticism, 4, 157
Auto-orientalism, 4, 159
AVAZ International Dance Theatre, 8, 9, 12, 20, 117, 124, 130, 174, 175, 176, 177, 178, 179, 182
Azad, Parvaneh, 14, 90, 192, 195, 196
Azerbaijan and Azerbaijanis, 2, 18, 19, 22, 90, 97, 103, 142, 163, 165, 179

Baha'is, 2, 108, 112

Bahor (Uzbek State Folk Ensemble), 163, 179
Bakhtin, Mikhail, 138, 151, 154, 155
Baku, 19
Balanchine, George, 37
Balkans, 155
Ballet, classical, 7, 15, 17, 24, 37-41, 66, 113, 159, 164, 167, 179, 185, 186
Baluchis and Baluchistan, 18, 22, 58, 96, 97, 195
Baluchistan, 18, 22
Bandari, 123
Barthes, Roland, 5, 6, 21, 40
Bazi-ha-ye namayeshi (women's theatrical games), 49, 120, 125, 130, 152, 153, 155
Beeman, William O., 98, 116, 121, 135, 136, 137, 152, 154, 155
Beiza'i, Bahram, 28, 39, 76, 152, 162, 163, 165
Belly dance, 2, 3, 25-27, 87, 118, 127, 161, 164, 175
Berger, Bennett M., 134
Bosworth, Clifford Edmund, 86
Bouroujerdi, Mehrzad, 87
Bousseloub, Boualem, 88
Bozorgmehr, Mehdi, George Sabagh and Claudia Der Martirosian, 104, 106, 110, 112
Brend, Barbara, 63, 64
Bricolage and bricoleur, 28, 35-37, 39, 41-44, 48, 185
Browne, Edward G., 74, 75
Bukhara (city in Uzbekistan), 19, 50, 97
Buonaventura, Wend, 116
Byzantium, 10, 74, 184

California, 2, 9, 10, 12, 14, 19, 26, 40, 43, 49, 50, 52, 53, 66, 93, 102-105, 107, 108, 110-

156-159, 164, 165, 167, 169, 170, 172, 174, 175, 176, 178, 179, 180, 181, 182, 183; art of, 4, 5, 57, 73; dance in, 1, 7, 12, 43, 138, 164; ethnic groups, Baha'is, 2, 108, 112; Jews, 2, 108, 112; Moslems, 2, 3, 34, 63, 67, 74, 75, 83, 87, 88, 100, 101, 111, 112, 123, 124, 128, 132, 133, 143, 144, 149, 158, 159, 175, 183, 193; Zoroas-trians, 2, 56, 57, 102, 111, 190
Iranian cultural sphere, 18, 19, 26, 28, 35, 45, 48, 55, 57, 60, 62, 73, 74, 77, 80, 86, 90, 93, 95-98, 101, 103, 113, 115, 138, 140, 142, 152-175; definition of, 90; ethnic identity, 98; Islamic identity, 95, 102
Iranian-Americans, 7, 8, 11-13, 15, 33, 35, 38, 39, 41, 43, 48, 49, 52, 55, 80, 81, 91, 93-115, 116, 126, 128, 130, 142, 146, 149, 151, 160, 171-178, 181-183
Iranian Revolution, 102, 103, 108, 109, 113, 120, 165, 167, 192
Iranian-ness, 15, 95, 98, 179
Iranians, 2, 4, 5, 7, 8, 9, 10, 11, 13, 15, 19, 21, 26, 48, 55, 57, 59, 68, 69, 71, 78, 80, 81, 87, 93, 94, 96, 97, 98, 99, 100, 102, 103, 104, 105, 106, 107, 109, 110, 111, 112, 114, 115, 119, 120, 121, 123, 124, 127, 131, 132, 136, 138, 142, 145, 148, 149, 151, 156, 159, 161, 162, 164, 169, 170, 171, 172, 175, 176, 177, 178, 179, 182
Iser, Wolfgang (see also "Reception Theory"), 61, 62, 75, 76
Isfahan (city in Iran), 17, 74, 75, 163, 164, 198
Islam, 2, 3, 4, 6, 7, 9, 10, 26, 53, 63, 72, 73, 80, 81, 83, 85, 86, 87, 88, 96, 98, 100, 101, 102,

112, 128, 129, 165, 188, 190, 191
Islamic identity, 95, 102
Islamic Revolution, 103, 110, 169, 180
Issari, M. Ali, 147
Italy (see also Fermor, Sharon), 5, 61, 67, 68

Jamal (Khosrow Jamali), 13, 32, 42, 88, 90, 105. 107. 109, 113, 118, 121, 126, 133, 139, 145, 147, 162, 170, 175, 178, 184, 189, 190, 193, 194
Jauss, Hans (see also "Horizon of Expectations"), 10, 95
Jews, 2, 108, 112

Kaboli, Farzaneh, 186
Kaeppler, Adrienne L., 81, 82, 92, 161
Keal, E., 70
Kealiinohomku, Joann, 41
"Key Symbol" (see Ortner, Sherry), 191
Khaleqi, Ruhollah, 77
Khiva (city in Uzbekistan), 17, 19, 50
Khomeini, Ruholla, 87, 111, 132, 139
Khorasan, 18, 22
Kurdistan and Kurds, 18, 19, 58, 71, 97, 142

La Meri (Russel Merriweather Hughes), 81, 84
Lawler, Lillian, 61, 65, 66, 67
Lazard, Gilbert, 72, 99
Lentz, Thomas, 5, 65
Levi-Strauss, Claude, 28, 35, 36, 37, 38, 41, 42, 44, 48
Lewis, Bernard, 87
Lincoln, Bruce, 98, 102
Logari (Afghan version of solo improvised dance similar to mojassameh), 46
"Logic of Choice" principle, 24, 31-35, 36, 41, 177

Persian, language (farsi), 11, 72, 96, 97, 104, 190, 195-196; literature, 3, 57, 64, 75, 86, 96, 97, 99, 187, 191
Persians (see also Iranians), 16, 58, 66, 70, 75, 96, 97, 99, 138, 168, 182, 195, 196
Phelan, Peggy, 62
Poetry, Persian, 59, 101, 158
Polyakova, A. E. and Rahimova, Z. I., 62
Pope, Arthur Upham, 20, 48, 51, 52, 71, 72, 73, 189

Qashqa'i (Turkish speaking tribe from Fars prince), 97
Queen Farah, 176, 179

Radio Seda-ye Iran, 13, 85, 176, 183
Ramishvili, Nino, 25
Reception Theory (see also Iser, Wolfgang), 10, 61, 75
Religiosity (element of choreophobia), 132
Representation, 4, 5, 60, 62-65, 71, 151, 156, 160-163, 169, 170, 176, 180, 181, 186, 187, 189, 195
Rezvani, Medjid, 57, 58, 73, 80, 81, 84, 88, 90, 92, 156, 188
Rhythm dance (see also shish hashtom [six-eight]), 22, 48, 50, 51, 53, 65, 73, 81-84, 91, 113, 118, 123, 125, 138
Roaf, M., 70
Royce, Anya Peterson, 13, 82, 83
Ru-howzi (style of comic entertainment), 27, 49, 138, 152-155, 194, 195

Saba (dance company), 167, 196
Sabagh, George and Bozorgmehr, Mehdi, 104, 106, 110, 112, 192
Safavids (dynasty 1501-1722), 39, 59, 60, 61, 68, 74-76, 77, 78, 152, 164, 165, 167, 191,
193
Said, Edward, 4, 87, 105, 157, 158, 159, 160, 168, 195
Sama', definition of, 88
Samarqand, 17, 60, 97, 168, 186, 191
Sasanids (dynasty 224-650), 10, 59, 69, 71, 72, 78, 95, 97, 98, 99
Savigliano, Marta, 151, 160, 169
Schimmel, Annemarie, 53, 75, 165
Self-exoticism, 151, 156-157, 161, 166, 167, 169, 180
Seljuqs (dynasty 1037-1157), art of, 73
Sexuality, 25, 26, 128-131, 145, 152, 155, 173
Shahbazi, A. Shapur, 70, 71
Shahnameh (epic history of Iran, see also Ferdowsi), 68, 189, 194
Shalinsky, Audrey, 137, 192
Shateri (type of solo improvised dance), 26, 117, 123, 127, 132, 193
Shay, Anthony, 7, 34, 125, 133, 152, 155, 159, 174, 178
Shelton, Anthony, 38
Shepherd, David, 94
Shiloah, Amnon, 58
Shiraz (city in Fars Province), 14, 19, 183, 186, 191
Shish-hashtom (six-eight rhythm), 22, 118
Siegel, Neil, 122
Sima-ye Ashena (television program), 1, 163
Simultaneity (logic of choice principle), 31, 33-35
Siyah-bazi (black-face thatre), 49, 101, 138, 152, 153, 154, 155, 194, 195, 196
Soleimani, Yaffa, 177
Soudavar, Abolala, 65, 67, 69, 209
Spector, Joanna, 28, 191
St. John, Katherine, 18, 73, 173, 187, 188